Reproductive Rights Issues
in Popular Media

Reproductive Rights Issues in Popular Media

International Perspectives

Edited by WALTRAUD MAIERHOFER
and BETH WIDMAIER CAPO

McFarland & Company, Inc., Publishers
Jefferson, North Carolina

LIBRARY OF CONGRESS CATALOGUING-IN-PUBLICATION DATA

Names: Maierhofer, Waltraud, 1959– editor. | Capo, Beth Widmaier, 1973– editor.
Title: Reproductive right issues in popular media : international perspectives / edited by Waltraud Maierhofer and Beth Widmaier Capo.
Description: Jefferson, North Carolina : McFarland & Company, Inc., Publishers, 2017 | Includes bibliographical references and index.
Identifiers: LCCN 2017020235 | ISBN 9781476669403 (softcover : acid free paper) ∞
Subjects: LCSH: Family planning in mass media. | Family planning—Press coverage.
Classification: LCC P96.F32 R46 2017 | DDC 304.6/6—dc23
LC record available at https://lccn.loc.gov/2017020235

BRITISH LIBRARY CATALOGUING DATA ARE AVAILABLE

ISBN (print) 978-1-4766-6940-3
ISBN (ebook) 978-1-4766-3006-9

© 2017 Waltraud Maierhofer and Beth Widmaier Capo. All rights reserved

No part of this book may be reproduced or transmitted in any form or by any means, electronic or mechanical, including photocopying or recording, or by any information storage and retrieval system, without permission in writing from the publisher.

Front cover photograph by Willem Velthoven for Women on Web

Printed in the United States of America

McFarland & Company, Inc., Publishers
  Box 611, Jefferson, North Carolina 28640
    www.mcfarlandpub.com

In memory of Ingeborg H. Solbrig (1923–2016),
professor of German at the University of Iowa, 1975 to 1994

Acknowledgments

Beth Widmaier Capo thanks Nick Capo for his support and editorial expertise.

Waltraud Maierhofer is deeply grateful for the encouragement and conversations on contraception-related topics with David R. Sheff. Work on this project was inspired by all the highly engaged students in her seminars on "Contraception Across Time and Cultures" at the University of Iowa.

The editors would like to acknowledge Daniel Korunka for his editorial assistance.

Table of Contents

Acknowledgments   vi

Introduction: Representing Reproductive Rights   1
    BETH WIDMAIER CAPO

Part 1. Contraceptives in the Media: Spreading the Story

Propagating Progress and Circumventing Harm: Reconciling References to Contraceptives in British Television and Cinema of the 1960s   11
    JESSICA BORGE

Pill and Remote Control: Politics of Contraception in Contemporary U.S. Quality Television   29
    MARKUS SCHLEICH and JONAS NESSELHAUF

A Romantic Steroid or a Great Performance? Visual Culture and the Pill   48
    JAMIE WAGMAN

Sex Education and Social Media: Contraception in the Digital Age   65
    MANON S. PARRY

Part 2. Stories of Forced Adoption

In Search of the New Woman and the Best Mother: Unwanted Pregnancy in Gina Kaus' Literary and Filmic Work   82
    REGINA RANGE

Pregnant Girls in the Attic—No Choices: An Analysis of Patrice Toye's *Little Black Spiders*   100
    KIRSTEN E. KUMPF BAELE and SOFIE DECOCK

Part 3. From Unplanned to Planned Pregnancies

From Unwanted to Wanted Pregnancy: Pregnancy, Abortion and the End of the GDR in the Film *Jana and Jan* (1992)   117
BELINDA CARSTENS-WICKHAM

Finding Humor in Birth Control: Fiction and Film from Hugh Mills to Matthias Schweighöfer   136
WALTRAUD MAIERHOFER

Part 4. Abortion Across Cultures: Reproductive Choice, Duty or Crime

When Abortion Was Illegal: Remembrance and Advocacy in Recent Films from Romania and Mexico—and "I Had an Abortion" Storytelling on the Web   156
WALTRAUD MAIERHOFER

The Forbidden Pregnancy and the Abandoned Children: On Mo Yan's Fiction about the One-Child Policy and Abortion in China   174
SHELLEY W. CHAN

Part 5. Legacies

Woman Rebel: Margaret Sanger and American Popular Culture   190
BETH WIDMAIER CAPO

From the Pill to the Pen to the Pill, Again: Carl Djerassi's Discursive Constructions of Birth Control   206
WALTER GRÜNZWEIG

About the Contributors   223
Index   225

Introduction
Representing Reproductive Rights

BETH WIDMAIER CAPO

> "No woman can call herself free who does not own
> and control her body. No woman can call herself free
> until she can choose consciously whether she will
> or will not be a mother."

Almost 100 years later, Margaret Sanger's words still encapsulate ongoing debates about reproductive rights. The fundamental question of bodily autonomy and the ability to choose and plan reproduction are hotly debated even as technology invents new forms of contraception, including the hormonal vaginal ring and the contraceptive patch, pregnancy and childbirth enter the realm of science fiction with IVF and other interventions, and the reproductive health of transgender men complicates what were viewed as binary systems. Reproductive rights arguments occupy space in public discourse and news media and have infiltrated global popular culture. Film, television, fiction, and other genres variously represent birth control and abortion, mediating the issues for a wide-ranging global audience. Social and cultural conflicts are embedded in reproductive rights discourse, played out against international social histories including communism in China and Romania[1] or feminism in the United States.[2] This timely volume offers 12 essays investigating reproductive rights issues at the center of popular media around the world.

Birth control and contraception, the attempt by humans to regulate and control their fertility and prevent conception, have existed as long as recorded history (Riddle). Abortion, the conscious act of terminating a pregnancy, has likewise been recorded since ancient times (Riddle). People in every society have wanted and needed to control their fertility and plan their families for

1

2   Introduction

economic, social, and personal reasons, and since 1966 reproductive rights have been recognized by the Universal Declaration of Human Rights (United Nations). Despite this long history, the right to control reproduction is routinely contested.[3] Although "in 2015, 64 per cent of married or in-union women of reproductive age worldwide were using some form of contraception," according to the United Nations, "12 per cent of married or in-union women are estimated to have had an unmet need for family planning" ("Trends" 6). In a single week at the end of October 2016, a Google alert detected numerous online articles on contraception, abortion, and reproductive rights from the United States, Britain, Malta, Poland, Ghana, Nigeria, and Ireland. For instance, in the third U.S. presidential campaign debate Hillary Clinton supported abortion rights while Donald Trump revealed a misunderstanding of abortion, stating, "In the ninth month you can take the baby and rip the baby out of the womb of the mother just prior to the birth of the baby" (Gunter). Meanwhile, "Irish women report relief and gratitude after using abortion pills," read a headline in *The Guardian* (Boseley). In Poland, mass public protests and boycotts against an abortion ban continued (Eleftheriou-Smith).

On the contraceptive front, British scientists announced in that same week that they had developed a compound that stopped sperm from swimming by inhibiting their motility, and thus could serve as the basis for a male "pill" (Adams). In Malta, discussions about access to emergency contraception were in the news (Diacono), while the governor of one Nigerian state urged Nigerians to practice birth control during the current recession (Olowolagba). In the United States, where nearly half (45 percent) of pregnancies are unintended, according to the Guttmacher Institute, "the number of sexually active American teenagers using no contraception fell by 35 percent in just seven years. Meanwhile, the teen birth rate has fallen almost 50 percent since 1990" (Thompson). Although abstinence-only education rather than comprehensive sex education continues to be mandated in some schools, and only 24 states require sex education in the schools (Marrone), Denver, Colorado's, experiment offering free long-lasting birth control such as IUDs to teenagers has led to plunging teen birth rates and a dramatic decline in abortion (Tavernise). These are a few examples of the way birth control, abortion, and reproductive rights issues are unfolding worldwide.

Since reproductive rights are still so prominent in global media and political discourse, "why aren't there more depictions of birth control in pop culture?" asks Sarah Seltzer. Abortion may serve as a dramatic plot point in film, as several essays in this volume attest, but it "has always been relatively taboo on TV" and, when it does appear, "is almost always met with controversy" (Bradley). Given the ubiquity of depictions of sex in popular culture and the usage statistics for contraception, birth control, and abortion, conversations about and images of people using family planning should permeate popular media. So why don't they? Perhaps because we still hide what is most mundane, such as going to the toilet, and many forms of birth control usage, such as taking a daily pill, are boringly repetitive, while the IUD and the patch are forgotten after insertion or application and do their work unnoticed—how, then, can they further the plot? As Seltzer notes, "Something that by its very nature creates freedom—an absence of risk and worry—isn't easy to depict in genres that rely on conflict." But, as Rosenberg argues, "it's not as if contraceptive use would be difficult to incorporate into pop culture with a relative minimum of effort," simply by inserting birth control into the standard props and settings for visual media, acknowledging it as an expected piece of the background of daily life.

Perhaps ratings and reception are the reason for "pop culture's weird silence on birth control" (Rosenberg). Few television networks want to offend viewers or alienate sponsors, and film ratings systems still impose a censoring effect. And this holds true not only in visual media, but also in music: Loretta Lynn's song "The Pill" was refused airtime by many radio stations in the 1970s (Hilliard and Keith 96), but where are explicit birth control references in today's productions? More contemporary odes to female independence, such as Lil' Kim's "Don't Mess with Me" and Nikki Minaj's "I'm Legit," reference birth control pills along with explicit sexual acts. But these songs' graphic language, while in line with the hip hop genre, ensure limited airplay or the airing of "clean" edited versions that replace or cover ("bleep") the offensive language. Another reason for the relative dearth of depictions of reproductive rights issues in popular media is that these issues are still contested in moral and political debates and therefore "off limits" to some writers or producers who want to avoid their work being labeled as controversial or propagandistic. But this absence of depiction has serious consequences, as Seltzer and other feminist cultural critics have argued: without widespread representation of abortion, birth control, and other reproductive issues in popular media, these issues remain taboo and misunderstood.

This critical interest in the discourse of birth control and abortion in popular media and fiction led to the international symposium "Pill and Pen: Contraception and Unwanted Pregnancy in Literature and Popular Culture" at the University of Iowa in March 2014.[4] Scholars from a wide variety of disciplines, including sociology, history, and literary studies, convened to speak about the representation of birth control and unintended pregnancy in cultural, historical, and sociological contexts. The conference culminated with a keynote lecture delivered by the world-famous chemist and writer Carl Djerassi, whose work was crucial to the development of the oral contraceptive pill.[5] Unfortunately, Djerassi, who was originally to contribute to this volume, died at age 91 in January 2015 (McFadden). As we lose birth control pioneers such as Carl Djerassi, and as Planned Parenthood celebrates its 100th anniversary,[6] it is time for a volume on the intersection of reproductive rights and global popular culture.

Growing out of the initial symposium, this volume offers a comparative and international perspective on reproductive rights discourse in popular media. While several books and collections have been published focusing on contraception, abortion, or reproductive rights in literature and the mass media,[7] this volume's breadth of international perspectives and forms of popular culture is unique. Together, these essays help us understand the ways popular culture influences reproductive rights discourse.

The first part, "Contraceptives in the Media: Spreading the Story," features an investigation of the ways birth control manifests for purposes of entertainment and education in the media. Jessica Borge uses archival research to explore the position of censors and regulators who oversaw references to contraception in 1960s British film and television. "Propagating Progress and Circumventing Harm: Reconciling References to Contraceptives in British Television and Cinema of the 1960s" demonstrates that a utilitarian rather than moral model guided regulatory decisions, offering new insights into how contraception was appraised in terms of its imagined impact on audiences, and, significantly, how this shaped the appearance and non-appearance of contraception on screen. Markus Schleich and Jonas Nesselhauf offer a brief history of the birth control pill and its liberating potential for sexual politics before turning to an analysis of the pill in contemporary U.S. television shows in "Pill and Remote Control: Politics of Contraception in Contemporary U.S. Quality Television." They identify a central theme connecting both serious and comedic shows—the ambivalent prospect of parenting a child—and reflect on how these shows stage decisions over reproductive control in the context of relationship power dynamics.

In "A Romantic Steroid or a Great Performance? Visual Culture and the Pill," Jamie Wagman analyzes birth control pill advertisements in the United States from the 1960s to today, charting a shift in visual rhetoric of the pill as "romantic" and liberating to feminine, infantile, or sexy. While early images depict a clinical environment without women's bodies, later images caricaturize white women's sexuality. This analysis of the visual culture of birth control pill marketing illuminates the ways in which the pill stood for contrasting symbols that helped shape a national understanding of birth control and women's physical embodiment. The final piece in Part 1, Manon S. Parry's "Sex Education and Social Media: Contraception in the Digital Age," considers how family planning promoters are using new digital platforms such as websites, Twitter, and SMS messaging to circumvent censorship and controversy and to reach young people. This essay examines how the Internet is transforming not only the form but also the content of contraceptive media, as the diffusion of material online shifts from informing to exchanging. Increasingly, contraceptive users are being reimagined, no longer seen as passive audiences in need of professional advice, but as individuals with experiences that also constitute a form of expertise.

Reproductive rights encompass a woman's right to control her fertility using contraception, to end pregnancy with abortion, to choose when to have children, and to keep them. Part 2, "Stories of Forced Adoption," focuses on the denial of these rights through state mechanisms of forced adoption and how they frame judgments of women. Regina Range probes the oeuvre of Gina Kaus (1893–1985), an Austrian-Jewish novelist, dramatist, essayist, and screenwriter, in "In Search of the New Woman and the Best Mother: Unwanted Pregnancy in Gina Kaus' Literary and Filmic Work." Kaus' work explored themes of gender inequality, reproductive rights, adoption, and motherhood. Range analyzes the trajectory of this writing to trace a discourse of reproductive rights and social attitudes in the mid–1920s Vienna magazine *Die Mutter* (*The Mother*), the 1927 play *Toni*, the film script *All Children* (1949), and the 1950 Hollywood melodrama *Three Secrets*. These works explore the responses of state institutions and individual women to unwanted pregnancy, adoption, and motherhood. In their essay, Kirsten E. Kumpf Baele and Sofie Decock analyze a 2012 Belgian film portraying an involuntary adoption scheme for unwed mothers in Belgium in the 1970s. "Pregnant Girls in the Attic—No Choices: An Analysis of Patrice Toye's *Little Black Spiders*" offers a brief overview of international involuntary adoption and "child removal" policies as well as recent films and books that bring light to this practice before turning to an analysis of Toye's 2012 *Little Black Spiders*. The authors demonstrate how Toye's choices underline the naiveté, imagination, and self-discovery of adolescence even in the dark circumstance of sexual oppression, religious intolerance, and control of the female body. These works exhume the hidden stories of women and girls denied reproductive rights, their choices stripped by social authority and custom, pressured to give up their child for adoption, and the means they employ to resist.

In Part 3, "From Unplanned to Planned Pregnancies," continues this exploration of rights, autonomy, and identity. In "From Unwanted to Wanted Pregnancy: Pregnancy, Abortion and the End of the GDR in the Film *Jana and Jan* (1992)," Belinda Carstens-Wickham examines a film set in a youth detention center during the last months of the German Democratic Republic. Contextualizing the film in the history of East German social policy and cultural attitudes toward unmarried pregnancy, contraception, abortion, sexuality, and gender roles, the essay offers a close reading of not only the film's exploration of rights for marginalized youth, but for the future of a newly unified nation. In "Finding Humor in Birth Control: Fiction and Film from Hugh Mills to Matthias Schweighöfer," Waltraud Maierhofer investigates representative works of 20th- and early 21st-century writing and film that take a lighter approach to birth control: the British novel *Prudence and the Pill* (1966), the Croatian film *Svecenikova djeca* (*The Priest's Children*, 2013), the 2011 American independent romantic comedy *The Pill* directed by J.C. Khoury, and the German film *Vaterfreuden* (*Joys of Fatherhood*, 2014). This essay asks whether such humorous depictions of failed birth control represent part of a backlash against the acceptance of birth control in the West or rather postmodern, lighter approaches to telling stories which include those of unintended pregnancies but also of desperately wanted parenthood.

The next part is "Abortion Across Cultures: Reproductive Choice, Duty or Crime." Waltraud Maierhofer discusses film and social media in "When Abortion Was Illegal: Remembrance and Advocacy in Recent Films from Romania and Mexico—and 'I Had an Abortion' Storytelling on the Web." She examines several recent films on abortion, focusing on the 2007 Romanian film *4 luni, 3 săptămâni și 2 zile* (*4 Months, 3 Weeks and 2 Days*) and two 2002 Mexican films, *El Crimen del Padre Amaro* (*The Crime of Father Amaro*) and *Punto y Aparte* (*Fresh Start*). These films use various techniques to raise issues of reproductive rights, including women's access to contraception and abortion. Maierhofer ends with an outlook to a new form of personal storytelling: women using the web to share their abortion stories, a new medium for global advocacy and access. Shelley W. Chan's "The Forbidden Pregnancy and the Abandoned Children: On Mo Yan's Fiction about the One-Child Policy and Abortion in China" was originally offered as a keynote address at the "Pill and Pen" symposium. Chan considers how 2012 Nobel Prize in Literature winner Mo Yan weaves China's One-Child Policy into his fiction. Through the themes of abandoned children, unplanned birth, and forced abortion, Yan explores the effects of the One-Child Policy. The essay culminates in an interpretation of *Frog* (2009, English translation 2015) as a political allegory for China's lost youth.

This volume's final part, "Legacies," contains two essays that discuss the lasting legacies of two important figures in the history of reproductive rights and the birth control pill. In "Woman Rebel: Margaret Sanger and American Popular Culture," Beth Widmaier Capo examines the split legacy of the leader of the American birth control movement, Margaret Sanger, as a feminist crusader for reproductive rights and as a racist eugenicist. Examining depictions in recent fiction, film, television, and graphic novels, the essay parses the ways various representations reproduce Sanger as a cultural icon and symbol malleable enough to serve divergent political and ideological positions. The final contribution by Walter Grünzweig, "From the Pill to the Pen to the Pill, Again: Carl Djerassi's Discursive Constructions of Birth Control," analyzes the Austrian-American chemist-turned-author's nonfiction writing for its usage of surprising metaphoric discourse of the pill. Djerassi, the "father of the pill," was a strong proponent of reproductive rights throughout his long career. His keynote address at the "Pill and Pen" symposium at the University of Iowa is representative of his active involvement until his death in educating the public about birth control and its interrelation with population demographics and political issues such as global health and migration. The piece concludes with Grünzweig's translation of an article Djerassi published in the leading Austrian daily newspaper, *Der Standard*, reacting to gains by the Austrian right-wing Freedom Party, as well as Djerassi's "Rebuttal" to a piece that misinterpreted Djerassi's stance on contraception, and a small translated selection of verbatim online comments that were posted immediately following the publication of the article.

The wide-ranging essays in this volume provide valuable insights into the many ways reproductive rights are reflected in film, television, and other popular media around the world, and how these representations influence wider debates and attitudes.

NOTES

    1. See Chan and Maierhofer, "When Abortion Was Illegal" in this volume.
    2. See Capo in this volume.
    3. This includes the right to choose to reproduce as well as the right to limit or end reproduction; for instance, poor and minority women in the U.S. have been coerced into taking contraception, and some women charged with drug use or child abuse have been offered long-lasting contraception as an alternative sentence to jail time, thereby denying their rights to reproduce (see ACLU). Similar measures have been suggested in Australia (see Medhora).
    4. This conference was sponsored by the Division of World Languages, Literatures, and Cultures; the departments of German, Chemistry, Cinematic Arts, Pharmacology, and Gender, Women, and Sexuality Studies; Global Health Studies Program; the Obermann Center for Advanced Studies; the Center for Human Rights; the Center for Asian and Pacific Studies; the College of Liberal Arts and Sciences; the Honors Program; and International Programs at the University of Iowa. It was organized by Waltraud Maierhofer (German; University of Iowa), Walter Grünzweig (American Studies and Comparative Literature; University of Dortmund, Germany); Elizabeth Heineman (History and Gender, Women, and Sexuality Studies; University of Iowa), and Steve Choe (Cinema Arts; University of Iowa).
    5. See Grünzweig in this volume.
    6. Sanger opened her first birth control clinic in the Brownsville neighborhood of New York City on October 16, 1916, and Planned Parenthood used this event to mark its 100th anniversary. See also Crockett on Margaret Sanger's grandson, Alexander Sanger, and Planned Parenthood.
    7. On fiction and/or film, see Boswell, Capo, Craig, Weingarten, Wilson, and Wilt. On media, see Parry. On contraceptive practices internationally, see Russell et al.

WORKS CITED

ACLU. "Norplant: A New Contraceptive with the Potential for Abuse." *ACLU: American Civil Liberties Union*. ACLU, 2016. Web. 26 Oct. 2016.
Adams, Stephen. "'Male Pill' Moves a Step Closer: British Scientists Discover Way to Stop Sperm Swimming—and Men Could Take It Just Before Sex." *The Daily Mail*. Daily Mail, Associated Newspapers, 22 Oct. 2016. Web. 24 Oct. 2016.
Boseley, Sarah. "Irish Women Report Relief and Gratitude After Using Abortion Pills." *The Guardian*. Guardian News and Media, 17 Oct. 2016. Web. 21 Oct. 2016.

8 Introduction

Boswell, Parley Ann. *Pregnancy in Literature and Film.* Jefferson, NC: McFarland, 2014. Print.
Bradley, Laura. "*Jane the Virgin* Has Set Itself Up for the Perfect Abortion Storyline, But Will It Go There?" *Vanity Fair.* Condé Nast, 17 May 2016. Web. 26 Oct. 2016.
Capo, Beth Widmaier. *Textual Contraception: Birth Control and Modern American Fiction.* Columbus: Ohio State University Press, 2007. Print.
Craig, Layne Parish. *When Sex Changed: Birth Control Politics and Literature Between the World Wars.* New Brunswick: Rutgers University Press, 2013. Print.
Crockett, Emily. "Margaret Sanger's Grandson Hopes for a Future Where We Don't Need Planned Parenthood." *Vox.* Vox Media, Inc., 16 Oct. 2016. Web. 24 Oct. 2016.
Diacono, Tim. "Updated: Medicines Authority Chief Urges Mater Dei to Stock Emergency Contraception for Rape Victims." *Malta Today.* MediaToday, 22 Oct. 2016. Web. 24 Oct. 2016.
Eleftheriou-Smith, Loulla-Mae. "Polish Abortion Protests: Women Dress in Black and Take to Streets to March Against New Restrictive Proposals." *Independent.* Independent, 24 Oct. 2016. Web. 25 Oct. 2016.
Gunter, Jennifer. "Donald Trump Confuses Birth with Abortion. And No, There Are No Ninth Month Abortions." *Huffington Post.* TheHuffingtonPost, 20 Oct. 2016. Web. 21 Oct. 2016.
Guttmacher Institute. "Unintended Pregnancy in the United States." *Guttmacher Institute.* Guttmacher Institute, 2016. Web. 18 Oct. 2016.
Hilliard, Robert L., and Michael C. Keith. *Dirty Discourse: Sex and Indecency in Broadcasting.* Malden, MA: Wiley Blackwell, 2008. Print.
Lil' Kim. "Don't Mess with Me." Written by Cliff Wade, Deric Michael Angelettie, Geoff Gill, Kanye O. West, Kimberly Jones. The Notorious K.I.M. 2000. *Lyrics.* STANDS4 Network, 2016. Web. 25 Oct. 2016.
Marrone, Katherine. "State Programs Take the Lead on Long-Acting Birth Control." *Bitch Magazine* 72 (Fall 2016): 5. Print.
Medhora, Shalailah. "Welfare Recipients Should Be Forced to Take Birth Control, Says Ex-Labor MP." *The Guardian.* Guardian News and Media Limited, 29 Dec. 2014. Web. 26 Oct. 2016.
McFadden, Robert D. "Carl Djerassi, 91, a Creator of the Birth Control Pill, Dies." *New York Times.* New York Times, 31 Jan. 2015. Web. 18 Oct. 2016.
Minaj, Nikki. "I'm Legit." Written by Ciara Princess Harris et al. Pink Friday: Roman Reloaded Re-Up. 2012. *Lyrics.* STANDS4 Network, 2016. Web. 25 Oct. 2016.
Olowolagba, Fikayo. "Surviving Recession: Aregbesola Tells Nigerians to Practice Birth Control, Shun Foreign Goods." *Daily Post Nigeria.* Daily Post Nigeria, 21 Oct. 2016. Web. 24 Oct. 2016.
Parry, Manon. *Broadcasting Birth Control: Mass Media and Family Planning.* New Brunswick: Rutgers University Press, 2013. Print.
Riddle, John M. *Contraception and Abortion from the Ancient World to the Renaissance.* Cambridge: Harvard University Press, 1992. Print.
Rosenberg, Alyssa. "The Contraception Debate and Pop Culture's Weird Silence on Birth Control." *ThinkProgress.* Think Progress, 17 Feb. 2012. Web. 24 Oct. 2016.
Russell, Andrew, Mary Thompson, and Elisa J. Sobo, eds. *Contraception Across Cultures: Technologies, Choices, Constraints.* New York: Bloomsbury Academic, 2000. Print.
Sanger, Margaret. "A Parents' Problem or Woman's?" *Birth Control Review* Mar. 1919: 6–7. *The Margaret Sanger Papers Project.* The Margaret Sanger Papers, New York University, 2003. Web. 17 Oct. 2016.
Seltzer, Sarah. "Why Aren't There More Depictions of Birth Control in Pop Culture?" *Flavorwire.* Flavorpill Media, 23 June 2015. Web. 24 Oct. 2016.
Tavernise, Sabrina. "Colorado's Effort Against Teenage Pregnancies Is a Startling Success." *New York Times.* New York Times, 5 July 2015. Web. 24 Oct. 2016.
Thompson, Derek. "The Pill, the Condom, and the American Dream." *The Atlantic.* The Atlantic Monthly Group, 31 Aug. 2016. Web. 2 Sept. 2016.
United Nations Department of Economic and Social Affairs Population Division. "Reproductive Rights." *United Nations.* United Nations, 2016. Web. 26 Oct. 2016.

_____. "Trends in Contraceptive Use Worldwide 2015." *United Nations*. United Nations, 2015. Web. 26 Oct. 2016. PDF.
Weingarten, Karen. *Abortion in the American Imagination: Before Life and Choice, 1880–1940*. New Brunswick: Rutgers University Press, 2014. Print.
Wilson, Aimee Armand. *Conceived in Modernism: The Aesthetics and Politics of Birth Control*. New York: Bloomsbury Academic, 2015. Print.
Wilt, Judith. *Abortion, Choice, and Contemporary Fiction: The Armageddon of the Maternal Instinct*. Chicago: University of Chicago Press, 1990. Print.

PART 1. CONTRACEPTIVES IN THE MEDIA:
SPREADING THE STORY

Propagating Progress and Circumventing Harm
Reconciling References to Contraceptives in British Television and Cinema of the 1960s

JESSICA BORGE

When the pill was made available in 1961, Britain was already experiencing a shift in social and cultural life. The nascent oral contraceptive contributed to newly-opened conversations about family planning as part of this shift, but it also coincided with a new, exciting era in the public consumption of information via screen media. Television ownership boomed in the 1950s and the BBC monopoly on broadcasting was broken by the 1955 launch of the commercial channel ITV. National coverage expanded to 95 percent (Hand 5). Conversely, as subject matter expanded, cinema audiences reduced in number (Docherty 3). The progressive ex-educator John Trevelyan was installed as the secretary of the British Board of Film Censors (BBFC) in 1958. Thereafter, sexuality-driven content in the cinema pushed against traditionally enforced (but unwritten) codes, pressing certification to its limits. Despite financial difficulties in the industry, historians feel this period marked a "coming out" of intimate life in British film (Hargreaves 53). However, despite the progressive intent of many filmmakers and broadcasters, tension over the depiction and discussion of intimate matters remained. Notwithstanding the gradual proliferation of topics tangential to contraception in the mass media (such as abortion and marriage), the question of reproductive rights in the period before the British Women's Liberation Movement took shape was given less priority than the possible isolation of viewer groups through offense, or the likelihood of harm done to vulnerable youth.

This essay unpacks the intent behind the reserve practiced in 1960s British screen media by triangulating contraception, television, and film. In so doing it contributes to growing interest in the depiction and citation of reproductive issues in time-based visual media, which, as well as this volume, includes recently published work (Parry) and symposia ("Pill and Pen," University of Iowa, 7–9 March 2014; "Reproduction on Film," Cambridge, 23–25 October 2015). While this essay acknowledges the richness of new conversations about reproduction in visual cultures, it does not aim to unpack contraception, television, and film in a strictly cultural sense. Rather, it investigates case studies of contraception dealt with on screen from the speculative position of contemporary censors and regulators, using contemporary evidence relating to regulatory codes, broadcasts and feature films, and primary source material from the Family Planning Association (FPA) and BBFC archives. The first section deals with television. It offers much needed clarification on how contraception was controlled by discussing advertising regulation in the first instance, before moving on to a case study of the first TV documentary on oral contraception. The second section examines censorial practices in relation to the filmmaking process before discussing two case studies using evidence from the BBFC Archive.

Restrictive practices that were applied to the 1960s British screen are often colored as stemming from an essential censorial fear of moral degradation (Thompson; Aldgate). This essay takes the overall view that TV and film censorship and regulation operated not so much on a moral model at this time but rather a utilitarian one and that, as such, censorial and regulatory decisions made over the appearance and indeed non-appearance of contraceptives should be re-evaluated. New insights explain how contraception itself was appraised in terms of an imagined impact on viewers and audiences, and, significantly, how this shaped the representation of contraceptives on screen.

Television

TV Advertising

From the beginning of independent television broadcasting in the United Kingdom in 1955 to the AIDS crisis in the 1980s, contraceptives were barred from brand advertising on screen. The prohibition was first outlined in *Principles for Television Advertising*, 1955 (reproduced in Gantzias, Appendix 2). *Principles* was the first formal code governing practice for what was then a brand-new commercial publicity medium (Payne). In the code, contraceptives were cited alongside products and services deemed unacceptable for TV advertising, including moneylenders, matrimonial agencies, fortune-tellers, undertakers, gambling tipsters, unlicensed unemployment bureau, slimming or bust development aids, smoking cures, and products for the treatment of alcoholism.[1] The code incorporated a supplement related to medical advertising. The Advertising Advisory Committee (formed to devise *Principles*) was required by the 1954 Television Act to include among its members experts on medical advertising (Paulu 68). In practice, this medical component was represented as an appendix to the code, which reproduced the British Code of Standards in Relation to the Advertising of Medicines and Treatments and, after 1961, in the British Code of Advertising Practice (BCAP), which also guided non-screen media (reproduced in Wilson 203–19). The appendix restated the unsuitability of contraceptive advertising, this time conflating birth control with contact lenses, scalp clinics, and hemorrhoid treatments. Contraception was therefore doubly classified for television advertising. On the one hand, it was an unregulated, non-medical service like fortune-telling.[2] On the other, it was a medical item vulnerable to misuse or used to exploit persons who were themselves vulnerable in the manner of quack medicines, such as cancer cures. Either way, contraception was construed as potentially harmful and not within the remit of responsible television advertising.

Under section 4 (5) of the Television Act, classes of advertisements prohibited from broadcast advertising were established in consultation with the postmaster-general (Gantzias 324). Lists of prohibited items were also arrived at by speculation over potential audience attitudes. As decreed by the act, the Independent Television Authority (ITA) was required to ensure that any programs broadcast did not "offend against taste and decency, encourage crime or disorder, offend public feelings or refer offensively to any living person" (Lloyd 167). The medical component, which prohibited televisual recommendations of over-the-counter products by doctors or by persons appearing as doctors, was concerned with the prevention of harm. The BCAP cited the Independent Code of Advertising Standards and Practice, which laid out the remit for harm prevention under "Medicines and Treatments" as "the harm to the individual that may result from exaggerated, misleading or unwarranted claims" (Wilson 211). Certain of the medically-oriented prophylactic measures also had a statutory basis. For example, the 1941 Pharmacy and Medicines Act made it an offense to advertise anywhere articles which purported to treat incurable diseases (Wilson 216–17). The 1917 Venereal Diseases Act made it an offense "to advertise in any way any preparation or substance of any kind as a medicine for the prevention, cure or relief of venereal diseases" (Wilson 203–19).[3] These legal statutes were therefore necessarily included in television advertising regulation.

As the first TV advertising code pre-dated the general availability of pharmaceutical contraception, it initially referenced mechanical and chemical contraceptives, which included condoms, caps, creams, vaginal pessaries, and foams. The sale, advertising, or distribution of such contraceptives was not illegal in mid-century Britain, despite earlier attempts to restrict it (Jones; Borge). Benevolent provision was made by the FPA and Marie Stopes clinics (the equivalent of Planned Parenthood clinics), but most contraceptives were distributed commercially by retail channels such as mail order, in vending machines, in specialist surgical or rubber stores, in barbershops, and in pharmacies which chose to stock them (Peel and Potts 58). Thus it was commercially-retailed contraceptives that were initially prohibited from being advertised in the mainstream and on television. The oral contraceptive "pill," available from 1961, was not an over-the-counter contraceptive but a prescription-only (Rx) medication. As such, the Association of the British Pharmaceutical Industry's Code of Marketing Practice already covered it for Medical Specialties (1958). The ABPI was a lobbying group and a self-regulating body made up of ethical pharmaceutical manufacturers. In the voluntary code, manufacturers elected not to advertise Rx medicines directly to the public, meaning the organization had itself already curtailed the possibility of advertising the pill on domestic television screens or to non-medical audiences.

Factual TV

Although contraceptives could not be advertised on television, free discussion of birth control as a philosophy and practice was permitted, providing brand names were avoided outside of news programming. In 1958, for example, ITV screened two factual pieces relating to birth control, *Sex Education* and *Unmarried Mothers*. Far from being an anathema to broadcast, contraception was regarded as central to the public interest trend for discussing love and marriage. Indeed, this viewpoint was actively encouraged by the FPA, whose Public Relations Sub-Committee tracked mass media coverage and sought to create new publicity opportunities for the cause by badgering television companies, as my dissertation investigates in detail. Coverage occurred in tandem with the staggered roll out of the pill in the UK, which saw early private prescriptions available from January 1961, restricted National Health Service availability from October that year, and distribution through FPA clinics the following January. The decision to include discussion of contraceptives was essentially a matter for producers and networks, who weighed each case against the likely public response and were influenced by social organizations with a stake in public discussion.

TV Case Study: *The Pill* (1961)

Oral contraceptives had been investigated in newspapers and on radio before the first television documentary, *The Pill*, was broadcast from Granada's Manchester studios on June 28, 1961. Transcripts were circulated in advance, and the ITA pre-approved the script (see Granada TV). The peak-time program was offered to all 13 regional broadcasters on option but was rejected at the last minute by Anglia, Southern, Westward, and Ulster. Tom Merrin, of the *Daily Sketch*, attributed refusals to a 40 percent Catholic audience (Ulster) and the likelihood of teenagers watching (Anglia), while Marc Alexander reported in *Television Mail* that Southern had not received their transcript in time and that Westward simply had nothing to say on the matter whatsoever. Viewer-wise, there was scant evidence of actual offense or harm following broadcast. Granada claimed a zero complaint rate, while the BBC's Television House noted, "We had only one call from a man in Ipswich—complaining that the program wasn't screened in his area" (Merrin). Industry-wise, *The Pill* was viewed as a *coup d'état*. Commentators saw fit to imbue the technologically-sophisticated pill with the qualities of television, the new modern medium, and vice versa. "Good for ITV and good for Granada," Alexander wrote; "the vitality of television depends on programs such as this." Merrin was equally captivated, saying, "The most impressive thing about this extremely well-researched program was that it shows the importance of TV in reaching a mass audience." Regional stations may have been wary of audience rebellion, but *The Pill* proved a successful test for what would become a common object of discussion on British television.

The Pill was formatted around a studio-based discussion featuring celebrities and commentators from the birth control world, including Gregory Pincus, Griselda Rowntree, and the FPA's Eleanor Mears. In the interests of presenting an ostensibly balanced debate, it also included a psychiatrist, an endocrinologist, a fertility specialist, and "mothers from Birmingham and London" supplied from the FPA's clinical trials (Granada 2). *The Pill* benefitted the non-profit and socially-interested FPA by giving it an inexpensive means of platforming its position on contraception which, as well as being respected, was woman-led and feminist (Cook 275–77). Following the program, it recruited 150 volunteers for London pill trials and received 50 enquiries from doctors. It had also sold Granada 35 feet of live sperm footage for £8.15 (Granada TV and FPA, Correspondence). However, it should be noted that commercial manufacturers, such as the London Rubber Company (Britain's biggest condom maker), were and would continue to be excluded from TV debate. This was because the direct representation of commercial enterprises on TV, particularly those who made well-known brands of contraceptives such as Durex, could easily be construed as advertising. While the FPA went on to act as a TV consultant for oral contraceptive matters, commercial companies (and their customers) remained disbarred (Borge).

In the decade following Granada's program, televisual discussion of contraceptives and related issues, such as abortion, marriage, and teenage sex, increased year after year. Contemporary listings in *Radio Times* and *TV Times* show that the conversation was, broadly speaking, divided into news coverage, factual discussion, and, by the early 1970s, pedagogically-oriented debates about the nature and future of sex education. As historians have noted, the pill provided a particularly useful proxy for discussing sexual matters, removed as it was from the outward functions of the body (Asbell xvi, Cook 48). This facet, which was not shared by other contraceptives, greatly added to the pill's TV-friendly persona as it did not particularly conjure up intimate bodily imagery.

Film

The Certification Process

There was no concrete ban on referencing contraceptives in the British cinema. Unlike its Hollywood counterpart, the Motion Picture Association of America, the BBFC did not follow a written production code in the 1960s. Rather, the British censor's purpose was to assess films on their own merits and make individual recommendations. This process took into account the cumulative effect of various filmic components in the treatment of subject matter, such as film style, genre, interpretation (including the quality or stature of casting, direction, or screenwriting), target audience, and precedents set elsewhere in the arts. Classification, sometimes called "certification" or "rating," was the system used to sort films following consideration of the above criteria. A certificate was essentially a permit that allowed entry to a film screening based on a person's age and implied capacity for dealing with content. The certificate was not so much a means of inflicting moral conformity upon audiences, although this inevitably happened, but a way of protecting the film industry from criticism and enabling distributors to target screenings. During the 1960s, three certificates were used: "U" for Universal (suitable for all), "A" for Adult (prohibiting unaccompanied children) and "X" for age 16 and up. In 1970, the age for an "X" was raised to 18, and an "AA" rating, for those aged between 14 and 18, was added.

The problem with British cinema in the 1960s was that attendance was at a record low, meaning it was difficult to make money from films (Docherty 29). The group most likely to attend cinemas on a regular basis was the newly-affluent teenager (Barclay Committee 13). Attracting and retaining teenagers was therefore essential for sustaining film production and exhibition, meaning that an A-rated film (or AA from 1970) was more likely to repay investors. The X certificate was a riskier bet, but it had the advantage of buffering the Board against criticism when dealing with colorful material. This contrary state of affairs and the focus on films for children led to much tension between producers and the Board, particularly when sex reared its inquisitive head. As it stood, classification was a long and involved process, although it was designed to aid producers rather than to hinder them. Advance scripts were assessed prior to production with the view that producers might avoid the unnecessary expense of shooting scenes that would inevitably be cut. Completed films would then be viewed and certificated, subject to further changes as deemed necessary. The BBFC's censors, which included women, would file reports independently and make recommendations, which were confirmed by a senior examiner.

BBFC's Remit as Censor

The BBFC was a non-governmental regulator funded by the film industry through fees charged for the Board's services. Though obliged to comply with the law, the BBFC was ostensibly free in its censorial capacity to classify films in line with industrial or societal change, as was the case under the leadership of John Trevelyan, BBFC secretary from 1959 to 1971. Under Trevelyan, the Board was packaged as a utilitarian rather than proselytizing overseer. For example, although the early 1960s witnessed a number of sensational landmark cases relevant to the public consumption of sexuality such as the *Lady Chatterley* obscenity trial and the Profumo scandal, the BBFC's official position on moral outrage was dispassionate. Trevelyan insisted that the Board "could not assume responsibility for the guardianship of public morality, or refuse for exhibition films that contravened the accepted moral code" ("The 1960s and Liberalisation"). In 1958, Trevelyan laid out the BBFC's remit in lieu of an official code of practice: "Can the Board's policy be defined? I think it can. I would say that in censoring films the board tries to reflect intelligent public opinion as far as it can be judged, and tries to avoid the showing on cinema screens of anything that might do positive harm, especially to children and young people, anything that might be likely to offend or disgust reasonable people" (Aldgate 38).

Trevelyan saw the Board as both an advisor for the film industry (guiding producers away from unnecessary expense or litigation) and as an intermediary for the protection of audiences from exposure to harmful material, which might psychologically impair individuals, or inspire them to harm themselves or others (Braden). While the BBC was chartered to inform and educate and had a responsibility to report on current affairs, the BBFC was under no obligation to provide a sounding board for social organizations such as the FPA, or to other stakeholders in reproductive or sexual rights. By the same token, any rejection of contraceptive references (below) could not be made on a moral basis alone. In the light of the increasingly permissive arts and entertainment environment, which provided a backdrop to creative industry in the 1960s, a utilitarian stance on progressive matters could be considered a form of censorial oppression. On the other hand, it might also be interpreted as a means of preserving liberties that already existed. Recourse to John Stuart Mill's Harm Principle offers an alternative interpretation for the BBFC's behavior in respect to contraceptives. According to Mill, "the only purpose for which power can be rightfully exercised over any member of a civilized community, against his will, is to prevent harm to others" (8). In practice, Trevelyan's application of the Harm Principle, or an unspecified proxy thereof, intermingled with overseeing the commercial interests of film producers and kept the Board's public image intact. The difficulty here was that while damage to the individual productions was predictable to a degree, injury to living, breathing audiences was less easy to measure or foresee. Combined with the absence of a defined code, this meant that, under Trevelyan's reign, the censorial process was necessarily speculative.

Tension over potential harm is especially apparent in the treatment of contraception in 1960s British film. This is partially because of the low incidence of contraceptive referencing in films during Trevelyan's administration. Contraception was a problematic theme for BBFC examiners and producers alike, as correspondence and examiners reports for each film in the BBFC Archive reveal. Examiners were opinionated about the social role of film as a medium for representing personal intimacy, which reflected a common view that reproductive agency was a private choice rather than a human right. In particular, there was a concern that imitation of free sexual behavior could put teenagers at risk.[4] Producers who dared tackle birth control increased the precariousness of their investment because, code or no code, the discussion or depiction of contraceptive practice usually resulted in a precautionary X certificate, excluding the biggest audience group from their films.

FILM CASE STUDY: *A KIND OF LOVING* (UK, 1962)

The precedent for including contraception in British film narratives was set with *A Kind of Loving*, the first British feature to make explicit reference to condoms. The foundation text, Stan Barstow's original 1960 novel of the same name, had been a literary hit. Following on the coattails of the X-rated 1959 feature *Room at the Top*, which had courted controversy over extramarital sex scenes but was still a resounding international success, the producer of *Loving*, Joseph Janni, felt that a film version of the new novel should be hastened. "I liked this book," Janni wrote to Trevelyan in October 1961, "because though it may not appear to be another Room at the Top, for a change it is not a story of a rebellious young man but about normal, decent youngsters."

Loving details the awkward coupling of a young draughtsman, Victor (Alan Bates), and a typist, Ingrid (June Ritchie), who work in the same Northern factory. In the film's most famous scene, Vic attempts to purchase condoms in a chemist's shop in anticipation of sex with Ingrid but, confronted with a female counter assistant, fails to make the crucial purchase. Later, on the brink of their first sexual union on her mother's sofa, Ingrid asks, breathlessly, "Did you get anything, you know…?" Vic replies, "No, I couldn't." "We'd better not go too far then," says Ingrid. Inevitably, the pair *do* go too far, resulting in a cloud of post-coital gloom, an unexpected pregnancy, hasty nuptials, and a rocky start to married life further overshadowed by a disappointed and protective mother-in-law (Thora Hird).

Files in the BBFC Archive describe a production that was both refreshingly frank and peppered with problems, not least of which was the inclusion of young people discussing and purchasing contraceptives. Neither Trevelyan nor Janni had been under the illusion that *Loving* would secure anything other than an X certificate due to its sexual content. But in the early 1960s, the X had already broken its limits with *Room at the Top* and *Saturday Night and Sunday Morning*, which both foregrounded older women enjoying extramarital sex with younger men. Contraception, it seemed, represented one step too far. Trevelyan repeatedly expressed concern that "once a door opens, it is difficult to close it again" (Braden; Trevelyan), and the birth control door, it was felt, should remain firmly locked. In November 1961, Trevelyan warned Janni: "I am worried about the introduction of contraceptives into films. You think that this can be done in a way that is quite acceptable and inoffensive, and you may be right, but, after further discussion with our Examiners, I think it is likely that we shall find this material unacceptable."

The suggested cut was highly problematic as Vic's intention to prevent a pregnancy is of pivotal import to the narrative, setting up the entire second half. Via the chemist's shop scene, contraception and sex are inextricably linked with fatalism; failure to manage contraception in the inevitable act of pre-marital lovemaking is posited so as to determine the course of the characters' future lives. For Victor, lack of reproductive agency leads ultimately to emasculation and humiliation as a trapped husband. For Ingrid who, in common with many pre–Liberation women, "adopted a sexual identity which prized sexual innocence and passivity" (Fisher 200), instant pregnancy and marriage removes the courtship ritual and theoretically places her in Vic's guardianship. Nonetheless, despite the centrality of the chemist's shop scene, the BBFC persistently asked for it (and any other mention of contraceptives) to be removed (BBFC and *A Kind of Loving*).

The first *Loving* screenplay was submitted to the BBFC for comments in February 1961. By October, Trevelyan cut the line "I've got this bint all lined up, and she's all ready for it. Only I don't want to take any risks" from the screenplay. By November he had stressed categorically, "We would not be prepared to have any talk or action about the purchase of contraceptives."

The feeling that contraception was an unacceptable subject matter for the medium of film was prevalent at the BBFC at this time. One censor felt that "what can be done in a book … may not come off on the screen" while another, after viewing a cut of the film in February 1962, expressed concern that "there is a limit to the intimacy the screen should pry upon between lovers." Trevelyan agreed with his examiners overall. Though feeling that the basic story was acceptable, he firmly felt that "there are several things in ordinary human life, and in normal conversation, that would be unacceptable for a film shown under the conditions of public entertainment." Contraceptive practice was evidently one of them. BBFC examiners felt an X certificate for *Loving* would protect young people from what was likely a "dangerous and irresponsible" filmic discussion about sex. To modern eyes, "offense," "embarrassment," "unsuitability for the medium," and "danger to young people" seem like sentententious reasons for attempting to cut contraception from *Loving*. For future BBFC examiners classifying the first home video release in 1988, it was the very *absence* of truthful scenes about contraceptive practice that appeared irresponsible. However, in terms of harm prevention in the early 1960s, offense and embarrassment might equally be read as the possibility for audiences to leave the film with incorrect and potentially injurious misinformation.

Unlike television programs of the time, which dealt with contraception in a factual way in viewers' own living rooms, the BBFC image of narrative film was an entertainment that was enjoyed away from home and in mixed company. As such, narrative films were unlikely to include a summation of the facts and fallacies of contraceptives at some strategic point, or to present balanced testimony from experts as factual television programs attempted to. It was also no secret that the cinema was the site of many young persons' pre-marital sexual experiences. In 1965, teenagers purchased 28 percent of all cinema admissions, and 51 percent of teenagers' first dates were at cinemas. Eighteen percent had their first sexual kiss in a cinema, and there was a strong correlation between sexual activity and teenagers attending with a steady partner (Schofield 25, 57, 143). Trevelyan felt that teenaged audiences might feel acute embarrassment at consuming risqué storylines in public spaces where they might also feel pressured to have sex (Braden).

Trevelyan was keenly aware of how media and messages define one another. He was also aware of what Marshall McLuhan would later call "the personal and social consequences of any medium" (McLuhan 7). "It's perfectly true," said Trevelyan in 1958, "that things have been shown on television that would not have been passed in a film to be shown in a public cinema, although I believe that most things have a lesser impact on the small television screen in the home than they would have on the large screens of cinemas with a crowd of people producing a mass response" (Aldgate 38). In this sense, the medium dictated the format, which, in the treatment of contraception, was as different as night and day for television and film. If film entertainments were interrupted by embarrassment or outrage or excessive pleasure (all factors potentially enhanced by the narrative shape, size, and public circumstances of a feature film), then information that might be applied in real life situations could become blunted, incomplete, or corrupted.

In the case of *Loving*, the result could be that the lessons of a failure to use contraception might be missed. Thinking speculatively, as censors necessarily did, even if the film was absorbed and understood on a completely rational level by intelligent, reasonable, and engaged audiences, this in itself could lead to the conclusion that, had Vic been able to procure condoms, all might have been well. This duplicitously suggests that sex is devoid of the potential for physical or psychological harm providing that pregnancy is avoided, while also reinforcing the message that store-bought contraceptives guaranteed the prevention of pregnancy. In fact, British condoms were not regulated until the 1964 British Standard 3704. This is not to say they were unreliable, but rather that there were known variations in quality. The FPA Archive at the Wellcome Library, London, contains numerous complaints about broken condoms. It was also possible to purchase low grades of product, which were perhaps not quite as reliable as more expensive items. Le Brasseur Surgical Manufacturing Company, for example, sold a "Third Quality" product under its Perfection brand (Consumer's Association 40). While some couples enjoyed the "surprise" element of unplanned pregnancies (Fisher 92, 108), this could hardly be encouraged for unmarried youngsters in a society mostly intolerant of abortion and single parenthood (Thane and Evans 121), and where teenage gonorrhea was on the increase (Hall 152).

Despite repeatedly requesting changes, the BBFC passed the producer's cut of *Loving*, including two contraceptive references they had wanted removed. Joseph Janni and director John Schlesinger essentially ignored the Board's warnings and produced the screenplay largely as planned. A complete cut was screened for the Board in February 1962, and the censors were converted by the film's "exceptional mood." Although still mildly concerned about partial nudity and vomiting, examiners "agreed that this was an exceptional British Picture." In any event, *Loving* did not open the floodgates to voluminous depictions of contraceptives in British cinema. In line with the trend for realist adaptations, films that sought to include reference to conception control usually included frank sexual content or discussion, which attracted X classifications anyway.[5] Although the Board's overarching embargo against the introduction of contraception into films had been somewhat nullified with *Loving*, a cautionary attitude against pushing the limits of certification remained among filmmakers.

22   Part 1. Contraceptives in the Media

FILM CASE STUDY: *PRUDENCE AND THE PILL* (UK/USA, 1968)

Prudence, a lavishly produced comedy starring Deborah Kerr, David Niven, and Judy Geeson, was the first British feature film to deal with oral contraceptives. The plot revolves around several interconnected couples, detailing their extra-marital affairs, pre-marital sex, pill-swapping, and, ultimately, a clutch of happy accidents in the shape of several bonnie babies. As Ian Wright commented in the *Guardian* in 1968, "It is a conclusion that a cardinal could not object to: the pill is plainly seen not to prevail." Hugh Mills, who wrote the original novel, claimed he was inspired by a *Guardian* story of pills swapped for aspirins. Such tales had become common tabloid fodder in the 1960s, meaning the BBFC could not be accused of introducing new and potentially harmful notions to audiences for passing a film version of an already well-circulated urban myth (Brunvand 42, Hobbs 74–86). Unlike condoms, access to oral contraceptives was restricted to married women with a prescription. Although reports on the dangers of the new pill were widely circulated, they were also inconclusive. It was not until the very end of the decade that the Committee for the Safety of Drugs reported that only high-dose oral contraceptives were potentially unsafe. *Prudence*, which opened production in 1966, therefore came at a time when there was a gap in the market for the filmic exploitation of the pill, a lack of clarity over public safety concerns, and controlled availability through a doctor's office.

On the whole, the BBFC and *Prudence and the Pill* files (cited hereafter) record Trevelyan's positive feeling toward the project, but individual examiners were less positive. Reading through the first draft screenplay in January 1966, one examiner praised *Prudence* for being "very funny" and "done with delicacy," but nonetheless expressed disapproval. "As against this, it is not only completely immoral, but immoral in such a pointless way; there was no reason whatsoever … why all these couples should not have been happily married." Another examiner expressed concern at the distasteful "basic attitudes" presented in the story, while lamenting that "they are not within the province of censorship by today's standards." In terms of harm prevention, the Board was mostly concerned with the presentation of pre-marital sex among youth. The threat of cheap titillation, examiners felt, was somewhat neutralized by the casting of household-name actors, and by the unlikely luxurious circumstances of key characters who appeared sophisticated and wealthy and therefore inimitable in real life. Given that the contraceptive theme would likely divide critical reception, it was sensible to make *Prudence* as polished as possible. It was also felt that the teenage characters should be at least 18 and should generally be fully clothed. "We think that in a film on this subject it would be helpful if Geraldine and Tony are not in an advanced state of undress," wrote Trevelyan to producer Kenneth Harper in April 1967.

"The material is tricky enough without presenting possible complications of this kind." The same rule applied to Kerr's "voluminous" nightgown, which was exchanged for a less titillating "opaque" one. Put simply, contraceptives and sex and the potential problems they threw up were intentionally offset by a starchy, old-fashioned treatment of the body, which was itself sugared with a highly colored, ornamental *mise en scène* and an overall sense of jollity. According to Fielder Cook's widow, Sally Chamberlain, Cook was invited over from America to direct "because of the great sense of visual style he would bring to the film." High production values, prestige casting, privileged characters, and a bar on nudity and bad language were felt to balance difficult content, an effect that was heightened by Cook's light and playful direction.[6] *Prudence* passed without cuts and was released in August 1968, but although its distributors, Twentieth Century–Fox, had willingly complied with the Board's suggested revisions, their request for an A certificate fell on deaf ears; *Prudence* was predictably given an X. Trevelyan was sympathetic, but the decision reflected a desire to protect the Board. "I have seen *Prudence and the Pill*. I do not think we can give it an A without our being open to possible criticism," he wrote to Percy Livingstone, a member of the British production team, in May 1968. To Ken Harper he wrote, "I have talked to our Examiners who saw this film, and I find that they are quite decided in their view that it should be in the X category. After all, the theme is not really one for children."

In the end, *Prudence* was a critical failure not because of the contraceptive theme but because of obvious attempts to obscure it. "When you come to think about it," wrote Margaret Hinxman in the *Sunday Telegraph*, "comedies being as uninhibited as they are these days, there's no reason why a frolic about the pill, its use and misuse, shouldn't be acceptable. But the leaden touch of Prudence and the Pill pretty well kills that joke." Patrick Gibbs, of the same newspaper, concurred. "Sex, one is reminded by *The Graduate*, is a wonderfully inexhaustible subject for comedy. Contraception, as part of the same subject, might seem equally promising, but to judge from *Prudence and the Pill* the comic possibilities are few and very quickly exhausted." Although most critics agreed that, in theory, *Prudence* was at least topical, particularly in the light of the "Humane Vitae" encyclical issued by Pope Paul VI in July of that year (which clarified the Catholic Church's prohibition of artificial contraception), the film was generally viewed as unfunny, unrealistic, and crass.[7]

Times had changed since *Loving*, even in the two years between *Prudence* opening production and being released. For one thing, the NHS (Family Planning) Act 1967 had enabled local health authorities to give birth control advice regardless of marital status, on social or medical grounds if they wished. The concept of reproduction as a right and not a privilege was taking shape. For another, privilege itself was culturally under attack. Nineteen sixty-eight was a significant year for human and civil rights, as exemplified by the many global protests gathering pace as *Prudence* was released. Laboring under the misapprehension that a contraceptive comedy should appear inimitable (as encouraged by the BBFC), *Prudence* clashed with the new cultural mood of mobility, empowerment, and realism. According to Madeline Harmsworth of the *Sunday Mirror*, the film was "wretchedly implausible, desperately unfunny, astonishingly tasteless and disastrously timed." Tom Milne of the *Observer* called it "an affair of sickening archness," while Claire Hirschorn of the *Sunday Express* simply found the experience too painful to speak about. "I will not embarrass you with the details," she wrote in her review, "and shall instead draw a tactful shroud over the whole misbegotten enterprise."

Conclusion

Restrictions on citing contraception on 1960s British screens were not ubiquitous, but where they did occur a primary concern was the prevention of potential harm, although probable offense was also an important factor. The treatment of contraception was also media-specific. Television programs and feature films were consumed in radically differing environments, under different conditions, and by dissimilar combinations of audiences. Regulatory and censorial measures took account of these different environments. Television programs were free to debate contraceptives providing that discussions did not amount to advertisements, which were linked with the irresponsible sale of goods and services such as cancer cures. In cinema, the depiction of contraceptives on film was more precarious because, although narrative cinema potentially allowed for more creative interpretation than factual TV programming, the long processes involved in producing film meant that it was less quick to respond to rapid social change in the 1960s.

The case studies examined in this essay look at responses to the ability to exercise reproductive choice, but what is the importance of choice in terms of the programming or censorial decisions made? *The Pill* was well received and was praised for achieving a balanced discussion in its choice of guests, but it nonetheless represented stakeholders with the loudest voices, such as the FPA. What this association lacked in funds it made up for in persistence. This saw its aims and methods (which favored contraceptives for women, thus marginalizing men) taken up and used to inform popular broadcast programming at a time when branded contraceptives could not even be advertised. Not all attempts at piggybacking popular programming were successful, however. *The Pill* was rejected by four regional stations excluding an estimated four million viewers from the debate (Alexander), and other programs, such as the commercial channel's *Emergency Ward 10*, were reluctant to support the FPA's propaganda campaign, citing the possible offense of viewers (Granada TV and FPA, Correspondence). Nonetheless, examination of British television's treatment of reproductive issues in this period needs to take into account the stakeholders who sought to utilize public broadcasting for the benefit of their particular cause.

This case for stakeholder coercion is less easy to make for commercial feature films, which, according to the available evidence, were not seen as an obvious channel for propaganda. Feature film was as much a money-making pursuit as an artistic one. Films needed to draw in younger audiences in order that the industry might survive. Unfortunately for producers, the young person in 1960s Britain was construed as vulnerable and at risk. Filmmaking could certainly work in conjunction with political or social causes,[8] but the gamble was that X-rated tracts might not recoup their investment. Rather than being included for political agitation, the use of contraception in 1960s British film was necessarily wrapped up in cultural cues that were recognizable by average viewers, for narrative purposes. Such cues included embarrassment at buying condoms and the distrust engendered by female-controlled contraceptive pill (Marks 198). In other words, contraceptives were employed because they were topical and recognizable and fed back into existing discussions. This begs the question as to how censorial variations on contraceptive references in film were reasoned. Given that Vic left the chemist's empty handed, and that the oral contraceptives in *Prudence* bore no resemblance to the unit-dose calendar packed pills used in real life, it would seem that visual representation was considered particularly potent. In *Here We Go Round the Mulberry Bush* (1968) a shot of Jamie, the teenaged lead, reaching for Durex brand condoms before venturing out on a sexual adventure was removed from the theatrical cut (see DVD extras). Gerry and Sylvia Anderson, of *Thunderbirds* fame, also suffered when a shot of a futuristic once-a-month pill packet, used to denote infidelity, was removed from the otherwise impenetrable *Journey to the Far Side of the Sun* (1969) (BBFC and *Journey to the Far Side*). The latter example was the last of a long list of cuts made to strip *Journey* of its adult content, thereby taking it from an unmarketable X to a teenager-friendly A. The *Mulberry Bush* cut, in a film entirely about a teenager trying vainly to have sex with any of the young Stevenage women who will have him, is less easy to reconcile particularly as, by this time, Durex was fully regulated by the 1964 British Standard. The effect of removing the condom from the scene is to remove reproductive and prophylactic agency from the young Jamie. In June 1964, the *Daily Mirror* reported that Dr. Alex Comfort, future author of *The Joy of Sex*, had advised boys to use condoms because it was "manly" ("Tell Boys It's Manly"). Without his censored condom stash, the sexually active Jamie is rendered little more than a child. Removal of the condoms in this instance does not ruin the story as it would have done in *Loving*, but it may have left viewers wondering why none of the girls in his circle who are having sex with other people become pregnant. In this way, censorial cuts designed to protect young audiences indirectly reinforce a popular mythology that the pill was as widely used by young British women as it was by their American counterparts.

Today, investigations of how family limitation and sexuality appear on screen are dominated by cultural readings. Contraceptives have come to serve as a symbol of women's liberation insomuch as the ability of women to control their own reproductive futures is seen as enabling greater freedoms in everyday life. Such readings would benefit greatly by taking into account the specificity of the medium, format, and production interests involved in creating and controlling these representations as well as the stakeholders who shape them and the male contraceptive users that are so often excluded. Regulation and censorship in the British 1960s shaped how contraception was presented to a degree comparable with the creative intentions of program makers and film producers. To this end, the referencing, discussion and depiction of contraceptives on screen cannot, and should not, be separated from the circumstances of production that facilitated it.

Notes

1. With thanks to Alison Payne for bringing this to my attention.
2. The FPA undertook contraceptive regulation and periodically issued a much respected "Approved List." However, while manufacturers clamored to be included (it was an excellent means of publicity) the list was by no means equivalent to statutory regulation.
3. Repealed November 19, 1998.
4. The BBFC Archive files are named according to the film. My use of "BBFC Archive" indicates the file for the film being discussed in the preceding text.
5. Some examples are *The L-Shaped Room* (directed by Bryan Forbes, British Lion Film, Romulus Films, 1962); *Georgie Girl* (directed by Silvio Narizzano, Columbia Pictures, 1966); *Up the Junction* (directed by Peter Collinson, BHE Films, 1967); and *Joanna* (directed by Michael Sarne, Laughlin, 1968).
6. According to Chamberlin, in conversation with the author, February 11, 2015, Cook was asked to leave the production when principal photography was around two-thirds complete. This is why *Prudence* feels disjointed. Cook had pursued a running disagreement with producer Darryl F. Zanuck over the casting of Irina Demick, Zanuck's lover.
7. This aspect is discussed in more detail in the essay by Maierhofer on humor.
8. See, for example, *Victim* (directed by Basil Dearden, Allied Film Makers, 1961).

Works Cited

Aldgate, Anthony. *Censorship and the Permissive Society: British Cinema and Theatre, 1955–1965*. Oxford: Clarendon, 1995. Print.
Alexander, Marc. "Censorship? 'The Pill' Affair Is Not That Sinister." *Television Mail* 7 July 1961. FPA Archive clippings file A17/98A, Wellcome Library, London.
Asbell, Bernard. *The Pill: A Biography of the Drug That Changed the World*. New York: Random House, 1995. Print.
Barclay Committee, and McAlley Associates. *The Cinema and Its Customers (a Pilot Study)*. 1968. Print.
Barstow, Stan. *A Kind of Loving*. London: M. Joseph, 1960. Print.

BBFC and *A Kind of Loving* producers and distributors, correspondence and examiners reports, 1961–1962, video examiner's reports, 1988. BBFC Archive, British Board of Film Classification, London.
BBFC and *Journey to the Far Side of the Sun* producers and distributors, correspondence and examiners reports, 1968–1969. BBFC Archive.
BBFC and *Prudence and the Pill* producers and distributors, correspondence and examiners reports, 1966–68, video examiner's reports, 1988. BBFC Archive.
Borge, Jessica. "The London Rubber Company, the Condom and the Pill: 1915–1970." PhD Thesis, Birkbeck College, University of London, 2017.
Braden, Bernard. "Braden Opinion Poll." Interview with John Trevelyan. *BFI InView*. British Film Institute, 1967. Web. 5 Sept. 2016.
British Standards Institution. "Specification for Rubber Condoms: BS3704." 1964. Print.
Brunvand, Jan Harold. *Encyclopedia of Urban Legends*. Updated and Expanded Edition. Santa Barbara: ABC-CLIO, 2012. Print.
Comfort, Alex. *The Joy of Sex: A Cordon Bleu Guide to Lovemaking*. New York: Crown, 1972. Print.
Committee on the Safety of Drugs. "Report for 1969 and 1970." London: Her Majesty's Stationary Office, 1971. Print.
Consumer's Association. "Which? Supplement: Contraceptives." 1963. Print.
Cook, Hera. *The Long Sexual Revolution: English Women, Sex, and Contraception 1800–1975*. Oxford: Oxford University Press, 2004. Print.
Docherty, David, et al. *The Last Picture Show? Britain's Changing Film Audience*. London: British Film Institute, 1987. Print.
Fisher, Kate. *Birth Control, Sex, and Marriage in Britain 1918–1960*. Oxford: Oxford University Press, 2006. Print.
Gantzias, George. *The Dynamics of Regulation: Global Control, Local Resistance: Cultural Management and Policy. A Case Study of Broadcasting Advertising in the United Kingdom*. Aldershot: Ashgate, 2001. Print.
Gibbs, Patrick. "No Sugar in This Pill." *Sunday Telegraph* 9 Aug. 1968. *Prudence and the Pill* press clippings, Reuben Library, British Film Institute, London.
Granada TV. "The Transcription of *The Pill*: One of Granada's *Life in Action* Programmes." Booklet, 1961. FPA Archive file A17/44.
Granada TV, and FPA. Correspondence, Apr. to July 1961. FPA Archive file A17/44.
Hall, Lesley A. *Sex, Gender, and Social Change in Britain Since 1880*. Houndmills: Palgrave, 2013. Print.
Hand, Christopher. "Television Ownership in Britain and the Coming of ITV. What Do the Statistics Show?" Unpublished paper. Department of Media Arts, Royal Holloway, University of London. 2002. Web. 20 Sept. 2012.
Hargreaves, Tracy. "The Trevelyan Years: British Censorship in the 1960s." *Behind the Scenes at the BBFC: Film Classification from the Silver Screen to the Digital Age*. Ed. Edward Lamberti. London: Palgrave Macmillan, 2012. 53–72. Print.
Harmsworth, Madeline. Review of *Prudence and the Pill*. *Sunday Mirror* 11 Aug. 1968. Press clippings, Reuben Library, British Film Institute, London.
Here We Go Round the Mulberry Bush. Dir. Clive Donner. Giant Film Production, 1968. BFI Flipside, 2010. DVD.
Hinxman, Margaret. Review of *Prudence and the Pill*. *Sunday Telegraph* 11 Aug. 1968. Press clippings, Reuben Library, British Film Institute, London.
Hirschorn, Claire. Review of *Prudence and the Pill*. *Sunday Express* 11 Aug. 1968. Press clippings, Reuben Library, British Film Institute, London.
Hobbs, Sandy. "The Folk Tale as News." *Oral History* 6.2 (1978): 74–86. JSTOR. Web. 9 Sept. 2016.
Jones, Claire L. "Under the Covers? Commerce, Contraceptives and Consumers in England and Wales, 1880–1960." *Social History of Medicine* (2015). Web. 11 Oct. 2016.
Journey to the Far Side of the Sun. A.K.A *Doppelganger*. Dir. Robert Parrish. Century 21 Television, 1969. Film.
A Kind of Loving. Dir. John Schlesinger, Vic Films Productions, 1962. Film.

28   Part 1. Contraceptives in the Media

Lloyd, Dennis. "Some Comments on the British Television Act, 1954." *Law and Contemporary Problems* 23.1 (1958): 165–74. *JSTOR*. Web. 9 Sept. 2016.
Marks, Lara. *Sexual Chemistry: A History of the Contraceptive Pill*. New Haven: Yale University Press, 2010. Print.
McLuhan, Marshall. *Understanding Media: The Extensions of Man*. London: Routledge, 2001. Print.
Merrin, Tom. "Granada's Bitter Pill." *Daily Sketch* 3 July 1961, FPA Archive clippings file A17/98A.
Mill, John Stuart. *On Liberty and Other Essays*. Oxford: Oxford University Press, 1991. Print.
Mills, Hugh. *Prudence and the Pill*. Philadelphia: Triton Books, 1965. Print.
Milne, Tom. Review of *Prudence and the Pill*. *Observer* 11 Aug. 1968. Press clippings, Reuben Library, British Film Institute, London.
"The 1960s and Liberalisation." *British Board of Film Classification*. BBFC, n.d. Web. 9 Sept. 2016.
Parry, Manon. *Broadcasting Birth Control: Mass Media and Family Planning*. New Brunswick: Rutgers University Press, 2013. Print.
Paulu, Burton. *British Broadcasting; Radio and Television in the United Kingdom*. Minneapolis: University of Minnesota Press, 1956. *Project MUSE*. Web. 9 Sept. 2016.
Payne, Alison. "'It hit us like a whirlwind': The Impact of Commercial Television Advertising in Britain, 1954–1964." PhD Thesis, Birkbeck College, University of London. Department of Film, Culture and Media Studies, 2016. Web.
"The Pill." *Life in Action*. ITV. 28 June 1961. Television.
Prudence and the Pill. Dir. Fielder Cook and Ronald Neame. Twentieth Century Fox, 1968. Film.
"Radio Times 1923–2009." *BBC Genome Project*. BBC, 2016. Web. 9 Sept. 2016.
Room at the Top. Dir. Jack Clayton. Romulus Films, 1959. Film.
Saturday Night and Sunday Morning. Dir. Karel Reisz. Woodfall Films, 1960. Film.
Schofield, Michael. *The Sexual Behaviour of Young People*. London: Penguin, 1968. Print.
"Sex Education." *People in Trouble*. ITV. 1 Jan. 1958. Television.
"Tell Boys It's Manly—Says Doctor." *Daily Mirror* 26 June 1964. FPA Archive clippings file A17/99.
Thane, Pat, and Tanya Evans. *Sinners? Scroungers? Saints? Unmarried Motherhood in Twentieth-Century England*. Oxford: Oxford University Press, 2012. Print.
Thompson, Ben. *Ban This Filth! Letters from the Mary Whitehouse Archive*. London: Faber & Faber, 2013. Print.
Trevelyan, John. *What the Censor Saw*. London: Michael Joseph, 1973, 1977. Print.
"TV Times Listings from 1955–1985." *The TV Times Digitisation Project 1955–1985*. British Universities Film & Video Council, n.d. Web. 9 Sept. 2016.
Unmarried Mothers. ITV, 30 Apr. 1958. Television.
Wilson, Alexander. *Advertising and the Community*. Manchester: Manchester University Press, 1968. Print.
Wright, Ian. Review of *Prudence and the Pill*. *Guardian*. 9 Aug. 1968, press clippings, Reuben Library, British Film Institute, London.

Pill and Remote Control
Politics of Contraception in Contemporary U.S. Quality Television

MARKUS SCHLEICH
and JONAS NESSELHAUF

The 1960s, the decade of various social changes, started with a major revolution which today is either forgotten or taken for granted: The invention of the oral contraceptive pill. Carl Djerassi, one of the major chemists involved, opens his autobiography *This Man's Pill* (2003) with remarks on this event: "In terms of socio-cultural impact, ranging from religions to women's rights, the Pill must surely rank close to the top. By separating the coital act from contraception, the Pill started one of the most monumental movements in recent times, the gradual divorce of sex from reproduction" (4).

From now on, women were finally able to actively "participate" in both their sexuality and fertility, simultaneously emancipating themselves within the relationship and from patriarchic role concepts—a radical and revolutionary improvement, reducing the number of unwanted pregnancies around the world. In this regard, Austrian-American chemist Carl Djerassi criticized the German term *Anti-Baby-Pille* (anti-baby pill) suggesting *Pro-Baby-Pille* (pro-baby pill) as a better naming in order to emphasize the newly gained women's choice (Djerassi, *Der Schattensammler* 37). Simultaneously, the example of Djerassi illustrates the interesting relation between the birth control pill and works of fiction—the subtitle of his fourth and final autobiography *In Retrospect* (2014) reads "From the Pill to the Pen"—both in Djerassi's own biography (from a chemist to a writer) and as a topic of socio-critical potential in literature.

This essay focuses on the birth control pill, the most popular form of oral contraception, in contemporary television series which debate contraception and birth control and its impact on the female-male relationship.

Hierarchies of Sex and Gender: The Politics of Contraception

In December 1966, readers browsing through the current edition of the *Canadian Medical Association Journal* found a double-page advertisement for the *Oracon* birth control pill, showing a young woman next to a large white flower: "The association of the birth control pill Oracon with nature in the imagery of the advertisement not only indicated its safety but also reassured the reader that the so-called natural menstrual pattern would remain" (Molyneaux 72). The caption claims: "So close to nature that it simulates the natural menstrual pattern." It is no coincidence that the pill was advertised as a "natural" complement to women's health because many people perceived it as an "unnatural" interference in female sexuality.[1]

But the chemical composition of the active pharmaceutical ingredient itself was a chance discovery by American chemist Russell Marker in the early 1940s. His Syntex SA was the first-ever company to create progesterone, a central hormone involved in the menstrual cycle (Benson 39f.). On this basis, chemists like Carl Djerassi and George Rosenkranz were working since the 1950s on an ovulation-suppressing oral contraceptive. In June 1960, the pharmaceutical company G.D. Searle filed an application for Enovid, which became the first hormonal birth control pill, followed by similar medicaments like Schering's Anovlar in Australia and parts of Europe in 1961.

This marks a historic date, not only for the history of medicine: Until today and compared to other methods of (a "female") birth control (e.g., sterilization, post-intercourse pills or abortion), only the pill stands out due to its availability, accessibility, and acceptance (David 9). The importance and influence can be seen in contrast to previous "sexual politics"—as Shulamith Firestone and Kate Millet work out in their feminist books *The Dialectic of Sex* and *Sexual Politics*, both published in 1970. The traditional and patriarchal role model is an unequal one (Firestone 81), "whereby one group of persons is controlled by another" (Millett 23): "Woman is still denied sexual freedom and the biological control over her body through the cult of virginity, the double standard, the proscription against abortion, and in many places because contraception is physically or psychically unavailable to her" (Millett 54).

While the control of fertility is inseparably linked to the control of female sexuality (Nusser 340), the availability of oral contraception in the early 1960s marked an act of radical freedom: Women now gained access to a safe, effective, and affordable form of birth control and were simultaneously able to separate sexual intercourse from (the risk of) reproduction, leading to new "hierarchies of sex and gender" and thereby to a changed balance of power within the relationship or the marriage: "The widespread use and acceptance of contraception today truly constitutes a revolution" (Lee 213).

In general, the feminist perspective on oral contraception was positive—and, together with legal changes concerning abortion and divorce, sometimes even considered as a powerful tool to "undermine" the traditional concept of marriage (Millett 208): "a shifting of emphasis from reproduction to contraception ... would provide an alternative to the oppressions of the biological family" (Firestone 230; see also 220).

So, already in the 1960s, feminist theory and gender studies emphasized the now closed "gender gap"—"Indeed, biological reproductive roles are the likely origin of most social distinctions involving sex and gender" (Shanner 405)—and perceived oral contraception as the end of the "*barbaric*" female pregnancy (Firestone 226; italics in original). Claims for an equivalent "male pill" or rejections of this "patriarchic repression" (Sichtermann 59) were an exception.

Pill and Pen: Introductory Remarks

It is no surprise that the pill soon became a permanent topic of literary works—from the beginning of Don DeLillo's novel *White Noise* (1984), where "birth control pills" are brought back on campus by students after the summer break, carried equally next to "tennis rackets, soccer balls, hockey and lacrosse sticks" (DeLillo 3), to Christian Grey's instruction that Ana should "ensure that she procures oral contraception ... to prevent any pregnancy" in E.L. James' bestselling novel *Fifty Shades of Grey* (170). But interestingly, television series were not as liberal as literature when it came to contraceptive issues: Highly popular family sitcom productions like *Leave It to Beaver* (CBS/ABC, 1957–1963), *Family Affair* (CBS, 1966–1971), or *The Brady Bunch* (ABC, 1969–1974) remained rooted in the traditional nuclear family structure of postwar America.

One of the main reasons is the so-called Motion Picture Production Code, a set of moral guidelines for film studios installed in 1930 (and legally binding until 1969). Besides other regulations for the visual presentation of "crimes against the law," "vulgarity," "dances," "religion," and "national feelings," it also defines "the sanctity of the institution of marriage" and bans any depiction of "sex hygiene" (Green and Karolides 361). With regard to television broadcasting, the Federal Communications Commission (FCC) marks a similar instance when it comes to such content-related censorship (Parry 68–69). Free-to-air broadcasting channels are regulated by the FCC—and it was only at the end of the 1980s when networks like CBS, NBC, and ABC first referred to delicate subjects like birth control at all. Coincidentally, during the 1986–1987 season, the prime-time television productions *Dallas* (CBS, 1978–1991), *Dynasty* (ABC, 1981–1989), and *The Colbys* (ABC, 1985–1987) "were simultaneously featuring story lines involving unplanned pregnancies"—an issue that only "has been broached on *Cagney & Lacey* [CBS, 1982–1988], *Kate & Allie* [CBS, 1984–1989] and ... *Heart of the City* [ABC, 1986–1987]" in the months before (Margulies). So, for instance, in the episode "Getting Ahead" (Season 5.15) of the NBC medical drama *St. Elsewhere* (1982–1988), an unmarried pregnant college student remarks: "I should have had Seth condomized." Other examples of a prime-time use of the "c-words" (condom and/or contraception) include the *Cagney & Lacey* episode "Rites of Passage" (Season 6.08) or the episode "Bad Timing" (Season 2.14) of NBC's comedy series *Valerie* (1986–1987)—although this very episode had to air "three hours later than usual" (Polman).[2]

Georgia Jeffries, the executive story editor of *Cagney & Lacey* and the writer of the episode "Rites of Passage," stated after the airing: "Television is always showing premarital sex but it won't talk about contraceptives. That's very hypocritical" (qtd. in Margulies). And Thomas Miller, one of the executive producers of *Valerie*, added: "What's real disturbing to me about this is not the threat of censorship, it's how far behind the times we are. I look back at *The Brady Bunch*, one of the first shows I worked on, and wonder how far we've come. It's like the Dark Ages" (qtd. in Margulies).

Pill and Remote Control: Introductory Remarks on "Quality Television"

What seems like a "normal" and "eligible" topic for a television series today exemplarily shows the difference between "regular" television and what Robert J. Thompson calls "quality television." In his 1996 monograph *Television's Second Golden Age*, he develops a set of 12 general criteria to define "quality TV" (13–16), including the transformation of traditional genres (such as *St. Elsewhere*), a large cast, and an aspiration toward "realism"; additionally, these formats discuss controversial topics, are self-conscious and have a memory, and the productions are "writer-based" and "enthusiastically showered with awards" (e.g., *St. Elsewhere* or *Cagney & Lacey*).

In general, Thompson predicates a new generation of television productions: Compared to rather superficial programs before, even family drama series were increasingly becoming "more realistic," for instance when a show like *Picket Fences* (CBS, 1992–1996) featured "complex discussions about the issues surrounding abortion, fetal tissue transplants, birth control, date rape, euthanasia, prejudice of many stripes, guns and drugs in school, religious freedom, sexual freedom, and many other contemporary ethical topics" (Thompson 171).

But Thompson's 12 categories hardly work for television sitcoms, and these formats are largely ignored in recent academic television studies with their focus on shows like *The Sopranos* (HBO, 1999–2007), *The Wire* (HBO, 2002–2008), *Mad Men* (AMC, 2007–2015), *Breaking Bad* (AMC, 2008–2013), or *Boardwalk Empire* (HBO, 2010–2014). This proper "canon" gains the main attention in public and research, along with ongoing productions like *The Walking Dead* (AMC, since 2010), *American Horror Story* (FX, since 2011), *Game of Thrones* (HBO, since 2011), and *Homeland* (Showtime, since 2011). But all of these epic stories have one thing in common—they are told on (premium) cable networks, which are subscription-based and thereby not regulated by the FCC, allowing the producers more creative freedom and offering the writers a certain "drastic" and "realistic" approach to their stories.

In contrast, popular sitcoms usually air on commercial broadcast networks like ABC, CBS, NBC, and Fox; recent shows like *30 Rock* (NBC, 2006–2013), *The Big Bang Theory* (CBS, since 2007), *Modern Family* (ABC, since 2009), or *New Girl* (Fox, since 2011) usually have only half the running time of a drama series and are shot in a multi-camera setup or sometimes even still in front of an actual audience (alternatively there is a laugh track added in post-production). In the past two decades, sitcoms as well as animated sitcoms like *The Simpsons* (Fox, since 1989), *South Park* (Comedy Central, since 1997), or *Family Guy* (Fox, since 1999) are broaching socially critical and controversial issues "wrapped" up in the comedy. Therefore, we elsewhere suggest an extended definition of "quality television" and would also include sitcoms which are as innovative, drastic, aesthetic, and meta-referential as the canonic "quality" drama series (Nesselhauf and Schleich).

Interestingly, especially topics like birth control, unwanted pregnancy, and abortion can help to close this "gap" between quality drama series and comedy, cartoon, and sitcom formats. The birth control pill as a *tertium comparationis* can show how contraceptive products have an immense impact on our definitions of gender and sex: In order to stabilize male hegemony and maintain traditional gender roles, some men try to keep women from taking the pill—both in television drama and sitcom.

Tragedy: "All family. All business"— Brotherhood *(2006–2008)*

The examples of the first category include drama television series usually considered as "quality television": Showtime's *Brotherhood*, AMC's *Mad Men*, and Netflix' *House of Cards*.

When *Brotherhood* first aired on Showtime in 2006, Alesandra Stanley, a television critic from the *New York Times*, noticed that "*Brotherhood* revels in the kind of politics that are rarely seen on television shows." She refers to the darker side of Politics with a capital P but also the politics of the criminal underbelly. The plot centers on the rivaling Caffee brothers and their attempts to come to power: "In a fictional neighborhood called 'the Hill,' the Caffee brothers claim authority, Tommy a Democratic seat in the state legislature, and Michael, his nemesis, from a middle-management perch in the local mob" (Bellafante). At first sight, *Brotherhood* is about complicated men, like so many quality television series nowadays are (cf. Martin 4–5), about "alpha males" struggling with the world that surrounds them and at the same time coping with their inner flaws. Tommy Caffee is a prime example for such a character: A husband, a politician, brother to a mobster, prone to taking moral shortcuts himself and too often caught up in his inner turmoil. He invites comparison to Tony Soprano, the protagonist and anti-hero of HBO's mafia series *The Sopranos*, a man who also cannot cope with the many social roles thrust unto him (Stanley; Bellafante). Tony Soprano has always been the center of attention, while his wife Carmela Soprano has often been the target of criticism:

> She lives a comfortable upper-middle-class existence partly paid for by prostitution…; she continues having sex with her adulterous spouse despite knowing about his sexual indiscretions; and she holds traditional, even conservative moral views while turning a blind eye to what her husband does for a living and enjoying the lifestyle he provides for her and her family. We have no quarrel with Cassidy's basic assessment that Carmela is an embarrassment to the feminist struggle [Akass and McCabe 39–40].

Carmela cannot compete with her spouse in matters of emotional depth, because she remains too stagnant within her social role as wife and mother.

In *Brotherhood* there is no Carmela. Eileen Caffee, the wife of Tommy Caffee, is not just a foil for her husband's moral misdemeanors: "The women of *Brotherhood* are no less complicated…. Tommy's wife, Eileen, the perfect helpmate, except that she is unhappy and hiding a problem with drugs and extramarital sex" (Stanley). Eileen Caffee is a troubled character herself. In the first season, she takes refuge from her role as a mother by starting an affair with the mailman. In the second season, after coming clean to Tommy, she returns home and, for the final installment of the show, actress Annabeth Gish, who portrays Eileen, stated in an interview—quite tellingly titled "Politics and Motherhood"—that it "was really about her trying to do the right thing, and about trying to find a purpose in her life outside of her role as a mother" (qtd. in Shattuk). By the third season, she has found this purpose and is working outside of the home and enjoys her entry-level job at a local community center. From a gendered perspective, Eileen frees herself from the limits of the socially established female role—thrust upon her by her hyper-conservative Irish environment—and explores male territory. Male territory in *Brotherhood* refers to a "purpose in her life outside of her role as a mother" (Shattuk). While reality does not necessarily render community work as "feminine" anymore, the fictional world of *Brotherhood* does (cf. Season 3.02).

However, Eileen is pregnant with their fourth child, a son, and her pregnancy causes problems. It pushes her back into the gender role she was trying to escape. Raising a toddler while working in an office is not exactly how the Irish community pictures the wife of an aspiring politician, or any woman for that matter. Her supervisor for instance passes her over for a promotion due to her pregnancy, as this renders her unreliable and turns her into a liability in his eyes (Season 3.02).

This is where *Brotherhood* explores themes of sexual politics: Based on her religiously conditioned value system—Eileen is a woman of Catholic Irish descent—the birth control pill has never been an option (Season 3.01). One key argument of many critics—including Pope John Paul II's encyclical *Evangelium Vitae* (1995) and his critique of the "contraceptive mentality"—is the believe that "contraceptive products encourage young people to engage in sexual activity, and that these products also induce abortion" (Sison 185).³ For Tommy and his side of the family, Eileen's pregnancy itself is neither unwelcome, for Tommy "brings Eileen home a glider, where she can sit comfortably and milk the baby" (Narkunski)—unlike the pregnancy of Kath, Michael's girlfriend; as Michael believes "that a career criminal suffering from a mild form of brain damage would not exactly make for an ideal father" (Bellafante), he has Kath abort the baby (Season 2.07)—nor a surprise (see Season 3.01). It actually corresponds with the designated gender roles: "Even in societies that promote women's equality and opportunity, though, 'real women' are expected to want children and to experience pregnancy. Men typically have other avenues of social and economic success outside of parenting, but stereotypes of masculinity still emphasize a man's ability to father a child" (Shanner 407). But when Eileen informs her husband about her desire to keep working after the pregnancy, she is stunned to learn that Tommy—a dominant male stereotype who refuses "feminine tasks" such as cooking or picking up the dry cleaning, and who is unwilling to explore what for him is "female gender territory" such as buying diapers or feeding the newborn with formula—is himself surprised that she would want to keep working outside of the house.

Not only does her pregnancy force Eileen out of her job, it later confines her to bed (Season 3.07)—a quite symbolic setting. *Brotherhood* examines the aftermath of an unwanted pregnancy, which makes it an exception "on television, where women are typically saved from unwanted children by the

36   Part 1. Contraceptives in the Media

convenient and politically neutral plot device of the miscarriage" (Bellafante). The example of Eileen in *Brotherhood* shows that contraception gives "real women" the choice *if* and *when* they want to become pregnant. Thus, *Brotherhood* implies that women have a choice to not let their sex dictate their gender roles, but the show also investigates how men—and a society created and ruled by men—interfere with these choices.

Tragedy: "I See You Are Not Married"— Mad Men (2007–2015)

AMC's *Mad Men* is probably the most prominent television show exploring the relationship of men and women embedded in a network of complex power relations:

> *Mad Men* investigates how discourses, practices and institutions are intertwined, forming this network, how patriarchal institutions—i.e. the husband, the gynecologist, the psychiatrist, the State—channel power through collaboration. The female body proves a key site of this power struggle, for those institutions read women as bodies, reducing "femininity" to "physicality," a logic that, on the one hand, objectifies women, and, on the other hand, evokes the Foucauldian notion of "the indocile body" [Seibert 54–55].

Foucault offers the following definition for the "indocile body": "A body is docile that may be subjected, used, transformed, and improved" (Foucault 180). Peggy Olson, one of the main characters of *Mad Men*, learns what it means to have an indocile body early on, and quite obviously, it is men who do the "teaching." Peggy appears to be shy and her appearance is rather low-key. Obviously overwhelmed with her new life in New York City, she enters the world of Sterling & Cooper, an advertising agency on Madison Avenue that is "populated by twentysomething men with license to drink, smoke and harass women" (Dean). At her first day at work, Joan Holloway, who introduces her to this "harem" (Dean), advises her to "go home, take a paper bag and cut some eye holes out of it. Put it over your head, look in the mirror and try and evaluate your strengths and weaknesses. And try and be honest" (Season 1.01: 08:58 min.). Thus, Joan instructs Peggy to see herself as an object of sexual desire, to be less of a subject but more of an object. Later in that episode, Pete Campbell—a young account executive at Sterling Cooper and sexual predator—makes some harsh remarks to Peggy. By asking her whether she was Amish, Pete attempts to lower her self-esteem. Later, Peggy visits Joan's doctor for necessary precautions that are, according to Joan, crucial for Peggy's new working environment: Contraception. However, the gynecologist is a representative of a disciplinary system that seeks to maintain male hegemony. The gynecologist offers male guidance, even though Peggy does not appear to be an infant in need of male supervision (Seibert 55). His monologue says more about society than about women: "Although, as a doctor, I'd like to think that putting a woman in this situation is not gonna turn her into some kind of strumpet.... I'll warn you now I will take you off this medicine if you abuse it. It's for your own good, really. But the fact is, even in our modern times, easy women don't find husbands" (Season 1.01: 20:25 min.). Under these circumstances, the contraceptive pill becomes a device of male authorities—for instance her co-workers—to gain control over female sexuality and hence the female body. Since the pill enables women to have a say in matters of reproduction, male hegemony socially incapacitates them.

During the night which follows Peggy's consultation with the gynecologist, Pete visits her to have sex with her. Pete obviously expects Peggy to be "on the pill," like every other woman who works at Sterling Cooper apparently. He shows a more vulnerable side of his personality which is in stark contrast to his earlier behavior—and apparently she is drawn to him because she does not refuse his advances but actively encourages him by inviting him into her apartment. It is unclear why Peggy does not ask him to use a condom or some other form of contraception. However, Peggy's insecurity is highlighted throughout the show's pilot. When she goes into labor at the end of the first season, she wonders where the strong abdominal pains come from. The series is quite ambiguous whether she is in denial or simply did not realize that she was pregnant. The latter would add substance to the claim that her rural upbringing did not include any sex education.

The baby resulting out of this one-night stand is Peggy's problem and the stigma of being a single mother would render her socially damaged—at the beginning of the second season, there is a lot of gossip about Peggy being impregnated by Don Draper and that Peggy went to a weight loss camp (Season 2.01). It is not hard to imagine how offensive the commentary would be if it was known that she actually had a child and gave it away.

The disciplinary system presented in *Mad Men* denounces pregnant women outside of standardized relationships—marriage—as abnormal outcasts but at the same time society "associates motherhood with 'naturalness' [and] marginalizes and sanctions women seeking abortion—legally, morally, politically" (Seibert 55). The fact that she can keep all this secret is the only reason Peggy's pregnancy does not hinder her to pursue a career: "Peggy's success is ... inextricably linked to her ability to control her reproductive capacities. She must, in fact, deny motherhood in order to succeed" (Arosteguy 144). The parallels to *Brotherhood* are quite striking: If Peggy's pregnancy became public, she would suffer the same fate as Eileen, but whereas the latter is quite literally locked into her own bedroom—again a very symbolic setting—to carry out her child, Peggy defies the mechanisms of male hegemony. Even though she succeeds where Eileen failed, this achievement comes at a price: Peggy has to give up her child.

What *Mad Men* achieves by staging Peggy's case is to highlight how men use the contraceptive pill to remain independent, while not sharing this independence with the other sex. Women are systematically stigmatized and reminded of their biological sex in order to deny them entrance to the realms of male hegemony. Interestingly, it is a show depicting the 1960s that counts as the prime example for television debating issues of sexism and questions of gender.

Historian Stephanie Coontz argues that the "authentic portrait of women's lives in the early 1960s makes it hard for some women to watch." Peggy and Joan are no heroines in the sense that they overcome sexism; quite the contrary. For the viewer of the 21st century this is at times unbearable and while it would be easy to claim that these are problems of an era long gone, *Mad Men* actually tackles problems of our time; Sady Doyle remarks that "the show portrays a long-gone era of gender relations—but it's not so different from our own." *Mad Men*'s cultural impact has been so powerful because it uses the past to illustrate problems of the present in a subversive way. A lot of what *Mad Men* says about gender politics of the past is still very valid for the realities of the present time.

Tragedy: "I despise children"— House of Cards *(2013–)*

At first sight, the critically acclaimed political thriller *House of Cards* does not ostensibly focus on questions of gender and contraception. Set in the 21st century, the show gives an account of the political power struggles within the White House before and during the presidency of a fictional Francis J. "Frank" Underwood—but *House of Cards* also refers to those schemes and plots on an interpersonal level. In the context of this discussion, the complex relationship of Frank and his wife Claire is especially of interest.

With the opening of the first season, Congressman and Majority Whip Frank Underwood is presented as a dangerous man—not when he coldly smothers a dying dog or the low camera angle when he does it, but rather as he breaks the fourth wall and lectures viewers on types of pain (Aken'Ova). Later in the first season, he directly addresses the viewer and claims: "I despise children. There, I said it!" (Season 1.09: 04:16 min.). This opens up an interesting link: Edward Cline among many others has dubbed Frank Underwood as an American Macbeth (Franzen 82). The original Shakespearean hero is described (and even more, characterized) by one of the play's characters, Macduff, with the words "He has no children" (Shakespeare 192). In Sigmund

Freud's reading of this sentence, Macbeth's childlessness only makes him able to kill the children of Macduff (Freud 242).

Similarly, Frank Underwood wants no children himself,[4] as they might soften him and disturb his political ambitions—and since the viewers "already know what Frank does to the young protégés he considers his substitute children" (Rosin), it is hard to imagine him as a caring father—or a father at all. Frank hated his own father—a recurring theme throughout the first two seasons—and he has no drive to father a child. He had Claire abort at least one child from him (see Season 1.13: 27:37 min.) and there is no apparent wish for an heir. His legacy is "America Works," a universal employment program (Season 3.01) that he pushes through Congress against opposition from both parties. However, while one could argue that Frank's not liking children does not mean not wanting children, there are a lot of scenes in which the series offers the viewer more insight into Claire and Frank's relationship to clarify this. When Claire visits her former bodyguard Steve at his deathbed—he suffers from terminal stage four pancreatic cancer—she informs him about Frank's proposal of marriage: He promised her to never put her on a pedestal, treat her as his equal, and that children are not part of this deal (Season 1.06). Given their almost professional relationship in all matters of power, it is natural to assume Claire shares Frank's feelings about having kids, for she is just as ruthless, complex, and unlikable as her husband: "The Underwoods' marriage is a rare thing in a political drama: It is an equal partnership.... Claire Underwood has her own storylines. She isn't just Lady Macbeth, pacing the floor while her husband does the deed" (Crampton). In the course of the series, it begins to show that she "formulates her own strategies for seizing power" (Crampton)—especially at the end of the third season (Landau 21).

Seen from a gendered perspective, Claire hardly fulfills the criteria of a caring mother. However, in the first season there is a softer, almost forgiving side of her that is absent during most of the political scheming. Later it is revealed that not only has she thought about children more than once in her life but also that Claire already had three abortions (Landau 24) and currently is "on the pill" (Season 2.04: 34:00 min.). So, when we follow Claire to her gynecologist in the last episode of the first season (Season 1.14), the viewer learns that she still has a chance to give birth, despite her age, which makes it harder to conceive but not impossible. The fact that she does not inform Frank about this doctor's appointment sheds a new light on their relationship. Although Frank's (dominant male) position has not changed—he needs Claire as a partner in crime, not as the mother of his children—this marks a turning point for the couple, especially with regard to the following seasons.

In the second season, Claire refrains from fertility treatment—necessary because of her age—in order to support Frank's cause to become president (Season 2.01). Later in the third season, this conflict reaches a climax. Claire gives up on maternity for Frank; for most of the season she has been "arm-candy to her husband in his re-election campaign" (Zheng). This results in a predicament for Claire as TV critic Sonia Saraiya states: "It's time to see how Lord and Lady Underwood resolve their marital strife, the strife of a marriage built on lies for the benefit of a political system where only one person—one man, usually—can be head of state." Frank reaches the highest office of the United States, but Claire comprehensively ponders whether there is a place for her at the top as well. One conversation between the Underwoods (Season 1.13: 25:15 min.) illustrates this:

> CLAIRE: I was thinking about ... when one of us dies ... what will we leave behind?
> FRANK: We've accomplished a great deal. And I intend for us to accomplish a lot more.
> CLAIRE: But for whom?

She is entitled to skepticism. Frank is the president of the United States and owes much of his success to Claire—who paid a price for this. At the end of the third season, Claire condescendingly and coldly remarks that she should never have made him president (Season 3.07: 51:15 min.). To "make" Frank what he is, she had to take up a subordinate role to him. She sacrificed motherhood for her husband to become the most powerful man in the world—just to realize how little power she has left.

House of Cards is about international politics just as much as it is about marriage, about being the father of a nation and being a mother without children. They discuss the predicament: Claire implicitly wonders whether Frank's presidency is actually a surrogate for children, because she is reduced to the role of a passive bystander while he actively governs the nation (Season 1.13: 25:40 min., Season 2.04: 21:50 min., Season 3.03: 21:30 min.). As Frank's wife, she cannot be the mother of the nation. The rift between the two—Claire walking out on Frank, hinting at her possible candidacy for presidency—is complete at the end of the third season. The show is about two individuals who appear to be equal, but when it comes to questions of reproduction, Frank appears to be "more equal."

Comedy: Scrubs *(2001–2010)*

Questions of gender roles and sexual politics can be illustrated using the example of the birth control pill, but the television series discussed so far also explored how intense such conflicts can become and how it can put stress on a relationship. In contrast to these rather "tragic" examples, we will now turn to more satiric approaches in *Scrubs*, *Desperate Housewives*, and *The Simpsons*.

The NBC medical comedy *Scrubs* follows the daily life of Dr. John Dorian and his colleagues at Sacred Heart Hospital, including the neurotic Dr. Elliot Reid, the sarcastic mentor and later chief of medicine Perry Cox, as well as the couple Christopher Turk and Carla Espinosa, a surgeon and a head nurse. As a procedural drama, the series combines both medical cases and the character's private issues—thereby, each episode consists of self-contained sub-plots (the so-called "monster of the week" or "case of the week") as well as character-related development over several episodes and even seasons. This format is typical for medical dramas such as *House* (Fox, 2004–2012) and *Grey's Anatomy* (ABC, since 2005), criminal drama series like *Law & Order* (NBC, 1990–2010) or *CSI: Crime Scene Investigation* (CBS, 2000–2015), legal drama series such as *Ally McBeal* (Fox, 1997–2002) or *The Good Wife* (CBS, since 2009), and mystery series like *The X-Files* (Fox, 1993–2002, since 2016). Additionally and in contrast to "epic" series like *Brotherhood*, *Mad Men*, and *House of Cards* discussed previously, this predictable and stable concept makes it, of course, easier for the viewer to skip one or even several episodes. Simultaneously, the viewer can literally "grow up" with the characters and witness their everyday life, their work routine, as well as the development of the characters and their relationships (especially of and between J.D. and Elliot)—for instance when Carla and Turk are about to get married at the end of season three (Season 3.22). Turk is delayed in the operating room, but finally the couple is married by a hospitalized priest at Sacred Heart. After their return from the honeymoon (Season 4.01), Carla starts her family planning at the beginning of the fifth season. Turk, in contrast, is not yet "ready" to become a father: "All this baby stuff, I feel like she rushed me into it" (Season 5.01: 09:56 min.). So, while Carla discontinues taking the birth control pill, Turk is secretly feeding her with it for more than a week, for example at night (Season 5.01: 10:06 min.) or baked in his "special homemade brownies" (Season 5.01: 12:09 min.); even a fig snack is "not only fat-free but [also] baby-free" (Season 5.01: 18:00 min.).[5] However, Turk gets caught and the couple engages in a war of words because Carla condemns the interference with her reproductive "rights" whereas Turk simply wants more time. Even though it is not directly addressed, the series does imply that in the end, time does not favor both sexes in the same way. Carla's biological clock is ticking, Turk's does not: he does not even have one. When a man uses the pill to prevent his partner's pregnancy, he forces her to obey his schedule and thus perverts the idea of what the pill means for women: empowerment. In the end, Carla flushes her remaining birth control pills down the toilet (Season 5.01: 17:55 min.),[6] and the couple agrees on family planning.

Interestingly, this very episode is the most direct one addressing contraception; being a medical drama, *Scrubs* depicts the hospital as a space of medical and bodily issues, daily tragedies and a predestined venue for controversial topics such as diseases and death, but topics like sexuality and birth control are rarely discussed. Although the story of Turk's interference in Carla's sexuality is a dramatic violation of her private life, the story is communicated with lightness and charm and for the viewer literally (in contrast to the self-made brownies) easy to digest. This surely may be due to the FCC rules, since *Scrubs* aired in NBC's prime time slot, either Tuesdays or Thursdays at 8:30 p.m. or 9:30 p.m. Eastern Time. Additionally, this rather satirical and simplified approach to the topic is in accordance with *Scrubs*' typical diverting depiction of diseases (ranging from cancer to Carla's later postnatal depression [Season 6.04/05]) and tragic losses (e.g., the death of Ben Sullivan [Season 3.14] or nurse Laverne [Season 6.15]), but nevertheless depicts males' attempt to re-influence female independence when it comes to contraceptives and, ultimately, sexuality.

Comedy: Desperate Housewives (2004–2012)

This male interference is reversed in ABC's Sunday prime-time series *Desperate Housewives*, running between 2004 and 2012 Sundays at 9:00 p.m. Eastern Time. The series is set around several couples and families on fictional Wisteria Lane and is told by the character Mary Alice Young; although she committed suicide in the pilot episode (Season 1.01), she seems to be still present in order to arrange the plotlines and to comment on the events in her off-voice monologues at the beginning and the end of every episode.

One of the couples from Wisteria Lane, Gabrielle and Carlos Solis, ostensibly agreed about their family planning—but while Carlos wishes for a baby, Gabrielle very clearly makes her point in the episode "Guilt" (Season 1.08): "Before we got married we made a deal, remember? No kids.... We're not negotiating my uterus" (Season 1.08: 16:55 min.). This crisis comes to a head in the episode "Fear no More" (Season 1.20): Already the "previously on..." segment at the beginning of the episode ties to earlier events and reminds the viewer of the conflict 12 episodes (after all, almost 500 minutes of screen time) ago. Now, Carlos tampers with his wife's birth control pills and replaces them with mints.[7] When Gabrielle becomes sick inside a new car and vomits on the premium Italian leather seats (Season 1.20: 6:37 min.), the car saleswoman indicates that she could be pregnant. When she does a pregnancy test right in the drugstore (Season 1.20: 13:30 min.), the result is positive. Gabrielle is stunned and approaches Father Crowley for a conversation: "It's impossible, I'm on the pill.... It's a 99.9 percent effective sin" (Season 1.20: 21:50 min.). After yet another sickness, Gabrielle discovers that Carlos has swapped her pills (cf. Season 1.20: 34:05 min.)—as the omniscient voice-over narrator, the dead Mary Alice Young, then summarizes: "In that moment, while looking at the pills that had been so obviously tampered with, Gabrielle's nausea was suddenly replaced by an even stronger sensation: Rage." She immediately slaps her husband during his farewell party—Carlos is about to go to prison for half a year—in front of the assembled guests (Season 1.20: 35:46 min.). Interestingly, after a short moment, Carlos is pleased and smiles about his successful plan.

The starting point is very similar to *Scrubs*—only reversed: Here, the male partner wishes for a baby, while the woman refers to their earlier (and mutual) agreement. The birth control pill enables Gabrielle to fully be in charge of both her sexuality and fertility, while Carlos' interference symbolizes a proper act of sabotage. It's another form of perverting the original idea behind the pill; no woman should be forced to carry out a pregnancy she does not wish for. For millennia, there was no reliable cure for the inequality of the sexes and the pill changed that in the 20th century. Carlos tampering with Gabrielle's birth control can be read as a male attempt to turn back time and it serves as a grim reminder of the past where women could not "negotiate the uterus" because they simply had no rights at all.

Comedy: The Simpsons *(1989–)*

This section on rather satirical and exaggerated approaches is finished with the example of an animated sitcom: The long-running Fox show *The Simpsons*, created by cartoonist Matt Groening, depicts an American middle class family in the fictional town of Springfield. Based on classic U.S.–American television series from *Father Knows Best* (CBS/NBC, 1954–1960) to *The Cosby Show* (NBC, 1984–1992), the "average" family consists of the parents Homer and Marge, their two daughters Lisa and Maggie, their son Bart, as well as the family dog, Santa's Little Helper, and the cat Snowball.[8]

In contrast to procedural series, the structure of *The Simpsons* is even more reduced and predictable, since all events and adventures which happen during an episode are reversed at the end—no matter if Homer works as a train conductor (Season 4.12), a union leader (Season 4.17), a blackjack dealer (Season 5.10), a NASA-astronaut (Season 5.15), at a bowling alley (Season 6.13), as a boxer (Season 8.03), on tour as part of a "freak show" (Season 7.24), as an outsider artist (Season 10.19), an opera singer (Season 19.02), and so on, no matter if Marge becomes the co-owner of Moe's Tavern (Season 16.07) or opens her own gym (Season 19.07), no matter if the car or the tree house get damaged.

This formalistic approach allows it to feature exaggerated (and—at least for a television show with actual human actors—"unrealistic") events, but also to address a huge variety of socio-critical topics, since none of the events have any consequences. As Jason Mittell states:

> Whereas the standard sitcom traditionally reaffirms the family through its weekly restoration of equilibrium, *The Simpsons* uses its cartoon form to pose problems, more akin to those of real life, that simply cannot be solved within a half-hour. The show then regularly solves these unsolvable problems in spite of itself, both parodying the artificiality of the sitcom tradition and demonstrating the power of animation to represent "realities" which cannot be captured in a three-camera studio before a live-audience [190].

The Simpsons regularly uses this Trojan horse-strategy (Danneil 144)—a satirical approach toward actual (scientific, social, political, familial, etc.) issues—to address controversial topics other family sitcoms usually suppress. So, for example, a "childlike" perspective on contraception can be found in the 2009 episode "O Brother, Where Bart Thou?" (Season 21.08): Here, Bart dreams of having a brother, just like Lisa and Maggie being sisters. He seeks ("medical") advice from Springfield Elementary School's bullies who suggest Bart should swap his mother's birth control pills with small mints (the fictional Tac Tics).[9] According to Mittell, the problem of Bart's interference in his mother's contraception as well as his wish for a brother is actually solved within the limits of the family's situation: Marge catches her son in the bathroom while exchanging the pills and talks to him about sexuality and family planning. However, the subtext of the episode sheds light on an interesting matter: Bart wishes for a little brother, male companionship, so to speak. In order to achieve his goal, he turns his own mother into a means to an end: a birth machine, an object that he can, by changing her pill, control and adjust to his needs. Even though his actions are guided by childish naivety, he represents male hegemony exercising power over the female body. Bart's discussion with the slightly older school bullies, who are all male, raises awareness that boys are from an early age onwards exposed to a doctrine that favors male needs over female rights. Hence, it is only fitting that it is Marge, Bart's mother, who has to educate Bart on matters of reproduction and not Homer, himself almost indifferent to the matter.

Conclusion

Contraception is not only a topic of individual health, but also became a central aspect in a relationship's power structure: "The availability of reliable ways to prevent pregnancy has a significant impact on individual heterosexual relationships and on the broader picture of male-female relations" (Lips 158). Especially due to oral contraceptives, "women taking the pill could control their reproduction, even without the knowledge and/or consent of their partners" (158–59).

The central theme that connects all these shows—which are not unified by genre—is the ambivalent prospect of parenting a child. A pregnancy brings a variety of social and economic changes to everyone involved and almost always threatens someone's independence. Thus, who controls the means of conception is in charge of the relationship and influences the hierarchy of genders. Contraception and—to some extent—the option of an abortion become symbols of power as they obliterate some of the biological differences between the sexes, which leads to a new balance of power: "The shift from condoms used by men to birth control that required female agency and responsibility altered both women's approach to sex and men's attitude towards women as sexual partners" (Schwartz and Rutter 84). These shows exemplify and explore how women have yet to adapt to the changing circumstances, while men still seek loopholes to exercise power, which seemed almost lost by women's control about the "ifs" and "whens" of a pregnancy. For us, it is not only the birth control pill or other means of contraception as a symbol for changing "sexual politics" within a relationship, but rather how individuals use them as means to an end that makes contraception in general such an interesting topic for creators of television series. And these are definitely controversial themes, which surely puts the "quality" into "quality television."

Notes

1. Cf. the essay on advertising by Jamie Wagman in this volume where this is further discussed.

2. The Federal Communications Commission permits "profane speech" only between 10 p.m. and 6 a.m. (cf. FCC 2015:1). It is obvious, though, that the so-called "late fringe" after the prime time as well as the "graveyard slot" between 2 a.m. and the start of breakfast television at 6 a.m. reaches proportionally fewer audience members.

3. While there are studies that say by 2000 Catholics in most countries use contraception about as much as other denominations (cf. Stanford), *Brotherhood* offers a potentially exaggerated perspective on the facts and plays with stereotypes of Catholic Irish-Americans.

4. See, for example, Season 1.08: 20:16 min., Season 1.11: 38:10 min., Season 2.04: 21:50 min.

5. Although contraceptive pills are supposed to be stored "away from direct heat and light," there are currently no studies about a possible change in the effectiveness after cooking or baking available. The baking-in can be seen as a satirical exaggeration and should not be tried at home.

6. Carla's behavior is, of course, environmentally very inconsiderate, since the EE2 content is blamed for effects on the environment (see McKie; Moore et al.); instead, surplus pills should be taken to a pharmacy which will dispose of them responsibly.

7. Interestingly, Gabrielle doesn't notice the different form, the dissimilar taste, or the opened packaging; see Maierhofer "Finding Humor in Birth Control" in this volume on the same trick.

8. This constellation is (with only minor modifications) typical for animated family sitcoms. It can also be found in *Family Guy*, *Bob's Burgers* (Fox, since 2011), and *American*

Dad! (Fox/TBS, since 2005), and dates back to *The Flintstones* (ABC, 1960–1966) and *The Jetsons* (ABC, 1962–1963).

9. Interestingly, Bart tampered with birth control pills before: In the episode "Itchy & Scratchy: The Movie" (S4.06), his teacher Ms. Krabappel accuses Bart of "replacing my birth-control pills with Tic-Tacs" (S4.06: 02:55 min.), as Marge learns at a parent-teacher night.

Works Cited

Akass, Kim, and Janet McCabe. "What Has Carmela Ever Done for Feminism? Carmela Soprano and the Post-Feminist Dilemma." *Reading the Sopranos: Hit TV from HBO*. Ed. David Lavery. London: I.B. Tauris, 2006. 39–55. Print.
Aken'Ova, Osi. "Netflix Pick of the Week: House of Cards." Blog. *OKC.NET*. OKC.NET, 22 Apr. 2013. Web. 1 Feb. 2016.
Arosteguy, Katie. "'It was all a Fog': Motherhood and the Birth Experience in *Mad Men*." *Mad Men, Women, and Children: Essays on Gender and Generation*. Ed. Heather Marcovitch and Nancy Batty. Lanham, MD: Lexington, 2012. 139–157. Print.
Bellafante, Ginia. "Mobster and Politician, Neither Rolling in Clover." *New York Times*. New York Times, 30 Oct. 2008. Web. 1 Feb. 2016.
Benson, Michael D. *Coping with Birth Control*. New York: Rosen, 1998. Print.
Coontz, Stephanie. "Why *Mad Men* Is TV's Most Feminist Show." Opinion. *The Washington Post*. The Washington Post, 10 Oct. 2010. Web. 1 Feb. 2016.
Crampton, Caroline. "Strong, Interesting Female Characters Are the Secret of *House of Cards*' Success." Blog. *NewStatesman*. New Statesman, 14 Feb. 2014. Web. 1 Feb. 2016.
Danneil, Sandra. "Lachen ohne Ende … Die Simpsons als transgressive Selbstüberbietung." *Quality-TV. Die narrative Spielwiese des 21. Jahrhunderts?!* Ed. Jonas Nesselhauf and Markus Schleich. Münster: Lit, 2014. 133–146. Print.
David, Henry P. "Overview." *From Abortion to Contraception: A Resource to Public Policies and Reproductive Behavior in Central and Eastern Europe from 1917 to the Present*. Ed. Henry P. David. Westport, CT: Greenwood, 1999. 3–22. Print.
Dean, Will. "Mad Men: Series One, Episode One." Blog. *The Guardian*. Guardian News and Media, 19 Apr. 2010. Web. 1 Feb. 2016
DeLillo, Don. *White Noise*. New York: Penguin, 2001. Print.
Djerassi, Carl. *In Retrospect: From the Pill to the Pen*. London: Imperial College Press, 2014.
_____. *Der Schattensammler. Die allerletzte Autobiografie*. Vienna: Haymon, 2013. Print.
_____. *This Man's Pill. Reflections on the 50th Birthday of the Pill*. Oxford: Oxford University Press, 2003. Print.
Doyle, Sady. "Mad Men's Very Modern Sexism Problem." *The Atlantic*. The Atlantic Monthly Group, 2 Aug. 2010. Web. 1 Feb. 2016.
FCC. "Consumer Guide: Obscene, Indecent and Profane Broadcasting." Blog. *FCC*. FCC, 25 Mar. 2015. Web. 1 Feb. 2016.
Firestone, Shulamith. *The Dialectic of Sex*. New York: Morrow, 1970. Print.
Foucault, Michel. "Disciplines and Sciences of the Individual." *The Foucault Reader*. Ed. Paul Rabinow. New York: Pantheon, 2010. 169–256. Print.
Franzen, Johannes. "'Conscience is a Killer.' Die Falschspieler in *The Shield* und *KDD*." *Gegenwart in Serie. Abgründige Milieus im aktuellen Qualitätsfernsehen*. Ed. Jonas Nesselhauf and Markus Schleich. Berlin: Neofelis, 2015. 79–95. Print.
Freud, Sigmund. "Einige Charaktertypen aus der psychoanalytischen Arbeit." *Bildende Kunst und Literatur*. Frankfurt: Fischer, 1969. 229–253. Print.
Green, Jonathon, and Nicholas Karolides. "Motion Picture Production Code." *Encyclopedia of Censorship*. Ed. Jonathon Green and Nicholas Karolides. New York: Facts on File, 2005. 361–364. Print.
James, E.L. *Fifty Shades of Grey*. New York: Vintage, 2011. Print.
John Paul II. "Evangelium Vitae." Encyclical. *Vatican*. Libreria Editrice Vaticana, 25 Mar. 1995. Web. 1 Feb. 2016.
Landau, Solange. "'I'm feeling hungry today.' Die Machthungrigen in *House of Cards* und

Borgen." *Gegenwart in Serie. Abgründige Milieus im aktuellen Qualitätsfernsehen.* Ed. Jonas Nesselhauf and Markus Schleich. Berlin: Neofelis, 2015. 19–32. Print.
Lee, Yoke-Lian. "Contraception." *Politics of Gender. A Survey.* Ed. Yoke-Lian Lee. London: Routledge, 2010. 213. Print.
Lips, Hilary M. *Gender. The Basics.* London: Routledge, 2014. Print.
Margulies, Lee. "Television Confronts the Contraceptive Issue." *Los Angeles Times.* Los Angeles Times, 3 Feb. 1987. Web. 1 Feb. 2016.
Martin, Brett. *Difficult Men.* New York: Penguin, 2013. Print.
McKie, Robert. "£30bn Bill to Purify Water System After Toxic Impact of Contraceptive Pill." *The Guardian.* Guardian News and Media, 2 June 2012. Web. 1 Feb. 2016.
Millett, Kate. *Sexual Politics.* Urbana: University of Illinois Press, 2000. Print.
Mittell, Jason. "Making Fun of Genres—The Politics of Parody and Genre Mixing in Soap and *The Simpsons.*" *Genre and Television: From Cop Shows to Cartoons in American Culture.* Ed. Jason Mittell. New York: Routledge, 2004. 153–195. Print.
Molyneaux, Heather. "Images of Women, Safety, Sexuality, and the Pill in the Sixties." *Gender, Health and Popular Culture. Historical Perspectives.* Ed. Cheryl Krasnick Warsh. Waterloo: Wilfrid Laurier University Press, 2011. 65–88. Print.
Moore, Kirsten, et al. "Birth Control Hormones in Water: Separating Myth From Fact." Editorial. *Contraception* Aug. 2011. *ARHP.* ARHP, 2011. Web. 1 Feb. 2016.
Narkunski, Michael. "*Brotherhood*: The Final Season Review." *JustPressPlay.* Just Press Play, 8 Oct. 2009. Web. 1 Feb. 2016.
Nesselhauf, Jonas, and Markus Schleich, eds. *Das andere Fernsehen?! Eine Bestandsaufnahme des 'Quality Television.'* Bielefeld: Transcript, 2015. Print.
Nusser, Tanja. "Reproduktion/Reproduktionstechnologien." *Metzler Lexikon Gender Studies. Ansätze—Personen—Grundbegriffe.* Ed. Renate Kroll. Stuttgart: Metzler, 2002. 340. Print.
Parry, Manon. *Broadcasting Birth Control: Mass Media and Family Planning.* New Brunswick: Rutgers University Press, 2013. Print.
Polman, Dick. "On Condom Commercials, Watchword Is Caution." *Philly.* Philadelphia Media Network (Digital), 7 Feb. 1987. Web. 1 Feb. 2016.
Rosin, Hanna. "More Than Sharks Love Blood." *Slate Magazine.* Slate, 18 Mar. 2013. Web. 1 Feb. 2016.
Saraiya, Sonia. "*House of Cards* Returns: Let the War between Frank and Claire Underwood Begin." *Salon.* Salon Media Group, 28 Feb. 2015. Web. 1 Feb. 2016.
Schwartz, Pepper, and Virginia Rutter. *The Gender of Sexuality.* Lanham, MD: Altamira, 2000. Print.
Seibert, Johanna. "'Let's Get Liberated!' Feminist Politics and Queer Subtexts in AMC's *Mad Men.*" *Journal of Serial Narration on Television* 1 (2013): 43–85. Print.
Shakespeare, William. *The Tragedy of Macbeth.* Oxford: Oxford University Press, 2008. Print.
Shanner, Laura. "Reproduction." *A Companion to Gender Studies.* Ed. Philomena Essed, David Theo Goldberg, and Audrey Kobayashi. Malden, MA: Blackwell, 2009. 405–414. Print.
Shattuk, Kathryn. "Drugs and Sex (and Politics and Motherhood)." *New York Times.* New York Times, 16 Nov. 2008. Web. 1 Feb. 2016.
Sichtermann, Barbara. "Die Frauenbewegung und die Pille." *Die Pille. Von der Lust und von der Liebe.* Ed. Gisela Staupe and Lisa Vieth. Berlin: Rowohlt, 1996. 55–66. Print.
Sison, Marianne D. "Gender, Culture and Power: Competing Discourses on the Philippine Reproductive Health Bill." *Gender and Public Relations: Critical Perspectives on Voice, Image and Identity.* Ed. Christine Daymon and Kristin Demetrious. New York: Routledge, 2014. 177–197. Print.
Stanford, Peter. "Roman Catholic Church." *BBC.* BBC, 29 June 2011. Web. 1 Feb. 2016.
Stanley, Alessandra. "In Showtime's *Brotherhood*, Crime and Politics Meet in Providence." *New York Times.* New York Times, 7 July 2006. Web. 1 Feb. 2016.
Thompson, Robert J. *Television's Second Golden Age. From Hill Street Blues to ER.* Syracuse: Syracuse University Press, 1996. Print.
Zheng, Marina. "Claire Underwood's Working Wardrobe." *Observer.* Observer, 1 Apr. 2015. Web. 1 Feb. 2016.

A Romantic Steroid or a Great Performance?
Visual Culture and the Pill

JAMIE WAGMAN

After several years of small- and large-scale pill trials, the Food and Drug Administration approved the first birth control pill, Enovid, in 1960. In the early years after the introduction of the pill, marketers and advertisers used images that revealed a shifting discourse in the field of sexuality over the female body. While early popular magazine images in *Time* and *Look* marketed the pill as an aesthetically pleasing object or an abstract symbol, later advertisements and even the pill packages themselves inserted women's hands, and then their bodies, into the photographs, showing that the concept of American sexuality had changed over time to include in-the-flesh, sexually-active women. These later images often patronized women, however, treating them as infantile or essentializing them as ultra-feminine.[1] I present the images in this essay as an archival collection of birth control pill visual culture, each image constructed and presented to the public with a specific intention.

Shawn Michelle Smith and Ann Laura Stoler illuminated the purpose and use of archives. Smith wrote: "archives are ideological; they are conceived with political intent, to make specific claims on cultural meaning" (7). Both she and Stoler understood primary sources as articulating emotions and feelings of the past. Stoler argued that "archives are not simply accounts of actions.... They are records of uncertainty and doubt" (4). This is true in this collection of visual culture, and the primary sources presented here articulate whose voices dominate the discourse on birth control—discussing who should reproduce, why, and when. In examining what is not present in this collection of images, we begin to think about the voices of minority and poor women who were the first women in the world to try the pill before its FDA approval. In *Along the Archival Grain*, Stoler wrote that when examining what is not present in archives, one can glean what constituted the common sense of a particular time. Material is unwritten for several reasons, Stoler explained; either "it could go without saying ... or it could not yet be articulated" (3). In this particular collection of visual culture, material is missing because of body anxiety and the mystique surrounding women's bodies and sexualities. The recovery of women's voices is at stake in the archive, and this collection of images exposes the consequences when men and women of privilege speak for other women and when women remain nameless.

Photographers and advertisers used images to instill the pill with meaning about women's bodies and sexuality. Pharmaceutical companies, advertisers, and marketers all debated the real meaning of the pill, and together these powerful institutions created narratives about the pill that dominated popular culture. To some pharmacists and advertisers, the pill was a "romantic" drug that allowed men and women a new freedom. At times the medical establishment told women that the pill would liberate them from their restrictive monthly cycles. At other times, advertisers marketed the pill as feminine, infantile, or sexy. To many photographers and marketers, the pill was tied to whiteness and beauty. Although the visual culture of the pill changed over time, the later images still failed to present the array of multicultural women who took the pill. Both the early and later images are troubling: the early images offer a sterile and clinical environment devoid of women's bodies, while the later images depict an overtly feminized caricature of white women's sexuality. Together this collection of visual culture, these photographs and advertisements of the pill, along with pill package images, illuminate the ways in which the pill stood for contrasting symbols to the parties with the power to shape our national understanding of birth control.

Despite the fact that the women in this selection of birth control images were white, public health physicians and family planning clinics often targeted minorities and working class women while first testing the pill. Although some people in positions of power and privilege did so because of their "liberal" values—they hoped the pill would help to alleviate poverty and control the country's population—these values were also laden with judgment. Yet this history of the pill is not the story most frequently told in the images in popular magazines, films, advertisements, and a pharmaceutical company's booklet. Instead of presenting a complicated history in which the medical establishment targeted women of little education and means to become test subjects, images often convey the medical establishment's respectability and authority. In focusing as much on what and who was not featured in advertisements and early photography of the pill, we have a means to understand the class and racial binary that existed throughout the birth control movement in the mid–20th century.[2]

Visibility and the Archive

My work is informed by Shawn Michelle Smith's and Richard Dyer's framework about aesthetics, memory, and whiteness. Smith explained the role of archival matter—such as photographs—in understanding historical narratives:

> The archive is a vehicle of memory, and as it becomes the trace on which an historical record is founded, it makes some people, places, things, ideas, and events visible, while relegating others, through its signifying absences, to invisibility. In this sense, then, archives have an ideological function not only in the moment of their inception but also across time, for they determine in large part what will be collectively remembered and how it will be remembered [8].

If we are to glean "how it will be remembered" from the earliest images of the pill in the 1960s, then we will see the pill as medicinal although disconnected from clinical trial participants, later patients, activists, and the many people who had roles in the pill's layered history. Later images in the 1980s render the pill as a capsule for the white woman of privilege. The popularity of using images of white women in advertisements and images reveals a tension between the historical reality and the narrative about birth control presented to consumers. As Dyer wrote, the association between whiteness and ordinariness "means that white people can both lay claim to the spirit that aspires to the heights of humanity and yet supposedly speak and act disinterestedly as humanity's most average and unremarkable representatives" (*White* 223). Whiteness presenting itself as average and ordinary in images falsely allows white people to act disinterestedly—although the white people who created and marketed the pill had a clear agenda in pushing the pill upon poor women of color. Legal scholar Kimberlé Crenshaw identified the problem with identity politics ignoring intragroup differences, and her theory of intersectionality also informs this project because the popular mainstream narrative that the pill empowered and empowers women ignores intragroup differences.

Birth control advertisements were not common in the early 1960s, but they had existed for decades in a covert manner. Because of the 1873 Comstock laws that made it illegal to send or advertise contraceptives through the mail or publish material considered obscene, including all contraception and sexually educational material, women's magazines stopped speaking in code about birth control once an overseeing body began regulating advertisements and banning women's magazines from publishing obvious birth control matter. Anthony Comstock, who founded the New York Society for the Suppression of Vice, led the organization for 40 years and attempted to rid the public of what his institution considered lewd or immoral (see Boyer).

These restrictions were overturned when a U.S. District Court of Appeals ruled in 1936 in *United States v. One Package of Japanese Pessaries* that birth control devices were exempted from restriction under the Comstock Law. Long before the advent of the pill, some women sometimes looked to household products—cleaning supplies—to assist them with preventing pregnancies. As scholar Amy Sarch observed, advertisements in women's magazines from the 1920s and 1930s for cleaning products (that some women used with a diaphragm to prevent pregnancy) spoke to women covertly about how to protect themselves from pregnancies. Sarch wrote that slogans such as "Lysol pursues germs into hidden folds and crevices," which ran in *McCall's*, a monthly women's magazine, in 1934, signaled a woman's body in ads that ran prior to the Pure Food and Drug law of 1938, a law requiring that drugs be proved safe before marketing (see U.S. Department of Health & Human Services).

The Earliest Pill Visual Culture

Prior to the pill, covert birth control advertisements did not typically focus on a woman's body. One of the earliest advertisements for the first pill, however, did precisely that. One of the first advertisements for the pill illustrated a woman with pronounced curvature, her hands bound by chains ripped apart, "Andromeda Freed from her Chains" (see reproduction in Junod and Marks 119). The ad appeared in *Enovid Bulletin* for medical professionals in May of 1964. The woman was not a real human figure, but instead a mosaic outline comprised of stone. She arched her back, one leg up, her body leaping forward with hands still in cuffs, the broken chain dangling. This woman seems an ethereal, athletic female. Because the illustration lacked any class or racial markers, this woman could be any woman, belonging to any race, ethnicity, and class. She could be married or single. She is on the cusp of a new life—freed from old barriers and constraints. The advertisement's accompanying text read:

> Unfettered. From the beginning woman has been a vassal to the temporal demands—and frequently the aberrations—of the cyclic mechanism of her reproductive system. Now to a degree heretofore unknown, she is permitted normalization, enhancement or suspension of cyclic function and procreative potential. This new medical control is symbolized in an illustration borrowed from ancient Greek mythology–Andromeda freed from her chains [Junod and Marks 119].

While a liberating message is often a popular one, the irony of a rescue narrative is that it assumed what preceded a rescue was a captivity narrative, and in this case, one of bondage. Also, the "rescue" implications in the text and illustration of Andromeda did not match the reality of marketing and disseminating the birth control pill in 1960. When the pill was approved by the FDA, it was not marketed to everyone. Enovid had to be prescribed, and most doctors would not prescribe it to unmarried women.[3]

The early Enovid advertisement's "every-woman" theme contradicted the references to ancient Greece, where bondage was common. In their scholarship, Ella Shohat and Robert Stam discussed a series of newspaper ads from 1991 appealing to Greece's ethnocentric "myth of origins" via a series of beautiful images. However, according to the authors, this series ignores "the slave-based nature of Greek 'democracy.'" The "Andromeda" advertisement's ancient Greece references also romanticizes this "myth of origins" (Shohat and Stam 56–57). The real mythic narrative provides an even starker contrast. As birth control historian Lara Marks, in her study of early attitudes toward Enovid, pointed out in her description of this advertisement, Andromeda was rescued from a rock by Perseus, who asked for her hand in marriage—the story implying that a woman must be married to take this new pharmaceutical. Junod and Marks argued in their 2002 article that the advertisement's rescue narrative did not account for women activists and consumers creating and purchasing this new technology.

"Andromeda" was somewhat of an anomaly in the earliest images and advertisements of the birth control pill because of its creative illustration, its storyline of marriage and femininity, and even its caption's contradictory suggestion of freedom and control, possibly because it was aimed at physicians. The word "control" is an important part of birth control discourse. Upon its introduction to the public in 1960, the pill was marketed solely as a tool to help women regulate their cycles for "ovulation control" (Marsh and Ronner 213). Because advertisements excluded plotlines about intercourse and pregnancy, if this new technology freed women, just what did it free them from? The 1964 "Andromeda" advertisement's accompanying text suggests that women's bodies are unnatural, their menstrual cycles binding them to unnecessary pains and compromises. Feminist scientist Anne Fausto-Sterling has studied this common trope in scientific literature and media. She asks why medical researchers have long used "syndrome" and "symptom" to describe the state of women's bodies throughout very normal stages of menstruation. The presence of early birth control advertisements like "Andromeda" reinforces a message to women—via their male doctors—about the problems associated with normal menstrual cycles. While the caption claims to free women, it also imposes control in the text's claim to "permit" women naturalization, indicating pharmaceutical power instead of free will.

Another one of the earliest images of the pill, in a book entitled *A Prescription for Family Planning: The Story of Enovid*, avoids any bodily reference. This image demonstrates the pharmaceutical manufacturer's avoidance of references to women's bodies. Taken from a book written for G.D. Searle & Company, the company that developed the pill, this 1964 image suggests the history of research behind the drug and asserts the pharmaceutical's efficiency and safety. The company assured readers that "everyone involved in the production and distribution of medicinal compounds has a twofold goal: to make them (1) effective; (2) safe" (G.D. Searle 44). The hardback book featured several small drawings, most of them sketches of chemical compounds or drawings of the female reproductive system. However, one larger illustration consisted of three images: a man in a white laboratory coat meeting with a woman, a table with men peering over papers, and another man in a white laboratory coat hunched over beakers with chemicals (G.D. Searle & Company 26; untitled image). Together these drawings represented the several steps that pill manufacturer G.D. Searle & Company wanted to convey to the public. Although the book explained that the drug was first tested on poor women of color before it received FDA approval, what the drawings do not show is the faces and bodies of these women in Port-au-Prince, Haiti, and San Juan, Puerto Rico. While the women were some of the first women in the world on the pill, they did not know the pharmaceutical had not yet received FDA approval (G.D. Searle & Company 12).[4] Also missing from both text and images were the mixed reactions from minority men and women once the pill began to be marketed to poor and minority neighborhoods in the United States. Instead, the montage created a sterile, clinical environment, a world in which test tubes and educated, white, male physicians in lab coats offered white women their best and brightest inventions.

Images Change in a Changing Culture

In contrast to the illustration in G.D. Searle's book, more common and typical images of the pill from the 1960s emphasized the pill itself and avoided the women taking it. The 1964 *Look* magazine feature story, "Catholics Take a New Look at the Pill" by Jack Star, grabs additional attention with a photograph by Archie Lieberman and a cutline describing "a cascade of birth control pills," a depiction of massive amounts of birth control pills being produced at G.D. Searle & Company (Star). The word "cascade," referring to a waterfall, is a common trope in discourse on women's sexuality and bodies—as though a reference to a waterfall does the job of conjuring a woman's form although the photograph does not (Caputi 321).[5] The black and white image was at once sterile—detached from any people or places—and may have been considered daunting or intimidating in number to some, especially at a time when social conservatives were critiquing the pill for "relaxing moral standards" (Tone 236). The magazine article, seemingly all too aware of these criticisms, frames oral contraception as a way to "greatly improve the rhythm method." The lack of human bodies in the photograph at G.D. Searle begs the question of what was beyond the frame: factory workers, other pharmaceuticals, or perhaps a photographer's assistant casting light upon the pills so they might look more symbolic. This early image of the pill cast it as a harmless abstraction—although the earliest form of the pill was far from harmless to many women. This abstract photograph also lacked people, time, and place, reluctant to link the pills to plotlines or bodies. The photographers seemed intent on capturing the pharmaceutical itself, as if a mere pill spoke for itself about a new era of sexual mores and standards. As birth control historian Andrea Tone explained in *Devices and Desires*, the FDA had approved Enovid for "gynecological disorders, such as infertility, habitual miscarriage, and excessive menstruation. But although the FDA limited legal licensure to gynecological disorders, nothing could prevent a woman from using the Pill for 'off-label' uses" (226). This stark stand-alone photograph lacking corporeality may have contributed to the "hype" that helped Enovid lose its pharmaceutical brand name and instead become iconic as "the pill," the only capsule that needed no name (Lieberman).

Archie Lieberman's photograph of G.D. Searle's cascade of birth control pills is part of the Library of Congress's collection of pill photography (see "Gallery" on *American Experience*). The archive's collection also includes a photograph of "the pill," which was held up by a hand that simulated the "okay" sign for viewers. After the Senate held hearings on the pill's side effects, *Look* magazine featured this same photograph in 1970 in an article by physician (Edward) T. Tyler, emphasizing the pill's safety, with the title "The Pill Is Safe" directly above the image (Tyler 65). The Library of Congress's Look Magazine Photograph Collection online description states that the accompanying 1970 photograph by Arthur Rothstein "shows a woman's hand holding a birth control pill between her thumb and forefinger" (Rothstein). Tyler in his article (with the lead "No medication is foolproof, but taken with your doctor's advice …") stressed the importance of following medical advice while taking the pill. Again, we see an absence of bodies in these early images of the birth control pill, with only a gradual introduction to the materiality of the woman's body through the insertion of the hand. Visually fragmenting the body reduced a viewer's gaze from the body and de-emphasized the role of that body as an active participant in the medical community.

The use of a white woman's hand in one of the earliest photographs of the pill has social significance. The popularity of using white images of women in advertisements unveils a tension between the historical reality and the narrative about birth control presented to consumers. In the 1960s, a critical time in abolishing discrimination, a connection between white femininity and birth control in photography did a disservice to women of color by not considering their sexuality, marital relationships, and family planning strategies. Scientists chose women of color as early subjects to test the side effects of the pill, but again these women's faces and bodies were not the images displayed in advertisements for birth control.

The lack of diversity in the earliest photos of the pill evidences the way in which the dominant culture in America suppressed discussion of racial difference. Not including women of color in early visual depictions of the pill meant not acknowledging their importance and lived experiences in American culture. Visual culture scholar Michael Harris's work discusses the many ways in which visual culture often associated whiteness with normality and blackness or darkness with "poor self-esteem and self-image" (19). Picturing white skin as typical, average, and ordinary has had powerful consequences. As Dyer wrote, "white power secures its dominance by seeming not to be anything in particular" ("White" 44). Not every audience may have had the same interpretation of the birth control images that showed only white women, but some may have interpreted them as alienating minorities. Since the 1960s, magazine advertisements increased the number of sexual illustrations, sexual portrayals, and visual depictions of, instead of verbal reference to, sexual intercourse. Researchers also argued that, in the absence of comprehensive sex education, the media has played a significant role in influencing young people's attitudes toward sexuality.[6] The boom of visual representations of contraception has led to a change in the ways in which the pill was portrayed in visual and material culture—from sterile photographs of the pharmaceutical to the sexualizing of in-the-flesh women's bodies.

Some pill packages associated the pill with the image of a young and attractive white woman. Searle's Ovulen 1 mg compact dispenser case, displayed in the exhibit "Virtue, Vice, and Contraband" at Dittrick Medical History Center at Case Western Reserve University in 2009, featured a young, white woman on its case.[7] The exhibit described the young woman as "a Caucasian woman with blonde hair in a blue dress, white gloves and shoes; the product name 'Ovulen 1 mg' is printed in blue on the cover below the illustration." The woman looked, dressed, and walked like a confident fashion model, similar to a Barbie doll with flaxen locks, and through this image the manufacturer marketed the pill to the young, beautiful, and fashionable white woman. While the exhibit itself is multifaceted in its presentation about ancient methods of birth control, what stood out was the gendered forms of contraception and the ways in which pill manufacturers tried to market the pill to women with images and symbols of femininity.

Gendering the Pill

The pill has also been repeatedly portrayed in films and storylines about "romance." In 1967, medical doctor J. Clifford Reid wrote about this very type of pill, Ovulen 1, in an article for a medical journal titled "Another Romantic Steroid—Ovulen." Reid's article welcomed the oral contraceptive as the "outcome of eleven years' research in the oral contraceptive field by G.D. Searle & Company" (57). He also documented the results of a clinical trial in 1964, explaining that the 77 patients did not experience any unplanned pregnancies (57). Except for the title, nothing in the article mentioned the idea of romance. Therefore, his suggestion of romance likely referred to the pill's purpose and its tie to sex, as though all sexual interludes spoke of romance.

Reviewing pill tablet dispensers provides a window into marketers' ideas about gender. Most pill tablet dispensers were simple, though some bore gender markers such as butterflies, flowers, and feathers on their covers. Printing botanical symbols of femininity on pill packages both stripped the pill of the notion that it had anything to do with sexuality and simultaneously associated sexuality with childlike symbols. As French philosopher Michel Foucault wrote, "bourgeois society repressed infantile sexuality to the point where it refused even to speak of it or acknowledge its existence ... one might argue that the purpose of these discourses was precisely to prevent children from having a sexuality" (120). By giving the impression that womanly sexuality is like a child's sexuality (which, as Foucault explained, is often denied to exist), the pill packaging thus communicated that the contraceptive device had no sexual role at all. Therefore, the pill was a safe, clean, medical prescription endorsed by the medical establishment and had nothing to do with intercourse.

Yet another pill tablet dispenser bore what became known as the "Blue Lady," a head profile of a young woman in blue (*American Experience*, gallery 10). Although the drawing of this woman lacked a natural skin tone, her profile and straight lustrous hair might be associated with whiteness. As Harris argued, not just skin color is associated with race. He explained, "What is not clear is what white is—what it looks like. It can include blue, brown, gray, or green eyes and blonde, red, or brunette hair color. It is usually not fragmented or undermined by national or ethnic subidentities" (19). The "Blue Lady's" "every woman" status must be assumed here, again emphasizing the disservice of one Westernized image of beauty standing for all women.

The pill packaging often communicated gender through color choice, design, and materials. Most of the pills were encased in gendered pastel shades of pink, yellow, and blue, although Ovex's 1968 Tab Stick dispenser was an actual lipstick container.[8] The tube of lipstick itself was an obvious signal to women that this is for them; it also signaled beauty, allure, and performance. Much has been made in feminist scholarship about gender as a social construct, from Fausto-Sterling's discussion of a lack of medical evidence about biological differences between the sexes to philosopher Judith Butler's idea that gender is a performance—in other words, women might perform their femininity by wearing lipstick. In this case, women might perform their gender and also their heterosexuality by holding an Ovex Tab Stick.

Although the pill packages themselves de-emphasized their use in sexual encounters, they simultaneously oversexualized women. Instead of looking at women as consumers with purchasing power or as patients of the medical establishment, those who designed the pill packaging and marketed Ovulen and Ovex conceived of women as receptacles for cosmetics and birth control pills.[9] Placing birth control pills in a lipstick container also sent the messages that the pill is something that should not be seen as such and that oral contraceptives are just another of the many gadgets to be found in a woman's purse. Such messages trivialized the chemical makeup of the pill and the side effects that some women suffered from taking it.[10] Although pill package designs may not be expected to pave the way for challenging gender norms and expectations, they did not need to adhere to sharp guidelines about the way women should look to appear attractive and acceptable to men.

A popular trope in birth control history has been the story about young, white women gaining control of their bodies, a storyline challenged by historian Beth Bailey. Her 1997 article, "Prescribing the Pill: Politics, Culture, and the Sexual Revolution in America's Heartland," discussed the introduction and use of oral contraceptives in Lawrence, Kansas, during the 1960s and 1970s. Her research disputed the notion that the pill contributed to women's sexual liberation; instead, she pointed to the federal government's concern over population growth and social welfare programs as inspiration for the proliferation of the pill. Bailey wrote about the significance of the American Public Health Association's reference to population growth in 1963 as "one of the world's most important health problems," a message received, understood, and promoted by President Lyndon B. Johnson, who backed federal support for birth control for the poor during his Great Society domestic program (830). Bailey's work subverted a national narrative that the pill was inspired by women and created for women to use as they pleased during the sexual revolution, a narrative also underscored in visual pill advertisements and ephemera.[11]

The Pill and Great Performances (Cycle After Cycle)

In contrast to several of the earliest images of the pill, some later advertisements used long, complicated storylines to sell the pill. In 1988, the Ortho Pharmaceutical Corporation, known today as Janssen Inc., sent an advertisement to physicians in a pink envelope marked with a pair of ballet slippers in the corner. The advertisement was for Ortho-Novum 7/7/7, a triphasic oral contraceptive created in 1984. Women who used Ortho-Novum took seven white pills, seven light peach pills, seven peach pills, and seven green pills that served only as "reminders" in each monthly pill package. By 1990, this particular oral contraceptive was noted as very popular (Reiter and Baer).

In this particular advertisement, calligraphy alerted the physician to the message on the envelope: "Great Performances Inside: One of ballet's most coveted roles!" Inside the envelope was a pop-up advertisement for the oral contraceptive, with a *Swan Lake* theme. A scene from the famous ballet *Swan Lake* was depicted above the advertising text for Ortho-Novum's 7/7/7, "Great Performances, Cycle After Cycle," and the Swan Queen Odette balanced on toe before an audience, performing one of the greatest ballet roles for any ballerina.[12] Like the lipstick tablet dispenser, the advertisement also chose to associate the pill with symbols of femininity: the color pink, ballet, the prima ballerina on pointe, her chin up, her clavicle bones jutting outward, her arms and left leg pointing outward delicately, her taffeta tutu encasing her, along with the arms of a man: perhaps her prince, or perhaps in the arms of the alluring villain, von Rothbart.

The illustration is explained in the left lower corner: "In Tchaikovsky's *Swan Lake*, the dual role of Odette, the Swan Queen, and Odile, daughter of the evil Rothbart, is one of the most challenging and prized a ballerina may dance. This part calls for 32 consecutive turns—more than any other classical ballet!" The advertisement then clumsily segued to the point in large print: "In oral contraceptive therapy, / Great Performances, / cycle after cycle / Unique ratios of low-dose norethindrone and ethinyl estradiol help maintain performance." The connection between *Swan Lake* and this new oral contraceptive, according to Ortho, was "great performances" time and time again. The advertisement also made a loose connection between a woman's typical 28- to 35-day menstrual cycle and the 32 turns called for by the featured ballerina. The main point was that Ortho-Novum777 performed well, cycle after cycle, with "low rates of breakthrough bleeding, low incidence of nuisance side-effects," and "low-dose norethindrone."

The text assumed that a community of gynecologists must have some awareness or first-hand knowledge of *Swan Lake*, or would have recognized the importance and grandeur of the ballet. Of course, most who have seen or know this piece also know its tragic ending: the swan dies. A poem about the ballet titled "After 'Swan Lake,' Act II at the San Francisco Ballet," ended with this final sentence: "The swan is doomed / in his embrace, enchanted and entombed" (Doyle). In the story, the swan princess, Odette, chose to die rather than to keep living without the love of her prince. One can only wonder whether those in charge of designing such a birth control advertisement considered the death of the Swan Queen. If taking the pill made one similar to Odette, then would consumers, too, suffer deadly consequences? In fact, some would. Women who have depression, migraines, high blood pressure, diabetes, high cholesterol, or a history of strokes or heart attacks, among other health problems, should not take these drugs (Ortho-Novum). Though this particular brand of oral contraception—still around today, 25 years later—was not directly linked to the early or most recent deaths of women on contraception or lawsuits, contraindications and precautions exist for many oral contraceptives, and many women still take the pill. Therefore, there are bound to be women suffering from complications, some of which may be deadly. While research on oral contraceptives was relatively limited when Ortho-Novum hit the market in 1984, today many academic papers and news articles have been written on the link between oral contraceptives and cervical cancer, breast cancer, and benign liver tumors, among other problems (National Cancer Institute). Few audiences would associate the pill with danger, however, when that audience's collective image of the pill includes a ballet stage.

Of course, death must not be dwelled upon—at least not by all audiences of literature and visual culture on the pill. Merging the pill with the story of the Swan Queen can have multiple meanings, as any dance piece may. Dance historian Selma Jeanne Cohen argued that *Swan Lake* should be open to multiple interpretations: "it may be presented as a simple, humanly touching love story or as a majestic declaration on the nature of good and evil. One era will conceive it as romance, another as melodrama, and still another will interpret it as classical tragedy." She explained that only "through its performances" has the ballet's essence been revealed to audiences (11). In other words, the directors and dancers of the ballet make choices that communicate the truth about the characters and the plot, and audiences of this advertisement could have therefore carried with them multiple interpretations of the true nature of this dance.

The nature of a performance must be emphasized; the advertisement itself performed a task to its audience. By associating oral contraception with a grand narrative about love and death, the advertisement performed ideas about womanhood and sexuality. Though likely unaware of such an interpretation, the pharmaceutical company associated women with a fairy tale, and in typical fairy tale fashion, the fulcrum of the story is the man, a prince. The woman in *Swan Lake* was not quite a woman. Instead she was caught between being a woman and a swan, morphing into a swan each day. The narrative in this advertisement reflects *The Journal of Consumer Research*'s claim that some advertisements feature only positive attributes about a product in order to create favorable attitudes about the product (Munch, Boller and Swasy 94).

Of course, if a woman doesn't take the pill at the same time every day or if she misses a dose, then the pill doesn't work, or "perform," and a woman's cycle is interrupted. Therefore, the advertisers emphasized regularity in taking the pill and in the menstrual cycle, suggesting the contradictory nature of freedom and control over a woman's ovulation. Because this particular ad was mailed to physicians, it implies that they have a role in the performance as director over a woman's cycle—the control being placed in their hands instead of the woman taking the pill. Her agency over her controlled and regulated body is then under someone else's control.

Conclusion

Together, the photography represented here must be treated as its own archive, one that reveals a layered tale about the ways in which the consumer is perceived. Sometimes she was not considered at all by an image; other times she was considered a naked pawn. Still other images used drawings of butterflies, flowers, and ballerinas to imply that women were childlike and easily impressed. Although the pill is not treated as profane in this later collection of images and material culture, the condescending treatment of women impresses upon the reader that this drug has to be something ultra-feminine and girlish, masking a supposedly darker narrative about sexuality. Depictions of the natural world or of pink ballet slippers cannot take away the fact that the pill allows women to have sex without worrying about pregnancy. The fact that images from nature and art are used to entice the viewer shows us that the real nature of the pill must not be mentioned for a reason—that the pill is, in fact, "profane." The study of this particular selection of visual culture of the pill allows us to gain an understanding of the gradual acceptance and inclusion of the woman's body in visual and material culture. The pill has been tied to many innocuous, playful, and feminine objects– cosmetics, butterflies, flowers, and ballet. As cultural studies scholar Stuart Hall asserted, "meaning is *not* in the object or person or things, nor is it *in* the world. It is we who fix the meaning so firmly that, after a while, it comes to seem natural and inevitable" (21). In other words, although the pill was not "natural," through the repetition of convincing advertisements and images, it became associated with ideas about what is natural and normal— and eventually many people became convinced that taking the pill meant having a "natural" menstrual cycle and maintaining a "normal" sexual relationship.

Whether the pill is being normalized or endowed with cultural meaning, studying the visual and material culture of the pill can provide us with deeper knowledge about the ways in which pharmaceutical companies, marketers, advertisers, and photographers viewed women consumers since the early 1960s. In the earliest advertisement for Enovid, women consumers were told that the pill was helping them—either by gaining control of their family planning or control of their monthly cycles. Young women consumers may have been considered by advertisers and marketers as impressionable, as shown by the overly feminine and infantile images such as butterflies and flowers on pill packages or by the vampy, sexy pill packaging of a lipstick container. We also can note that physicians were targeted to see, understand, and believe pharmaceutical companies' elaborate ideas about womanhood and birth control and simplistic ideas about *Swan Lake* and Tchaikovsky. By examining these cultural artifacts and images, it is easy to be confused about what a woman was supposed to stand for in a birth control narrative.

By looking at photography alone, we see that, with the insertion of the womanly hand into the frame, photography eventually featured fewer abstractions, letting readers and viewers know that a real woman consumes the pill every day. Finally, advertisements in popular women's magazines today market the newest and most improved oral contraceptives by using pictures of active, smiling women, yet the white woman is still often essentialized as representing all women in these ads. For example, a November 2008 issue of *Cosmopolitan* featured an advertisement for Yaz, a birth control pill whose manufacturer was at the time sued for its alleged side effects. No pills are present in the advertisement; instead a blonde, blue-eyed smiling young woman punches at floating phrases, "fatigue," "bloating," "moodiness," "acne." She wears a sporty tank top and poses against a backdrop of blue skies, as though with the help of a popular contraceptive, she will have blue skies ahead. Discussion of her sexuality is still absent from the plotline. Another 2008 birth control ad for the brand-name Seasonique from a June issue of *Glamour* magazine features two views of a young white woman— one holding a laptop, dressed in conservative office attire, another in a formal gown. She is the same woman, dressed casually and dressed for work. The caption reads, "Satisfy your need-to-know side. And your get-up-and-go side." Like all contemporary oral contraceptive advertisements, the accompanying text explains that while Seasonique is 99 percent effective, it does not protect from sexually transmitted diseases. These advertisements are more straightforward in their discussion of pregnancy and disease than advertisements of the past, and thereby speak to the bodily concerns of women today.

In contrast, a woman of color is finally featured in a 2012 print advertisement in a mainstream women's magazine, *Glamour*, for Plan B. On the one hand, women of color are finally receiving the attention they deserve as having bodies that count. On the other hand, Plan B is also known as the "morning-after pill," and only in a narrative about a woman's regular birth control having "failed" is a woman of color featured, as pointed out by an anonymous blogger ("Plan B Advertisement in Glamour Magazine") who heralded the advertisement for featuring a woman of color with natural hair.

However, magazine advertisements today still most often repeatedly portray a typical consumer of oral contraceptives as a young, white female. A culture that does not adequately address the contraceptive needs and sexual desires of women of color can be read as not deeming the needs of all women as important. The scope of visual culture in the images discussed in this essay raises the compelling question over whether birth control is more about birth—letting families choose when to have children—or control—fitting women into a larger narrative about race, class, and gender struggles.

Notes

1. The Smithsonian's National Museum of American History provides images of sample pill package designs. The Library of Congress houses a collection of early photographs of the birth control pill. Case Western Reserve University's Dittrick Medical History Center contains one of the largest collections of birth control pill packages in the world. Including illustrations was not possible but the respective images can easily be found on the web.
2. Birth control historians Andrea Tone and Elaine Tyler May have discussed the ways in which the first large-scale pill trials in Puerto Rico and Haiti included low-income women of color before the pill's FDA approval.
3. Collins writes about the ways in which state laws limited women's access to the pill after its FDA approval: "The law did not have much effect on middle-class married women, who could quietly get a prescription from the family doctor. But anyone who needed to go to a clinic—poor women or unmarried women seeking anonymity—was out of luck" (160).
4. The book states that "the area chosen for the study was a large slum clearance housing development in San Juan where over-population and poverty" were problems. See also Tone 220–225; May 32; Marsh and Ronner 207–8; *The Pill.*
5. Caputi writes about the many ways in which women water goddesses or women emerging from water conjure ideas about women's sexual power.
6. See, for instance, Soley and Kurzbard; Soley, American Academy of Pediatrics.
7. Image and description from PDF created from database of all the objects from contraceptive pill collection, supplied by Laura Travis, Assistant Curator of Multimedia and Communications, Dittrick Medical History Center, Case Western Reserve University.
8. A 1968 Ovex Tab Stick dispenser was part of the exhibit "Virtue, Vice, and Contraband."
9. According to Ortiz-Gómez and Santesmases, birth control pill packages were "designed to be attractive and discreet, often appearing indistinguishable from common makeup compacts, mirrors and lipstick dispensers" (117).
10. This led to "The Pill on Trial" as *Time* magazine headlined in 1970. See also Chalker, Schlesselman.
11. Linda Gordon also complicates this narrative in her study, arguing that birth control had always been central to societal perceptions of women and sexuality: "The Pill did not so much change women's lives as enable them to make changes they longed for" (288).
12. To my knowledge, this image has not been republished; permission to reproduce it in this volume was not granted.

Works Cited

American Academy of Pediatrics: Committee on Public Education. "Sexuality, Contraception, and the Media." *Pediatrics* 107.1 (2001): 191–194. *Academic Search Complete.* Web. 1 Nov. 2016.
American Experience: The Pill. PBS Online. PBS, 2002. Web. 30 June 2011.
Bailey, Beth. "Prescribing the Pill: Politics, Culture, and the Sexual Revolution in America's Heartland." *Journal of Social History* 30.4 (1997): 827–856. *Academic Search Complete.* Web. 1 Nov. 2016.

Boyer, Paul S. *Purity in Print: Book Censorship in America from the Gilded Age to the Computer Age*. Madison: University of Wisconsin Press, 2002. Print.
Caputi, Jane. *Goddesses and Monsters: Women, Myth Power, and Popular Culture*. Madison: Popular Press, 2004. Print.
Chalker, Rebecca. "Drug Companies Push Pill." *Guardian*, 14 Jan. 1981. Reproductive Rights National Network Papers, Box 1, Folder 7, Sophia Smith Collection, Smith College.
Cohen, Selma Jeanne. *Next Week, Swan Lake: Reflections on Dance and Dances*. Middletown: Wesleyan University Press, 1982. Print.
Collins, Gail. *When Everything Changed: The Amazing Journey of American Women from 1960 to the Present*. New York: Little, Brown, 2009. Print.
Crenshaw, Kimberlé. "Demarginalizing the Intersection of Race and Sex: A Black Feminist Critique of Antidiscrimination Doctrine, Feminist Theory and Antiracist Politics." *University of Chicago Legal Forum* 140 (1989): 139–167. Web. 1 Nov. 2016.
Doyle, Suzanne J. "After *Swan Lake*, Act II at the San Francisco Ballet." *Chicago Review* 35.1 (1985): 58. Web. 1 Nov. 2016.
Dyer, Richard. "White." *Screen* 29.4 (1988): 44–65. Web. 1 Nov. 2016.
_____. *White: Essays on Race and Culture*. London: Taylor & Francis, 2007. Print.
Fausto-Sterling, Anne. *Myths of Gender: Biological Theories About Women and Men*. New York: Basic Books, 1985. Print.
Foucault, Michel. *Power/Knowledge: Selected Interviews & Other Writings, 1972–1977*. Ed. Colin Gordon. New York: Pantheon Books, 1980. Print.
G.D. Searle & Company. *A Prescription for Family Planning: The Story of Enovid*. New York: Reference and Resources Program of G.D. Searle & Company, 1964. Print.
Gordon, Linda. *The Moral Property of Women: A History of Birth Control Politics in America*. Champaign: University of Illinois Press, 2002. Print.
"Great Performances." Ortho Novum 7/7/7. Advertisement. Print. Private Collection Jamie Wagman.
Hall, Stuart. "Representation, Meaning, and Language." *Representation: Cultural Representations and Signifying Practices*. Ed. Stuart Hall. Thousand Oaks: Sage, 2007. 13–74. Print.
Harris, Michael. *Colored Pictures: Race and Visual Representation*. Chapel Hill: University of North Carolina Press, 2003. Print.
Junod, Suzanne White, and Lara Marks. "Women's Trials: The Approval of the First Oral Contraceptive Pill in the United States and Britain." *Journal of the History of Medicine* 57.2 (2002): 117–160. Web. 1 Nov. 2016.
Lieberman, Archie. "Enovid—Contraceptive Pill." 6 photographs. *Look*. 29 June 1964. Look Magazine Photograph Collection, Library of Congress, Washington, D.C.
Look Magazine Photograph Collection 1937–1971. Library of Congress, Washington, D.C. Web. 3 Nov. 2016.
Marsh S., Margaret, and Wanda Ronner, *John Rock and the Reproductive Revolution*. Baltimore: Johns Hopkins University Press, 2008. Print.
May, Elaine Tyler. *America and the Pill: A History of Promise, Peril, and Liberation*. New York: Basic Books, 2010. Print.
Munch, James M., Gregory W. Boller, and John L. Swasy. "The Effects of Argument Structure and Affective Tagging on Product Attitude Formation." *The Journal of Consumer Research* 20.2 (1993): 294–302. Academic Search Complete. Web. 1 Nov. 2016.
National Cancer Institute. "Oral Contraceptives and Cancer Risk." Fact sheet. *National Cancer Institute*. National Cancer Institute at the National Institutes of Health. Web. 5 Sept. 2016.
"Ortho-Novum." *RxList*. RxList, 2011. Web. 18 July 2011.
Ortiz-Gómez, Teresa, and María Jesús Santesmases. *Gendered Drugs and Medicine: Historical and Socio-Cultural Perspectives*. Farnham: Ashgate, 2014. Print.
The Pill. Dir. Elise Swerhone and Erna Buffie. Women Make Movies, 1999. Film.
"The Pill on Trial." *Time*. Time, 26 Jan. 1970. Web. 14 Feb. 2011.
"Plan B Advertisement in Glamour Magazine." Blog. *Natural Hair in the Media*. Big Green Media, 22 May 2012. Web. 20 Oct. 2015.

"Planning Your Family." (Filmstrip. G. D. Searle & Company, 1965.) LC online catalogue. *Library of Congress*. Library of Congress. Web. 9 Aug. 2011.
Reid, J. Clifford. "Another Romantic Steroid—Ovulen." *Canadian Family Physician* (1967): 57–58, 60–62. *PubMed*. Web. 20 Oct. 2015.
Reiter, S.L., and L.J. Baer. "Initial Selection of Oral Contraceptives." *The Journal of Reproductive Medicine* 35.5 (1990): 547–48. Web. 1 Nov. 2016.
Rothstein, Arthur. "The pill." Photograph. *Look*. 30 June 1970. Look magazine photograph collection, Library of Congress, Washington, D.C.
Sarch, Amy. "Those Dirty Ads! Birth Control Advertising in the 1920s and 1930s." *Critical Studies in Mass Communication* 14.1 (1997): 31–48. Web. 1 Nov. 2016.
Schlesselman, James I. "Cancer of the Breast and Reproductive Tract in Relation to Use of Oral Contraceptives." *Contraception* 40.1 (1989):1–38. Loretta Ross Papers, Sophia Smith Collection, Smith College.
Seasonique. Advertisement. *Glamour* June 2008. N. pag. Print.
Shohat, Ella, and Robert Stam. *Unthinking Eurocentrism: Multiculturalism and the Media*. New York: Routledge, 1994. Print.
Smith, Shawn Michelle. *Photography on the Color Line: W.E.B. Du Bois, Race, and Visual Culture*. Durham: Duke University Press, 2004. Print.
Soley, Lawrence, and Gary Kurzbard. "Sex in Advertising: A Comparison of 1964 and 1984 Magazine Advertisements." *Journal of Advertising* 15.3 (1986): 46–64. Web. 1 Nov. 2016.
Star, Jack. "Catholics Take a New Look at the Pill." *Look* 8 Sept. 1964: 71.
Stoler, Ann Laura. *Along the Archival Grain: Epistemic Anxieties and Colonial Common Sense*. Princeton: Princeton University Press, 2010. Print.
Tone, Andrea. *Devices and Desires: A History of Contraceptives in America*. New York: Hill and Wang, 2001. Print.
Tyler, T., with Roland Berg. "The Pill Is Sage." *Look* 30 June 1970: 65. Print.
U.S. Department of Health & Human Services, U.S. Food and Drug Administration. "History." 18 June 2009. Web. 18 Oct. 2011.
"Virtue, Vice, and Contraband: A History of Contraception in America." 2009. Exhibit. Dittrick Medical History Center at Case Western Reserve University, Cleveland, OH.
Yaz. Advertisement. *Cosmopolitan* Nov. 2008. N. pag. Print.

Sex Education and Social Media
Contraception in the Digital Age

Manon S. Parry

Since the earliest years of the movement, birth control advocates have used every medium available to broadcast information about contraception, from pamphlets to posters, radio to film (Tone; Parry). In the digital age they are also using websites, Twitter, and SMS messaging (Lim, "Young").[1] In fact, in the United States, digital strategies are rapidly overtaking television, which was until very recently lauded by health communication experts as an "almost ideal" medium for sex education, due to its "accessibility, frankness, and appealing nature" (Ward and Friedman 134). Despite significant progress integrating sexual health messaging into mainstream programming since the 1960s, the majority of sexual content on television today includes a narrow range of representations of gender roles and sexuality, and only rarely references effective contraceptive use.

Of course the Internet also includes a great deal of negative and stereotypical sexual content, although new media can present a broader diversity of identities and activities because it can reach "niche" audiences rather than relying on broad mainstream markets. "Moral panics" regarding the influence of sexualized media on young people have accompanied the introduction of every new format, from silent film to home video, and the ease of distributing illegal, abusive, or extreme content over the Internet has created concern among researchers, policy makers, and advocacy groups. Certainly digital tools allow people outside of the formal networks of media production to create and distribute material on sex and reproduction.

This diversified landscape includes large quantities of *misinformation*, particularly regarding contraception and abortion. While some misleading material comes from organized sources with a long record of such activities (such as crisis pregnancy centers, who discourage abortion by linking it to negative health consequences on their websites, in the literature they distribute, and in clinic consultations), a large amount also appears to have been produced independently or by unknown individuals or groups, such as YouTube videos claiming to share personal experiences with particular types of contraception (Bryant et al.; Luttrell, Zite and Wallace). For some of those working in reproductive health, such developments create an urgent need for "expert" online information provided by medical professionals. They cite potential misuses of these newly accessible resources, such as unmonitored use of hormonal contraceptives despite personal risk factors, or even the attempted self-insertion of IUDs (Bryant-Comstock et al.). A wider group worries more simply about the accuracy of information online. Indeed, health communication professionals frequently cite misleading or missing information on the web as a core reason to move their own work there, especially given that 75 percent of Americans use the Internet to locate health-related information (Allen et al. 316). The Internet may be an especially important source of information for young people, particularly in regions where comprehensive sex education is not available in schools, such as Oklahoma and Alabama, with some of the highest rates of teen pregnancy in the United States and where sex education is not mandated in the curriculum (Strasburger and Brown E1–E2).[2] Despite federal measures to improve sex education countrywide, formal sex education declined between 2000 and 2014, with rural areas worst affected (Guttmacher Institute 2).

Despite the fears of some health professionals (and much to the chagrin of conservative opponents of comprehensive sex education), it is indeed possible to find accurate information and positive "testimonials" about the use of different types of contraception online (Paul, Duvet and Boraas 322; Allen et al. 316).[3] To a large degree, however, health professionals no longer control such material or serve as the gatekeepers to information and services. In the transition from television to the tablet computer as well as laptops and smartphones, activists and advocacy groups have joined health professionals in creating and sharing messages about contraception and sexual health online. I focus here on three types of digital projects—informal, entrepreneurial, and institutional—that are reshaping the presentation of the pill. All offer opportunities to reframe the narratives and images used to promote contraception in the media, including representations of the pill.

From TV to PC

Health communication researchers have consistently encouraged campaigners to go where audiences are already gathered and to adapt to the forms of media that they enjoy. For American audiences in the last 30 years, this primarily meant entertainment television. Since their initial breakthrough projects in the 1960s and 1970s, family planning promoters have successfully integrated contraceptive messaging into a range of mainstream programming. This includes shows targeting young audiences directly, such as *Moesha* and *Felicity*, as well as those marketed to older viewers but with a large contingent of adolescent viewers, such as *Friends* and *ER* (Parry 132–34; Collins et al.; "The Impact of TV's Health Content"). The emergence of HIV/AIDS gave a new legitimacy to such work, but also increased the likelihood that if any contraceptive was represented, it was most likely to be a condom, a barrier method that could prevent the transmission of HIV as well as unplanned pregnancy (although the pill has also been featured in American television, as Schleich and Nesselhauf discuss in this volume).

The relationship between family planning and public health organizations, and their collaborators in the entertainment industry, is therefore fairly well-established, if a little rocky at times. In the 21st century, references to contraceptive use, especially when tied to young adult characters, are rare compared to depictions of sexual acts, and are still controversial among media producers as well as media critics.[4] Some media producers have been happy to work with health professionals, but only in specific circumstances, and to a limited degree. While they might be willing to integrate health messages in a new program, for example, they tend to be less receptive as a program becomes increasingly popular. Although they may adopt aspects of a scenario proposed by their health communication colleagues (as a public service and in return for guidance on technical aspects of a particular storyline, for instance), they tend to opt for the most dramatic plot resolution rather than the most educational one. In some instances, this has even undermined intended messages (Collins et al.). Moreover, mounting evidence of the limits of such "entertainment-education" to promote sustained awareness or behavior change has undermined the use of TV as a core strategy for the promotion of contraceptive use, as has criticism of the "preachy" uses of drama to promote moral messages about sex for young audiences (Moyer-Guse; Buckingham and Bragg).

The relevance of television for family planning promotion was briefly revived by a shift from drama to so-called "reality" television with the launch of *16 and Pregnant,* however. The series was developed by MTV and the National Campaign to Prevent Teen and Unplanned Pregnancy, and launched in 2009. Episodes profile young women (and more rarely, their partners) as they deal with unplanned pregnancies. It has spawned three spin-off *Teen Mom* series, and by 2010 had become the most highly-rated cable show among female viewers 12–34 years of age ("MTV Greenlights Season Two"). Initially, commentators embraced the producers' claims that the show has a "contraceptive" power, given the depressing depictions of life as a young parent that it presents (Dolgen; The National Campaign to Prevent Teen and Unplanned Pregnancy; Dinh). While occasionally criticized for "glamourizing" teen pregnancy by making minor celebrities out of the participants, overall, media critics agreed that the young men and women featured are often in quite desperate and difficult circumstances (Henson; Grossberg; Montalvan). Yet most public health researchers are less convinced of the claims made for the impact of the series. Certainly, teen pregnancy rates, on the decline in America since the 1990s (but still significantly higher than in comparably wealthy nations), have decreased more sharply since 2008 (CDC; Kearney and Levine 3598). While this coincides with the period that *16 and Pregnant* has been shown on MTV, it also maps onto the economic downturn, and must surely reflect multiple factors that go beyond the persuasive power of a single television series. Moreover, while studies of Google Trends and Twitter suggest that airings of the show coincide with increased web traffic regarding contraceptive use and abortion (Kearney and Levine 3597),[5] any long-term impact on sexual behavior and contraceptive use has been harder to prove (Brewer; The National Campaign to Prevent Teen and Unplanned Pregnancy; Wright, Randall and Arroyo).

Recent research has even concluded that as a result of watching the show, young women, whether they identify with those featured or not, are likely to underestimate their own risk for unintended pregnancy (Martins and Jensen).[6] The more the viewers identified with the teen moms on the show, "the more they accepted myths about teen pregnancy, the less they believed themselves to be at risk for teen pregnancy, the more they perceived the benefits of teen pregnancy to outweigh the risks of teen pregnancy, and the more favorable their attitudes about teen pregnancy." Researchers concluded that while the reality-style format might be more popular with young viewers than traditionally scripted television, the approach nevertheless undermined the efficacy of any intended health message due to inconsistencies in the casts' statements: "the stories are told through the perspective of the young girls who have contradictory things to say about teen pregnancy, who might undersell the value of prevention and contraception, and who might convey the notion that teen pregnancy is a way to garner attention from others, if not the people in their lives who are featured on the episodes, then at least from MTV who put them on TV" (Aubrey, Behm-Morawitz and Kim 1156–57). As a result, the television series cannot be celebrated as an unequivocal success.

Informal Sex Ed

Yet *16 and Pregnant* is nonetheless a good example of the potential of the Internet to transform the way information about sex and contraception are developed for, with, and by young people themselves. Online platforms offer the opportunity to "talk back" to the messages of the show, either via organized social media campaigns or by following individuals who publicly share their own responses. As well as an MTV website to accompany the series, the show has inspired parody videos, produced primarily by teenage girls (with a smaller number made by boys), with between a few thousand to more than 100,000 views on YouTube (Cunningham). As well as offering insights on the reception of the original television show among members of the target audience, these videos and the online comments posted by those who watch them also reveal themes—such as misunderstandings about the use and efficacy of contraceptive methods—that could then become the focus of targeted education efforts via links and comments posted to the discussion thread. Fan forums (online communities where enthusiasts of particular books, shows, or films share comments and debate plotlines), are similarly being studied as a source of "peer-to-peer education," where young people are educating one another, with or without the input of "experts" sanctioned by public health professionals (Masanet and Buckingham). While such networks of informal sex education depend on their members' access to, and understanding of, reliable information, the same is true of the similar networks of exchange that preceded the Internet, from conversations in the school playground to discussions huddled around a library book. In fact, some new media theorists would argue that the scaling up of the groups involved in such activities, as made possible by the Internet, increases the likelihood of misinformation being discredited and accurate information being validated via the so-called "wisdom of crowds."

I define this kind of "informal" sex education as self-produced by an independent individual, often in response to more formally-produced media, as a celebration or critique of the messages contained therein. As an alternative to traditional sources of sex education such as school curricula, parents, and the mass media, as well as the narrow visions of appropriate sexuality they often provide, young men and women can thus choose their preferred sources of information from a wide array of material online. A large amount of informal sex education resources has been crafted by amateurs and activists, just as much health information produced by the women's movement was created by feminists without formal medical or public health training. Such diversification means that a far greater range of ideas about contraceptive use can now be found online, where researchers can filter information to safely locate material that "aligns with their values on sex and sexuality" (Edwards 273). Blogs commenting on representations of sexuality in the media, on reproductive health politics, and on personal experiences provide commentary and informal community-building around homosexuality, transgender issues, sexual expression, and sexual politics, often with an explicitly feminist or queer critique of mainstream sexual ideology.

These resources can be risky, however, for the people who produce them. Online and real-world harassment, including threats of sexual assault, violence, and death (known as "gendertrolling," in which women become the targets of organized and sustained intimidation),[7] are likely familiar to most women writing online, as well as to their readers, and campaigns of intimidation have been particularly vicious against women who have written about sex, abortion, and contraception.[8] It is not my intention here to minimize such challenges, but it is important to note that (a) aggressive campaigns have not driven women off-line, as producers of, or audiences for, sexual health resources, and (b) advocates for such activities are becoming increasingly adept at protecting and defending people and projects under attack (Edwards; Muise; Wood).

Entrepreneurial Sex Ed

Another influential form of online information, and one that is less vulnerable to online intimidation tactics, I characterize as "entrepreneurial," as this is developed by an individual or small team, with a specific educational goal, and usually financed from a mix of public funding and commercial profits. Popular examples of this sort of project include the website *Scarleteen*, as well as its predecessor from the 1990s, gurl.com, and the university-hosted sexual health site *Go Ask Alice* (1993).[9] As the website names suggest, the majority of this material is clearly aimed primarily at young women, mirroring the emphasis on female responsibility for preventing pregnancy common to sexual education campaigns since the 19th century. However, the tone has shifted from that traditional message of burden and responsibility, to instead emphasize female empowerment, particularly in the *Scarleteen* project. Moreover, the websites are undoubtedly read by young men, and indeed young men's questions and perspectives are often included.

Scarleteen was founded by activist and teacher Heather Corinna, who relates her interest in sexual health education to her own experiences as a young person who identified as bisexual from a young age and who has experienced sexual assault and abuse (McNeilly, "Scarleteen's Heather Corinna on the Future of Sex Education"). Corinna's sex-positive, often explicitly feminist, approach to "inclusive" and "comprehensive" information arises from the three main problems she identifies today—a highly sexualized media culture with unrealistic representations of sexuality, the legacy of abstinence-only education on sexual knowledge, and the negative fear or shame-based tone of much existing education (McNeilly, "Getting to Know Heather

Corinna"). At the time of writing, the main articles previewed on the home page included "D.I.Y. Sex Toys: Self-Love Edition," "When Sex 'Just Happened' and How to Make It Happen Instead," and "Driver's Ed for the Sexual Highway: Navigating Consent" (Scarleteen/Corinna). Throughout the tone is casual, often comedic, but with a recurring emphasis on consent, boundaries, and the wide range of preferences possible among readers. Speaking in 2014 about the future of sex education in an interview for the online magazine *Sex, etc.* (run by a foundation from Rutgers University and with teenage writers on staff, and using the tagline "By teens, for teens"), Corinna emphasized the importance of being an "ally," a term commonly associated with straight support for gay rights, saying that peer educators should be as supportive of all choices among friends, whether they do not want to have sex or are interested in doing so (McNeilly, "Scarleteens's Heather Corinna on the Future of Sex Education").

She concluded the interview with a call for young people to empower themselves to educate their peers. Noting that young people often get their messages from one another, regardless of the range of information and misinformation now circulating, she encouraged readers to "learn about sexuality from accurate sources and with a very open mind, so that when friends have questions, you have good answers. Get connected with all your local resources for sexuality and sexual health, and be the friend who everyone knows is the one to ask when they need help accessing resources—like a clinic" (McNeilly, "Scarleteens's Heather Corinna on the Future of Sex Education"). The reference to the clinic is an interesting one in the context of this collection's focus on the contraceptive pill and reproductive rights. It reveals the continued relevance of clinic services in the provision of contraception for young people, no doubt because the pill, the IUD, and other long-acting contraceptives remain important female-controlled options for young women still learning how to navigate condom use with perhaps unwilling partners.

In the website's "Birth Control Bingo," a 25-page guide to different contraceptive methods, the pill is presented as "one of the most popular methods of birth control" and "one of the most thoroughly researched and studied medications in history" (Scarleteen/Corinna). A lengthy textual overview includes references to positive and negative side effects, efficacy rates based on perfect or ideal versus typical use, and reasons why the pill might not be suitable or might be ineffective. The tone overall is fairly enthusiastic, with even limitations being framed in a positive way, as in "When Good Birth Control Does Bad Things," the title of a section on reasons the pill might fail. There is one section early on in the page that draws attention to the potential difficulties associated with teenagers using the pill reliably, saying,

> Some adolescent-specific studies on the pill have shown that it is less effective for adolescents in typical use than it is for *adults. One study* found that teens' ability to

use the pill properly was as low as only 45% with the first three months of use, and only 33% with one year of use. So, if you're going to use the pill, as with other methods, be sure you study up on what proper use means and make it a goal to stick to it as best you can. If you're not sure you can take it correctly every single day, you can always back up with condoms: that gives you nearly 100% *effectiveness* and *STI* protection the pill does not provide.

Words in italics are hyperlinked to additional information on the terms used or the issues described. It is notable here that the reader is encouraged to try their best, to "study up" on what that would mean, and encouraged to use condoms as a back-up method, rather than directed to choose an alternative method such as the IUD or implant. The implicit assumption is that young people can reliably evaluate their own capacity to follow the regimen and decide when they need to use a back-up or alternative method.

This website resists two of the most common assumptions of online communication to teenagers about sexual health—that it must be multimedia rather than text-heavy, and that it should avoid overloading young people with too much information that is too complicated. Firstly, this section, like most of the site, is decidedly text-heavy, relying on extensive explanations with catchy sub-titles. Although the tone is friendly, medical language and technical terms are frequently used, rather than simplified. Secondly, the site references and links to additional information such as the original reports by reproductive health agencies, rather than summarizing relevant information and excluding extensive additional resources (especially those written for medical professionals rather than the intended youth audience). The sense overall is that young people can understand detailed information and they should be given access to multiple sources to evaluate its credibility and applicability for themselves. Reviewing a sample of posts to the message boards, it appears that some of the site's users are older than the teenage audience implied in the name Scarleteen, as some identify themselves as college age or older. The myths and misinformation among many people posting on the message boards does suggest an active community of younger users too, although it is possible that some are using the message boards precisely because they find the information on the site difficult to follow. Of course no one solution would serve all visitors, and the blend of expert and peer-to-peer education that this project accomplishes is better integrated than in other projects, and surely a large part of its popularity.

Institutional Sex Ed

In 2011, the National Campaign to Prevent Teen and Unplanned Pregnancy launched a new initiative, this time entirely online. This "institutional" project (meaning one developed by a large, established organization, developed with major health organization and media partnerships, and secured by long-term funding) is a not-for-profit website and community called *Bedsider*. The site, developed with international design company IDEO, is branded as a "free birth control support network" on the home page and in promotional material (Swiader). The project focuses on adults aged 18–29 rather than adolescents, an emphasis chosen because seven out of ten pregnancies among women in their twenties are unplanned.[10] The website includes information about birth control methods and tools for locating services and providers, options to sign-up for email or text message reminders to use contraception or attend appointments, videos of women in the same age group discussing their experiences with contraception, short animations tackling myths about different kinds of birth control, and blog-type articles with comments from readers.

The approach was intended to be accessible (meaning less densely medical than other resources on the topic) and trustworthy (with a professional tone), and includes humor. Launching the campaign in 2011, CEO Sarah Brown stated, "we need to rebrand contraception as something that promotes self-determination, education and achievement" (Sessions Stepp). In contrast to much previous public health and sex education material, it is also deliberately sex-positive, emphasizing enjoyment rather than risk, and recognizing the role of emotion and "heat-of-the-moment" decision-making (Antonishak, Kaye and Swiader 3). The entrepreneurial efforts of projects like *Scarleteen* have thus clearly demonstrated the appeal and efficacy of such strategies, which were previously underutilized in "institutional" efforts.

The pill is one of 17 methods discussed on the site, including implants and IUDs as well as the withdrawal method and charting fertility over the menstrual cycle. The representation of the pill emphasizes its long history ("it's been around for 50 years") and positive as well as negative potential side effects (control over periods versus nausea and vomiting, for example). The text repeatedly emphasizes the importance of taking the pill every day, around the same time, as well as the gap between ideal use and actual usage and the resulting impact on failure rates: "You may have seen information about 'perfect use' stating that the pill is 99.7% effective, but the reality is that with typical use it's 91% effective. (That means that of 11 women taking the pill for a year, one will become pregnant)" (Jackson). In a comparison chart with each option graded great, decent, pretty good, or not at all in categories including effectiveness, mistake-proof, and effort, it ranks lower than the IUD and contraceptive implants. In fact, even though the site is purportedly aimed at an older audience, the implicit message is very similar to that traditionally proposed for younger women or others deemed "unreliable" or "non-compliant" in the recent history of family planning promotion in the

United States and around the world: that it is unlikely that they will be "perfect" users and should thus choose a professionally-inserted method that they cannot undermine through their own behavior. Under the heading "It Takes Discipline," the text emphasizes again, "you've got to remember to take your pill at the same time every day. Even on weekends. Even on vacation. So, ask yourself: how good are you with stuff like that?" The one innovation added to this traditionally paternalistic stance is the use of hyperlinks to connect the reader to a comprehensive explanation of what to do if they have missed a pill (depending on the type of pill and the stage in the cycle), and to sign up for email or text message reminders. The site also uses "Provider Perspectives" to cast expert opinions in a more individualistic light, presenting women working in reproductive health with social media-style identities including their name and an informal illustrated portrait. I have yet to find any male providers featured on the site, and although there may be some used occasionally, the overwhelmingly female presence reinforces the framing of this as a women's resource—by women, for women, as in the style of the women's health movement or other pro-women (even if not explicitly feminist) media.

The site reflects some recent trends in discussing contraceptive options with users, by emphasizing that non-hormonal options do exist and can be effective, for example. This includes the re-evaluation of the benefits of the withdrawal method—more usually represented in sex education materials as highly risky, but receiving more positive attention by family planning experts and their audiences since a 2014 study declared careful use "as effective as condoms at preventing pregnancy" (Shane).

There are also "Guy's Guide" videos where a male character named "Guy Nottadadi" describes how he remains not-a-daddy, by explaining contraceptive techniques. The videos appear to be tailored for a male viewership who are framed as largely ignorant and unconcerned, suggesting that the resource is designed for women using the website to share with their partners. In "Introduction," Guy begins by saying, "Most guys don't know jack squat about how birth control works," and "78% of guys admit that they don't know anything about the pill" ("Guy's Guide"). In a series of short videos (one to two-and-a-half minutes), Nottadadi argues men should know how birth control methods work, for their own benefit, for the women they have sex with, and in one instance, despite having been "written off" by "a million women who think that birth control information is best left in the hands of women and women alone" ("Guy's Guide: The Implant"). It is especially interesting that in this video, male lack of knowledge is blamed on women excluding them—not the health professionals who have targeted women as holding primary responsibility for preventing pregnancy for decades.

The videos revel in male stereotypes such as inclusion of frequent shots of women in swimwear or underwear and references to football and voracious appetite (for food and sex). Each is set in a masculine location, sometimes with links to the subject matter—the condom video in a barbershop, the IUD explanation in a garage (where viewers can learn the "mechanics" as Nottadadi rebuilds a car engine), and over the barbecue and in the kitchen where the chemistry of the pill is laid out. Some of the claims contradict information elsewhere on the site, as in the video on withdrawal, which is far less positive about its efficacy than the text on the site.[11] Although the videos present a more traditional view of masculinity than the site does of femininity overall, there are occasional exceptions. The concluding comments of the video on the pill, for example, focus on the idea that until there is a male version, "offering to help her with the costs or remembering when to take it could be very beneficial to your non-parental status" ("Guy's Guide: The Implant").

The project as a whole has been well received by media and health professionals. In 2011 it was selected by the Ad Council for nationwide promotion to media outlets, and in 2013 the Ad Council partnered with the National Campaign to Prevent Teen Pregnancy and the BET Networks to develop a second series of materials specifically targeting African American women aged 18 to 29 (Vega). The same year they launched "Thanks, Birth Control" day on November 12, a project which has generated submissions of testimonials and self-produced media from contraceptive users who send in their stories to *Bedsider*, and on Twitter with the hashtag #ThxBirthControl which won a Webby Award in 2015 (Duberman; Lucas).[12]

After a 2015 evaluation the *Bedsider* project reported a fairly small but demonstrable impact, the National Campaign to Prevent Teen and Unplanned Pregnancy declared the website "the first digital intervention in reproductive health in the U.S.—with adults as an audience—that has shown to prevent unplanned pregnancy" (Swiader; Sonalkar et al.). Other studies have concluded more tentatively that the website *may* be useful, especially in conjunction with the advice of a health professional (Jamshidi, Robinson and Burke).

Interestingly, one study found that clinic staff had very different reactions to the site than their clients. While clinic users were "very receptive" and described the website as "trustworthy, accessible and empowering," staff "had concerns regarding the website's legitimacy, accessibility, ability to empower patients and applicability" (Gressel et al. 588). Specifically, staff doubted that their community of users could understand terminology used, and thought that some of the representations of sex were "trashy," "smutty" or pornographic, and unsuitable for young people or promoted an unhealthy message about female sexual availability (Gressel et al. 592, 591). The concerns of the clinic staff limited their willingness to recommend the tool to their patients. The authors of the study ended by asking whether *Bedsider* "should be modified to make it more acceptable to providers or, instead, whether we should seek to broaden providers' openness to tools that young women find applicable and empowering" (Gressel et al. 593). The study's juxtaposition of the two disparate interpretations of the site, as trustworthy versus trashy, underlines the core issue at the center of debates over the pill in the digital age—namely who has the authority to inform and prescribe.

Conclusion

As the case studies here confirm, the low cost of producing and disseminating digital media, combined with the reach of the Internet and the power to search and filter results, have transformed the scale of contraceptive information available online (as well as giving broader access to contraceptive technologies). This model of communication and exchange differs significantly from the standard mode developed for the promotion of family planning since the pill was approved for use in the United States, which was based on a model of one-way diffusion, from medical expert to patient. Like public health campaigning more broadly, institutionally-produced material relies on the "diffusion of innovations" technique of delivering messages and services to various individuals or groups, usually with health professionals still serving as gatekeepers. Health communication experts have noted the limits of this model in the new media landscape, noting that "public health has embraced both mass media and interpersonal communication, but the field has not fully recognized the growing benefit of hybrid communication forms like YouTube that add fresh dimensions to interventions and appeal to a growing segment of the population" (Lillie 267). Some of the "interventions" implied here include a complete upheaval of expert-audience diffusion, to instead acknowledge audience input, co-creation, or even critique.

Public health professionals increasingly emphasize the need to meet health information "consumers" where they are already online, on social media sites such as Facebook and content platforms where health professionals are underrepresented, such as YouTube, although the use of the language of consumption reveals a limited understanding of this shift. Emerging public health uses of social media have also drawn on surveillance strategies that may well undermine their appeal to those already suspicious of digital methods of monitoring behavior.[13] At least one project has used publicly available information to warn teenagers that the behaviors they describe online (such as multiple sexual partners or having sex while drunk) put them at risk for sexually transmitted diseases (Moreno et al.), even as researchers caution against "disrupting" social networks by infiltrating them in this way (Byron et al.; Lim et al.).

Moreover, appealing to audiences increasingly means incorporating their input. Digital users are reframing or completely remaking the media that targets them, rejecting the hierarchy of expert and audience, and reaching out to underserved groups with messaging that respects a growing array of gender identities and sexual behaviors. Furthermore, institutional resources are well-utilized by individuals and entrepreneurs, as *Scarleteen*'s hyperlinks to published research and state and federal information demonstrates. The credibility of those drawing on these "official" resources comes precisely from their location outside of official institutional realms, and from their apparently authentic and spontaneous engagement with their peers (as opposed to a contrived and organized response). So far, entrepreneurial and individual efforts appear to have more quickly adapted to the expectations of the digital age, and most likely will drive changes in institutional approaches. Yet it may be a mistake for those in institutional projects to try to mimic the techniques of their competitors. In this diversified digital age, such competition may in fact prove entirely complementary.

NOTES

1. For more on digital strategies for sex education and the promotion of contraception see Albury, Allison, Bull, Gawron, both Jones entries, King, Kofinas, Madathil, Selkie, Simon, and Talukdar.

2. Teen pregnancy rates are from 2014, the latest comprehensive figures available at the time of submission. Strasburger and Brown also notes that "many sexually experienced teens (46% of males and 33% of females) report that they had not received any instruction about contraception before they began having sex" (E1).

3. Allen et al. also note the inclusion of negative comments about pain and side effects as part of the generally reliable information provided in 2012, apparently an improvement on research findings four years earlier (316).

4. See, for example, comments by the producer of *Modern Family* in 2012, regarding sending a female character off to college with a box of condoms (Rose).

5. The authors, both economists, overlook the entire field of health communications research on media for family planning, and unwisely conclude that their findings regarding web traffic also demonstrate the impact of the show on actual practices. Health communications literature is much more cautious in acknowledging a significant gap between knowledge, attitudes, and practice (KAP, in the terminology of the field).

6. The show's cast had also tended to underestimate the risk—one study of four years of episodes of *16 and Pregnant* and *Teen Mom* noted that while none of the participants reported that they were trying to get pregnant, only five of 47 mentioned trying to avoid a pregnancy, but failing, while three-quarters (36 of 47) acknowledged not using any form of contraception at the time they got pregnant, and 36 of 47 reported that they did not think that they would have sex or become pregnant (Kearney and Levine 3602).

7. On "gendertrolling," see Mantilla.

8. See, for example, McNeilly "Scarleteen's Heather Corinna on the Future." In this interview, entrepreneurial sex educator Heather Corinna notes that she no longer receives this kind of harassment as she did when first working in the field—presumably by becoming more well-known and better established within professionally-endorsed networks of sex education.

9. Gurl.com still exists today but had been sold by its founders and has taken on a far more commercial and mainstream perspective than in its early years, when it presented an explicitly feminist take on popular culture for young readers (Symonds).

10. Unintended pregnancies in this age group have not declined, unlike rates of teenage pregnancy which have been in decline since the 1990s (Antonishak, Kaye and Swiader 1).

11. In the video on withdrawal, for example, the character emphasizes the importance of skill and states that perhaps the level of skill required explains why one in five couples using this method for a year will become pregnant.

12. Planned Parenthood launched a similar effort to gather public stories titled "Birth Control Helped Me" on Twitter as #BirthControlHelpedMe in June 2015 (Castillo).

13. Public health researchers have matched increased online traffic on key topics to geographical clusters of seasonal allergies and flu outbreaks, as well as symptoms and self-medication (off-label uses of Benadryl for insomnia, for example). While results can be collected faster than by traditional methods of public health monitoring, so far the data collected conforms to the knowledge already gathered by more traditional means, although enthusiasts emphasize the "expressiveness" of tweets as well as the "public display" of information, especially behavior and opinions, that individuals are reluctant to discuss with healthcare workers as potential areas of interest (Dredze 82–830).

Works Cited

Albury, Kath. "Young People, Media and Sexual Learning: Rethinking Representation." *Sex Education* 13.supl (2013): S32–S44. Web. 25 Oct. 2016.

Allen, A., et al. "Social Media and the IUD—a YouTube Content Analysis." *Contraception* 86.3 (2012): 316. Web. 25 Oct. 2016.

Allison, Susannah, et al. "The Intersection of Youth, Technology, and New Media with Sexual Health: Moving the Research Agenda Forward." *Journal of Adolescent Health* 51.3 (2012): 207–12. Web. 25 Oct. 2016.

Antonishak, J., K. Kaye, and L. Swiader. "Impact of an Online Birth Control Support Network on Unintended Pregnancy." *Social Marketing Quarterly* 21.1 (2015): 23–36. Web. 25 Oct. 2016.

Aubrey, Jennifer Stevens, Elizabeth Behm-Morawitz, and Kyungbo Kim. "Understanding the Effects of MTV's *16 and Pregnant* on Adolescent Girls' Beliefs, Attitudes, and Behavioral Intentions Toward Teen Pregnancy." *Journal of Health Communication* 19.10 (2014): 1145–60. Web. 25 Oct. 2016.

Brewer, Tiffany. "Exploring the Impact of MTV's *16 and Pregnant* on Parents and Teenage Girls." MA Thesis, American University, Washington, D.C., 2011.

Bryant, Amy G., et al. "Crisis Pregnancy Center Websites: Information, Misinformation and Disinformation." *Contraception* 90.6 (2014): 601–05. Web. 25 Oct. 2016.

Bryant-Comstock, Katelyn, et al. "Information About Sexual Health on Crisis Pregnancy Center Web Sites: Accurate for Adolescents?" *Journal of Pediatric and Adolescent Gynecology* 29.1 (2016): 22–25. Web. 25 Oct. 2016.

Buckingham, David, and Sara Bragg. *Young People, Sex, and the Media: The Facts of Life?* Basingstoke: Palgrave Macmillan, 2004. Web. 3 Oct. 2016.

Bull, Sheana S., et al. "Social Media-Delivered Sexual Health Intervention." *American Journal of Preventive Medicine* 43.5 (2012): 467–74. Web. 25 Oct. 2016.

Byron, Paul, Kath Albury, and Clifton Evers. "'It would be weird to have that on Facebook': Young People's Use of Social Media and the Risk of Sharing Sexual Health Information." *Reproductive Health Matters* 21.41 (2013): 35–44. Web. 25 Oct. 2016.

Castillo, Stephanie. "Planned Parenthood's New #BirthControlHelpedMe Campaign to Remind Women Birth Control Is an 'Important Driver' of Stability." *Medical Daily* 24 June 2015: n. pag. Print.

Centers for Disease Control and Prevention. *Preventing Teen Pregnancy in the U.S. CDC.gov.* CDC Vital Signs, 2013. Web. 10 Oct. 2016.

Collins, R. L., et al. "Entertainment Television as a Healthy Sex Educator: The Impact of Condom-Efficacy Information in an Episode of *Friends*." *Pediatrics* 112.5 (2003): 1115–21. Web. 25 Oct. 2016.

Cunningham, Carolyn M. "Sixteen and Not Pregnant: Teen-Created YouTube Parody Videos and Sexual Risk-Taking in the United States." *Journal of Children and Media* 8.1 (2014): 53–68. Web. 27 Oct. 2016.
Dinh, James. "MTV's *16 And Pregnant* Credited for Decline in Teen Pregnancy Rates." *MTV.* MTV, 22 Dec. 2010. Web. 10 Oct. 2016.
Dolgen, Lauren. "Why I Created MTV's *16 and Pregnant.*" *CNN.* Cable Network News, 5 May 2011. Web. 10 Oct. 2016.
Dredze, Mark. "How Social Media Will Change Public Health." *IEEE Intelligent Systems* 27.4 (2012): 81–84. Web. 25 Oct. 2016.
Duberman, Amanda. "Bedsider's 'Thanks, Birth Control' Puts All Our Gratitude for Contraceptives into A Musical Number." *The Huffington Post.* TheHuffingtonPost, 12 Nov. 2014. Web. 10 Oct. 2016.
Edwards, Nichole. "Women's Reflections on Formal Sex Education and the Advantage of Gaining Informal Sexual Knowledge Through a Feminist Lens." *Sex Education* 16.3 (2016): 266–78. Web. 25 Oct. 2016.
Gawron, Lori M., and David K. Turok. "Pills on the World Wide Web: Reducing Barriers through Technology." *American Journal of Obstetrics and Gynecology* 213.4 (2015): 500.e1–500.e4. Web. 25 Oct. 2016.
Gressel, Gregory M., et al. "Patient and Provider Perspectives on Bedsider.org, an Online Contraceptive Information Tool, in a Low Income, Racially Diverse Clinic Population." *Contraception* 90.6 (2014): 588–93. Web. 25 Oct. 2016.
Grossberg, Josh. "*16 and Pregnant's* Abortion Special: Teachable Moment or Bad Example?" *E! News.* E! Entertainment Television, 29 Dec. 2010. Web. 10 Oct. 2016.
Guse, Kylene, et al. "Interventions Using New Digital Media to Improve Adolescent Sexual Health: A Systematic Review." *Journal of Adolescent Health* 51.6 (2012): 535–43. Web. 27 Oct. 2016.
Guttmacher Institute. "American Teens' Sources of Sexual Health Education." Fact sheet. *Guttmacher Institute.* Guttmacher Institute, 2016. Web. 10 Oct. 2016.
"Guy's Guide." *Bedsider.* The National Campaign to Prevent Teen and Unplanned Pregnancy, 3 June and 23 Oct. 2013. Web. 10 Oct. 2016. Video.
Henson, Melissa. "MTV's *Teen Mom* Glamorizes Getting Pregnant." CNN.com. CNN Entertainment, 4 May 2011. Web. 10 Oct. 2016.
"The Impact of TV's Health Content: A Case Study of ER Viewers." *Kaiser Family Foundation.* The Henry J. Kaiser Family Foundation, 2002. Web. 27 Oct. 2016. PDF. Excerpt from "Communicating Health Information through the Entertainment Media" by Mollyann Brodie et al. *Health Affairs* (Jan./Feb. 2001): 192–99.
Jackson, Andrea. "Late, Late, for a Very Important Pill?" *Bedsider.* The National Campaign to Prevent Teen and Unplanned Pregnancy, 12 Mar. 2011. Web. 11 June 2016.
Jamshidi, Roxanne M., Jennifer Robinson, and Anne E. Burke. "'The Effect of the Bedsider.org Web Site on Contraceptive Use Within an Urban Gynecology Clinic': *Obstetrics & Gynecology* 125 (2015): 79S–80S. Web. 27 Oct. 2016.
Jones, Rachel K., and Ann E. Biddlecom. "Is the Internet Filling the Sexual Health Information Gap for Teens? An Exploratory Study." *Journal of Health Communication* 16.2 (2011): 112–23. Web. 27 Oct. 2016.
_____. "The More Things Change…: The Relative Importance of the Internet as a Source of Contraceptive Information for Teens." *Sexuality Research and Social Policy* 8.1 (2011): 27–37. Web. 27 Oct. 2016.
Kearney, Melissa S., and Phillip B. Levine. "Media Influences on Social Outcomes: The Impact of MTV's *16 and Pregnant* on Teen Childbearing." *American Economic Review* 105.12 (2015): 3597–632. Web. 27 Oct. 2016.
King, N., et al. "A Quantitative Assessment of the Contraceptive Decision Aid Bedsider.org Among Low-Income Spanish-Speaking Women in New York City." *Contraception* 90.3 (2014): 344. Web. 27 Oct. 2016.
Kofinas, Jason D., et al. "Adjunctive Social Media for More Effective Contraceptive Counseling: A Randomized Controlled Trial." *Obstetrics & Gynecology* 123.4 (2014): 763–70. Web. 22 Feb. 2016.

Lillie, Sarah E. "Diffusion of Innovation in the Age of YouTube." *American Journal of Preventive Medicine* 34.3 (2008): 267. Web. 27 Oct. 2016.

Lim, M. S., et al. "Young People's Comfort Receiving Sexual Health Information via Social Media and Other Sources." *International Journal of STD & AIDS* 25.14 (2014): 1003–08. Web. 27 Oct. 2016.

Lim, M. S. C., et al. "SMS STI: A Review of the Uses of Mobile Phone Text Messaging in Sexual Health." *International Journal of STD & AIDS* 19.5 (2008): 287–90. Web. 27 Oct. 2016.

Lucas, Jillian. "LifeStyles Condoms Wants You to Thank Your Birth Control Today with #ThxBirthControl Campaign." *The Gloss*. The Gloss/Defy Media Lifestyle network, 10 Nov. 2015. Web. 10 Oct. 2016.

Luttrell, K., N. Zite, and L. Wallace. "Myths and Misconceptions About Intrauterine Contraception on YouTube." *Contraception* 78.2 (2008): 183. 27 Oct. 2016.

Madathil, K. C., et al. "Healthcare Information on YouTube: A Systematic Review." *Health Informatics Journal* 21.3 (2015): 173–94. Web. 27 Oct. 2016.

Mantilla, Karla. *Gendertrolling: How Misogyny Went Viral*. Santa Barbara: Praeger, 2015. Print.

Martins, Nicole, and Robin E. Jensen. "The Relationship Between *Teen Mom* Reality Programming and Teenagers' Beliefs About Teen Parenthood." *Mass Communication and Society* 17.6 (2014): 830–52. Web. 27 Oct. 2016.

Masanet, Maria-Jose, and David Buckingham. "Advice on Life? Online Fan Forums as a Space for Peer-to-Peer Sex and Relationships Education." *Sex Education* 15.5 (2015): 486–99. Web. 27 Oct. 2016.

McNeilly, Sarah. "Getting to Know Heather Corinna: The Activist Behind Scarleteen." *Sex, etc.* Answer and Rutgers University, 7 Aug. 2014. Web. 10 Oct. 2016.

_____. "Scarleteen's Heather Corinna on Feminism and Sex Ed." *Sex, etc.* Answer and Rutgers University, 14 Aug. 2014. Web. 10 Oct. 2016.

_____. "Scarleteen's Heather Corinna on the Future of Sex Education." *Sex, etc.* Answer and Rutgers University, 21 Aug. 2014. Web. 1 May 2016.

Montalvan, Renee. "Teen Pregnancy T.V. Shows Are a Bad Influence." *The Californian*. The Californian, 17 Mar. 2011. Web. 10 Oct. 2016.

Moreno, Megan A., et al. "Reducing At-Risk Adolescents' Display of Risk Behavior on a Social Networking Web Site: A Randomized Controlled Pilot Intervention Trial." *Archives of Pediatrics & Adolescent Medicine* 163.1 (2009): 35. Web. 27 Oct. 2016.

Moyer-Guse, Emily. "Entertainment Television and Safe Sex: Understanding Effects and Overcoming Resistance." PhD Diss., U of California, Santa Barbara, 2007.

"MTV Greenlights Season Two of Hit Series 16 and Pregnant." Press release. *TV by the Numbers*. Tribune Media Company, 30 June 2009. Web. 10 Oct. 2016.

Muise, A. "Women's Sex Blogs: Challenging Dominant Discourses of Heterosexual Desire." *Feminism & Psychology* 21.3 (2011): 411–19. Web. 27 Oct. 2016.

Parry, Manon. *Broadcasting Birth Control: Mass Media and Family Planning*. New Brunswick: Rutgers University Press, 2013. Print.

Paul, J., M. Duvet, and C. Boraas. "YouTube and the Contraceptive Implant: A Content Analysis." *Contraception* 90.3 (2014): 322. Web. 27 Oct. 2016.

Rose, Lacey. "Boyfriends, Condoms, Babies, Vasectomies: 'Modern Family' Cast and Creators Reveal 7 Spoilers for Season 4." *The Hollywood Reporter*. The Hollywood Reporter, 19 Sept. 2012. Web. 29 Apr. 2016.

Scarleteen/Corinna, Heather. "Birth Control Bingo: The Combination Pill." *Scarleteen*. Scarleteen/Heather Corinna, 13 July 2016. Web. 10 Oct. 2016.

Selkie, Ellen M., Meghan Benson, and Megan Moreno. "Adolescents' Views Regarding Uses of Social Networking Websites and Text Messaging for Adolescent Sexual Health Education." *American Journal of Health Education* 42.4 (2011): 205–12. Web. 27 Oct. 2016.

Sessions Stepp, Laura. "A Funny Approach to Birth Control for Young Adults." *CNN*. Cable News Network, 15 Nov. 2011. Web. 27 Oct. 2016.

Shane, Charlotte. "Pulling Out Is as Effective as Using Condoms." Blog. *Vice*. Vice Media, 10 Sept. 2015. Web. 10 Oct. 2016.

Simon, Laura, and Kristian Daneback. "Adolescents' Use of the Internet for Sex Education: A Thematic and Critical Review of the Literature." *International Journal of Sexual Health* 25.4 (2013): 305–19. Web. 27 Oct. 2016.

Sonalkar, Sarita, et al. "Does the Use of Bedsider.org Increase Long-Acting Reversible Contraception Uptake in Patients Presenting for Induced First-Trimester Abortion?" *Obstetrics & Gynecology* 125 (2015): 7S. Web. 27 Oct. 2016.

Strasburger, Victor C., and Sarah S. Brown. "Sex Education in the 21st Century." *JAMA: The Journal of the American Medical Association* 312.2 (2014): E1–E2. Web. 27 Oct. 2016.

Swiader, Lawrence. "Evaluation Results: Bedsider Works!" *The National Campaign*. The National Campaign to Prevent Teen and Unplanned Pregnancy, 9 June 2015. Web. 24 Feb. 2016.

Symonds, Alexandria. "The Forgotten Pioneer of Teenage Pop-Feminism." *Nymag*. New York Media, 14 Aug. 2014. Web. 10 Oct. 2016.

Talukdar, Joy. "The Prospects of a Virtual Sex Education: A Review." *American Journal of Sexuality Education* 8.1–2 (2013): 104–15. Web. 22 Feb. 2016.

Tone, Andrea. *Devices and Desires: A History of Contraceptives in America*. New York: Hill and Wang, 2001. Print.

"U.S. Teen Birth Rate Drops a Dramatic 9% in 2010." *The National Campaign*. The National Campaign to Prevent Teen and Unplanned Pregnancy, 17 Nov. 2011. Web. 10 Oct. 2016.

Vega, Tanzina. "Using Humor to Talk About Birth Control." *New York Times*. New York Times, 10 Nov. 2013. Web. 10 Oct. 2016.

Ward, L. Monique, and Kimberly Friedman. "Using TV as a Guide: Associations Between Television Viewing and Adolescents' Sexual Attitudes and Behavior." *Journal of Research on Adolescence* 16.1 (2006): 133–56. Web. 27 Oct. 2016.

Wood, E. A. "Consciousness-Raising 2.0: Sex Blogging and the Creation of a Feminist Sex Commons." *Feminism & Psychology* 18.4 (2008): 480–87. Web. 27 Oct. 2016.

Wright, Paul J., Ashley K. Randall, and Analisa Arroyo. "Father-Daughter Communication About Sex Moderates the Association Between Exposure to MTV's 16 and Pregnant/Teen Mom and Female Students' Pregnancy-Risk Behavior." *Sexuality & Culture* 17.1 (2013): 50–66. Web. 27 Oct. 2016.

PART 2. STORIES OF FORCED ADOPTION

In Search of the New Woman and the Best Mother
Unwanted Pregnancy in Gina Kaus' Literary and Filmic Work

REGINA RANGE

As an Austrian-Jewish novelist, dramatist, essayist, and screenwriter, Gina Kaus (1893–1985) moved in the literary and intellectual circles that would frequent the coffeehouses of Vienna and Berlin in the 1920s and 1930s. Kaus, along with her sons Otto (1920–1996) and Peter (1924–) and her partner Erich Frischauer, fled the country on the day of Austria's annexation in March 1938. The family first travelled to Switzerland, then to France before arriving in the United States in 1939. Kaus quickly found work as a screenwriter in Hollywood in order to provide for her family, using the restrictive Hollywood apparatus of the 1940s and 1950s as an effective means to call the normative and dominant discourses of the era into question, especially with regard to the understanding of "inherent" gender roles.

Gender Inequality, Reproductive Rights, Adoption and Motherhood in Kaus' Works

Kaus' concern with gender inequality, reproductive rights, adoption, and ideas of motherhood is particularly interesting, as her work not only covers a timespan of almost 40 years, but also because it deals with these concepts and discourses on two different continents. Her national as well as transnational oeuvre serves as an uncompromising portrayal of the social reality for women, and sheds light on the intersections between women's oppression and the socio-political climate of the 1920s, 1930s, and 1940s in Austria and Germany as well as the 1940s and 1950s in the United States. Reading the exile Kaus' work provides insight into the stringent gender expectations under which women labored prior to the pill.

This essay provides insight into Kaus' mid-1920s Vienna magazine *Die Mutter* (*The Mother*), and more specifically an advice column in which the topic of adoption is openly addressed. A discussion of Kaus' play *Toni: Eine Schulmädchen-Komödie in zehn Bildern* (*Toni: A Schoolgirl Comedy in Ten Pictures*), which premiered in 1927, demonstrates Kaus' ability to use the stage as a platform to criticize the inadequate education as well as limited social mobility of young women during the 1920s. The analyses of the film script *All Children* (1949), written in the United States more than 22 years after the premiere of *Toni* in Austria, traces Kaus' ongoing concern with gender inequality, family planning, adoption, and unwanted pregnancy.

All Children was reworked and made it to the silver screen as *Three Secrets* in 1950. A more in-depth investigation of *Three Secrets* allows further insight into Kaus' transnational view and understanding of unwanted pregnancy, and shows her reflection on women's oppression and the socio-political climate during the United States in the 1940s and 1950s. Prevailing attitudes on adoption in the United States began to change in the early 1950s; adoption practices were changing as well. The dilemma of the female protagonists in *Three Secrets* illustrates these changes without apology.

Adoption and Foster Care in Die Mutter

The concern Kaus clearly had with unwanted pregnancy, family planning, adoption, and construction of motherhood can be traced back to her first publication of a magazine entitled *Die Mutter*[1] (*The Mother*) in December 1924. As the subtitle "Halbmonatsschrift für alle Fragen der Schwangerschaft, Säuglingshygiene und Kindererziehung" indicates, the journal aimed to address *all* questions concerning pregnancy, newborn hygiene, and child rearing. As she recalled in her memoirs, Kaus regularly interviewed and collaborated with doctors, lawyers, social workers, and students of the psychologist Alfred Adler to educate young women and mothers with her journal (Kaus, *Von Wien nach Hollywood* 114).[2] She also volunteered with counseling centers for mothers to provide practical help and advice. As Kaus later recalls in her autobiography, her journal had no precedent neither in Vienna or Germany (Kaus, *Von Wien nach Hollywood* 113).[3]

Early evidence of Kaus' engagement with adoption can be found in the third volume of *Die Mutter*. A letter[4] in the "Briefkasten" section (advice column) indicates Kaus' involvement in helping a mother find a "Pflegemutter" (foster mother) for her twins. The letter contains information for the twins' mother as to who to contact should the placement of the children be unsuccessful. By directing the letter-writer to the Child Protective Services of the City of Vienna, Kaus is by proxy advising other readers who might be facing a similar situation. Addressing adoption openly and informing mothers about where and to whom to turn allows her to engage actively in the Viennese government's socialist endeavor and agenda of helping mothers in need.[5]

This advice column does not indicate that Kaus and her editors are necessarily looking for an adoptive family, as they initially use the term for foster mother. Post–World War I women were often the sole caretakers of their families, as most men had died in the war, were traumatized and unable to provide assistance, or were unemployed. The wording of the letter also makes it apparent that the editorial board is looking for a long-term arrangement in which the children remain with whoever accepts them for good. Furthermore, they explicitly state that they do not foresee any harm should the twins need to be separated as long as the families that take them in treat them lovingly. This understanding is different from the United States' discourse on adoption at that same time, which defined kinship on the basis of blood. Therefore, this construction of kinship stigmatized adoption as socially unacceptable. E. Wayne Carp points to this conception in his historical overview of American adoption, stating that during the late 19th and early 20th centuries, "a broad segment of the American public believed that adoption was an unnatural action that created ersatz or second-rate families" (9). According to Carp, social workers in the United States had to overcome widespread popular prejudice against adoption to convince potential adoptive parents that it was not abnormal (9). Kaus' magazine *Die Mutter* shows that the situation in Austria was rather different. World War I left Austria's economy in a disastrous state, causing food and housing shortages. Child welfare and the wish to place any child—regardless of gender, race, ethnicity, or mental or physical disability—in a caring home was a major concern in Austria during the 1920s. This socialist agenda remained in place until Austria was invaded by the National Socialists in March of 1938.

In 1926, after more than 40 issues of *Die Mutter*, Kaus, then an aspiring writer and dramatist, attempted to sell the rights to the journal to the German publishing house Ullstein. Instead, Ullstein offered Kaus an advance for writing a novel for them (Kaus, *Von Wien nach Hollywood* 126) which appeared under the title *Die Verliebten* (*The Lovers*, 1928). It was while working on this novel that Kaus also started writing her second play about the schoolgirl with the androgynous name *Toni*. It would premiere in 1927.

Growing Up as a "New Woman": Toni

Kaus' ongoing concern with gender inequality can also be observed in this play. The theater provided Kaus with a platform to candidly question and blur the existing class and gender limitations of Vienna and Weimar culture.[6] Kaus wrote *Toni* under the male pseudonym "Andreas Eckbrecht," crossing the border into the space of the male-dominated Weimar theater world. Once the play was performed, Kaus revealed herself on stage as the author. This is just one of many instances in which Kaus exposes her understanding that a critique of and resistance to oppression would need to be formulated within the format and the terms of that very oppression. This method of subverting oppression would resurface in her Hollywood work.

The play consists of ten scenes revolving around a young female protagonist named Toni who is coming of age during the Weimar period. The audience follows Toni on her path toward potentially becoming a "New Woman." As women "who voted, used contraception, obtained legal abortions, and earned wages," the "New Women" of 1920s Germany were more than a sheer construct or "bohemian minority or artistic convention" but rather women who indeed "existed in the office, factory, bedroom, and kitchen—just as surely as—in cafe, cabaret, and film" (Bridenthal 11). As argued in my dissertation, *Positioning Gina Kaus*, the play *Toni* provides a female perspective of the emerging tension and anxiety that both women and men encounter as they struggle with the blurring of traditional gender roles and the arising generational conflicts of the inter-war period (Range 12).

One such boundary is the source of strife between Toni and her mother, a representation of the rising conflicts between older and younger generations of women. The reading material available to Toni at the all-girl school she attends is based on the canon of the *Bildungsbürgertum*, the intellectual middle class, which fiercely clung to traditional gender roles and discourses. When Toni expresses her frustration with these constraints, her mother deems her daughter ungrateful, reminding Toni of the hardship the two suffer just "damit du alles lernst, ganz, als ob du ein Junge wärst!" (19) ("so that you learn everything, as if you were a boy!").

However, it is only through Andreas, a university student who rents a room in their apartment, that Toni actually accesses readings which enable her understanding of the limited choices for females within the class and gender hierarchy. Andreas' character represents an example of traditional male authority in the play. Through her interaction with Andreas, Toni constantly crosses geographical boundaries, invading spaces that are supposedly only reserved for men, and thus questions the legitimacy of the binary oppositions her society upholds. When Andreas catches her breaking into his room and reading Otto Weininger's book *Geschlecht und Charakter* (*Sex and Character*),[7] he acts appalled: "Dieses Buch gehört überhaupt nicht in Frauenhände, am wenigsten in die eines kleinen Mädchens" (30) ("This book does not at all belong in women's hands, especially not in those of a little girl"). As Toni protests, Andreas suggests 19th-century historical fiction such as *The Last Days of Pompeii* or *A Struggle for Rome* (39) as more suitable fare. Toni, however, wants to "etwas über das Leben erfahren" (40) ("learn something about life").

Toni's thirst for knowledge cannot be quenched. Curious to know more about relationships and sex, Toni attempts to have a conversation with her mother about her father. Toni wants to know: "Hast du ihm verziehen, was er—in der Hochzeitsnacht—und später mit dir gemacht hat?" ("Did you forgive him, for what he did with you—on your wedding night—and later?") Her mother is mortified and reacts by screaming: "Toni, das geht zu weit! Über so etwas darf man nicht sprechen. Und am wenigsten mit dem eigenen Kind" (59) ("Toni, this is going too far! One must not talk about such a thing. And especially not with one's own child"). The mother's reaction to Toni's query corresponds with what Helmut Gruber and Pamela Graves observe in their study on *Women and Socialism*: "Although there were public discussions on sex education in the 1920s, continuity between the Empire and the Weimar Republic in the working class existed regarding sex education in the family. The topic was taboo" (118).

The mother further elaborates that Toni's father had the right to do as he pleased and, therefore, there was no need for forgiveness. The mother's speech reveals that all women suffer the same fate; independent of their social background, "in der Hochzeitsnacht und im Wochenbett sind alle gleiche arme Kreaturen" (60) ("on their wedding night and during puerperium all are the same poor creatures"). As in so many of Kaus' works, the author presents the audience with an everyday experience and confronts them with the underlying power structures. She leaves it up to the audience to draw their own conclusions or to take action. *Toni* was a tremendous success. Not only did the play receive a prize from the Bremer Goethe-Bund in 1927, the year of its premiere, but it was also performed by more than 50 German theaters, as Kaus points out in her autobiography (124). Through Toni's character, Kaus points to the limited social mobility of young women during the 1920s and illustrates just how little equality women had actually gained by then. McCormick's observations on *Das kunstseidene Mädchen* (*The Artificial Silk Girl*) also apply to Kaus' play. Kaus endows her female protagonist with wit, desire, and skepticism, while simultaneously providing her with the "capacity to expose, to understand and even to revise in some ways the limitations … [of] dominant social discourses [which] shaped her" (McCormick 145).

Adoption in Postwar America and the Script All Children

Kaus' screenplay *All Children*[8] (1949) was written in the United States and in the English language more than 22 years after the play *Toni*. It reveals the émigré's undeterred engagement with discourses of family planning, adoption, and unwanted pregnancy.

The protagonist of the screenplay, Virginia, is wholly abandoned after bearing an illegitimate child. The story exemplifies the consequences of a society that does not allow for family planning and reveals how governmental as well as medical institutions sacrifice women's needs in their own interests. What's more, it demonstrates the ramifications of the dramatic change in discourse and practice of maternity homes taking place in postwar America.

The script of *All Children* revolves around two female protagonists: Virginia and Celeste. Virginia is a young woman who intends to give up her child for adoption at the maternity home, where Celeste works as an adoption agent. Most of the story takes place in and around the maternity home, The Children's Aid Society in Philadelphia. While living at the institution, Virginia pretends to be a married woman in order to maintain a superior position over the numerous girls who are also in the home to deliver their illegitimate children. As in the majority of Kaus' narratives, *All Children* exemplifies society's reaction to unmarried and single mothers.

The narrative of *All Children* illustrates the various phases Virginia experiences in her ever-changing decision to keep the child and bring it up by herself or give it up for adoption. Virginia's choices are heavily influenced by Celeste. Kaus' representation of the maternity home as well as the social worker Celeste parallel the social reality and changes which occurred in maternity homes during the postwar era.

Celeste constantly tries to convince Virginia that it would be best to give up Betsy, Virginia's illegitimate daughter. Celeste represents a new generation and understanding of adoption agents. Whereas prewar maternity homes were usually run by religious women and charity workers, the staff of postwar maternity homes consisted primarily of professional social workers. While the religiously motivated women saw themselves as sympathetic "sisters" and believed that motherhood would increase a woman's chances of living a good and proper life (Fessler 142), the influx of professional social workers were motivated by what they "considered to be more rigorous approaches to social problems, rather than basing their practices on religious perspectives" (Fessler 143). With regard to the change in the mission and philosophy of such homes that had occurred by the end of World War II, Fessler observes, "Maternity homes of the 1950s and 1960s were, to a great extent, places to sequester pregnant girls until they could give birth and surrender their child for adoption. If a young woman was unsure of or uninterested in relinquishment, the staff attempted to convince her that it was the best, and perhaps only, option" (143).

Celeste is relentless in persuading Virginia that she should give up Betsy for adoption. Virginia is reliant on the help the government provides. Not only is she unmarried with a child, she is also physically and psychologically deterritorialized and displaced. Further, she cannot return home to the small town where she grew up, as her father fears for his reputation. Nor can she be with the child's father because he has eloped with another, much richer woman. Virginia's father's fear and refusal to take his daughter in with an illegitimate child coincide with the behavior Ann Fessler recorded in her more than 100 oral histories of mothers who gave their children up for adoption. In her resulting book *The Girls Who Went Away*, Fessler (a scholar, author, filmmaker, and installation artist) argues that it was particularly the prosperity of the postwar era—and the fear of losing that newly gained status—which played a major role in these decisions. According to Fessler, this became a driving force in parents' desires to conform to the middle-class values of the time: "The parents' fears of being ostracized from their community or church ultimately led them to treat their daughters in precisely the same manner that they feared their neighbors would treat them" (102).

Working and being a single mother at the same time proves impossible in *All Children*. A disillusioned Virginia eventually decides to give her child up for adoption. The narrative clearly draws on Kaus' experience as a single parent of two, an exile, someone who worked in counseling centers for mothers during the 1920s, an editor of the magazine for mothers, and finally as someone who viewed postwar America's social and gender injustices with a transnational eye. Moreover, it reflects on the social practices of adoption and politics of reproduction in the United States during the 1940s and 1950s.

All Children is not only unpublished but also remains unfilmed. A rewrite of the script served as the final script for the movie entitled *Three Secrets*.

The Hollywood Movie Three Secrets *and Its Portrayal of Adoption*

Three Secrets, the reworking of *All Children* which made it to the silver screen, differs drastically from the original screenplay.[9] The final script for *Three Secrets* (1950) also incorporates the theme of unwanted pregnancy, but concentrates on three female characters who have to give up their children for adoption due to their individual circumstances and pressures. The script was the product of a collaboration between Gina Kaus and Martin Rackin, later head of production at Paramount, one of the major film studios in Hollywood.[10] Nonetheless, these deviations from the original script do not differ from the overall idea the writers indicated for the scenes. This demonstrates that Kaus' scriptwriting, and especially her dialogues, were adopted as they stand, and also that her ideas of presentation made their way onto the screen. This is only one example of many. As the following analysis shows, the scriptwriter's ideas found their way almost unchanged into the film.

Three Secrets dramatizes the story of a five-year-old boy who is the only survivor of a plane crash. An eager newspaper reporter reveals that the boy, whose parents passed away in the crash, was originally adopted. Upon hearing the news, three women, Phyllis, Susan, and Ann, begin to ponder whether the boy, Johnny Peterson, might be the son each had given up for adoption. The three women not only have to confront their past decisions, they also have to decide about the boy's—and hence their own—future. Unsure as to the identity of the boy's mother, the women first try to find the biological mother but slowly begin to decide which one of them will be the best mother for Johnny.

The first female character the audience encounters is Susan Connors (Eleanor Parker). Her character is representative of the dominant discourse on women at the time the movie was released, around 1950. With the end of World War II, women were again thought of as "homemakers": responsible for managing the household, caring for children, and promoting the happiness and well-being of their families. At first sight, Susan seemingly fits this 1950s "perfect housewife" ideal—considering herself "happier than any girl deserves to be." However, Susan alludes to a traumatic past event which haunts her present when she tells her mother: "The past is the past. We've decided that five years ago. I locked away my girlish grief, tied it in a ribbon and locked it away for good."

The idea of Susan as an exemplary homemaker is visually supported by her first appearance on the screen, in which she is packing a suitcase for her husband. When he comes home, he asks Susan whether there was anything new in connection with the Johnny Peterson case. Susan is completely oblivious to the news, to which her husband Bill immediately responds by saying, "Oh, you disappoint me. A good American housewife loves her radio first and her husband second." When Susan apologetically explains that she was busy packing for his trip, he sarcastically replies: "You poor overworked slave," and then gives her a kiss.

The dialogue between Susan and her husband is superficial, to the point that their lines ventriloquize advertisement slogans of the 1950s. Susan wears well the "perfect housewife" mask, while simultaneously struggling with her past, trying to cope by suppressing any memory of having given her child away. Through a flashback scene the viewers learn that Susan had fallen in love with a soldier who impregnated her. When she meets him at a San Diego base to inform him of her pregnancy, she finds out that he is about to leave for another deployment. Before Susan can even tell him that she is pregnant, he confesses to her that he cannot move past his childhood love for another woman and that he must therefore end his brief relationship with Susan. As a result, Susan attempts suicide which she tragically considers her only option as an unwed mother. Susan's mother discovers her daughter and promptly gets her medical attention. During her recovery, Susan shares with her mother the shame she encountered through her experience at the doctor's office to confirm her pregnancy. The mother devises a plan to protect Susan from further social scrutiny. She calmly explains to her daughter: "You made one mistake, a bad one, I will not let you make another. I've thought it all out. We will go away until it's all over. And then we will come back. Alone. No one will ever need to know."

The reaction of Susan's mother coincides with the sentiment of the 1950s. Whereas prior to World War II, single mothers could often count on the extended family to assist them in rearing their children, this was not the case in postwar America. The conformist culture of the white middle class of the postwar era demanded that unmarried individuals abstain from sexuality. The parents' fear of the stigma of having a pregnant and unwed daughter often resulted in them turning to maternity homes where their daughters could give birth and then give their child up for adoption unbeknownst to their community.

Susan's mother's reaction echoes the discourse at the time both on adoption as well as unwed mothers. According to Sarah Potter's study, *Adoption and Politics of Domestic Diversity*, there was a greater acceptance of adoption in American families during the 1940s, 1950s, and 1960s.

> Adoption was widely understood as a second chance for unwed mothers and their "illegitimate" babies [and] became a positive choice for solving a wide range of personal and social issues.... White middle-class unwed mothers were increasingly encouraged to relinquish their babies to the homes of infertile middle-class white couples and to move on to a new life in which they would supposedly remain chaste until marriage gave them the opportunity to have a "legitimate" family [18].

However, the increased acceptance of adoption at the time certainly should not be viewed as the increased acceptance or decreased stigmatization of unwed mothers. These seemingly positive trends pertained only to adoption. Adoption professionals had created a discourse which favored placing children for adoption with infertile, married couples as the "right" thing to do for the sake of these illegitimate children (rather than, as these professionals had previously believed, maintaining the integrity of the natal family at all costs). Following this logic, placing these illegitimate children with married couples, these children would be spared an otherwise inevitably doomed life with an "unmarried, emotionally unstable," and presumably immoral mother who could not "offer them real love or security" or possibly adequately provide for a child (Herman). This new societal acceptance of adoption applied only to the adoptive parents and adopted child; it did not equate with an increase in social acceptance of the unwed mother. She and her pregnant-out-of-wedlock condition were still shameful, proof of sexual immorality, to be hidden, and forgotten, if at all possible. The hope that the neighbors and relatives will not see or hear anything about Susan's pregnancy informs her mother's suggestion to come back when the adoption has been finalized.

In the film, a cut to a maternity hospital sign following this conversation between Susan and her mother indicates time has passed. Again, the viewer witnesses an exchange between mother and daughter. Susan is torn and declares: "I cannot go through with it. I won't let my child be adopted." The mother calmly replies that the arrangements have already been made. Susan is desperately trying to convince her mother that there might be an alternative solution: "But I cannot give him away... my own flesh and blood. It's wrong. Unnatural." Susan's mother responds: "Living with an illegitimate child will be wrong and unnatural, too, only it will last for the rest of your life. This will be over in a few months. It is right and natural for every child to be brought up in a normal home. You must realize that." The discourses on normalcy and ideas on kinship are brought to the foreground through Kaus' choice of dialogue. Ellen Herman's historical overview of adoptions in the United States attests to the fact that the idea of being a single mother at the time was perceived as *unnatural*. According to her findings, most adoption professionals, who earlier in the century had strived to preserve natal families, believed by the middle of the century that it was a mistake for unmarried women to keep their children. She reports that "childlessness and motherhood without benefit of marriage were both abnormal, but adoption was less abnormal than living in a female-headed family tainted by illegitimacy" (97). The discussion further emulates the 1940s-era idea that adoption spared "children who would otherwise have been condemned to the stigma of being born out of wedlock and raised by an unwed mother ... potential shame when they were placed with married adoptive parents" (Potter 19). It also provided the biological mothers of those children with an opportunity to have a "legitimate" family later on.

The implications of preserving the nuclear family at all costs become obvious as the scenes progress. Not only does Susan suffer at the hand of these, the dominant, moral standards, but her mother does as well. Even though the mother seems stern and uncompromising, a short exchange with a nurse indicates that her character is more complex than she might first appear. The mother stops the nurse who is just about to enter Susan's room with the baby boy: "Just a minute, nurse. You must be new here. This baby never goes to its mother." The instant the nurse is ready to leave with the baby, Mrs. Connors asks her whether she could hold the baby for a moment. As she does, a close-up shows that Susan's mother is nearly in tears. She hands the boy back to the nurse and walks to the window. The audience can hear her weeping as she is facing away from the camera and toward a window overlooking Los Angeles. Kaus is thus able to address how societal pressure wears heavily on both women.

The last scene of Susan's flashback takes place in the waiting room of an adoption agency. A few women and their companions are waiting to finalize their adoptions. This shot also serves to establish the characters of Phyllis Horn (Patricia Neal) and Ann Lawrence (Ruth Roman) who later too wonder whether they could possibly be the mother of Johnny Peterson. While Phyllis moves around freely and makes snarky comments about the representation of child welfare in the newspaper, Susan and her mother sit quietly on a sofa. Once called to enter the agent's office, a close-up of Susan's face indicates how conflicted she is about the adoption. This shot creates a stark contrast to the agent's objective and monotonous voice as she explains the legal consequences of the impending adoption. Susan signs reluctantly while the agent concludes: "There is no recourse through law to recover your child. And never, under any conditions, will his whereabouts be—or any information concerning him—available to you." This procedure reflects the actual processes at the time. As Sarah Potter points out, "adoption records and the original birth certificates of children placed for adoption went from being legally confidential, and thereby hidden from the public, to being inaccessible to even the very parties most affected—adoptive parents, adopted children, and birth parents" (23).

"I wasn't a woman": A Working Woman, a Troubled Woman and Motherhood

After the news of the plane crash, Susan drives to the crash site to observe the rescue mission for Johnny Peterson, who is trapped on a mountain. Phyllis is also present, although mainly in her function as a news reporter. Ann Lawrence is the last to arrive at the scene. Whereas Susan's flashback takes place on her way to the mountain, Phyllis and Ann's recollections begin at the cabin located at the bottom of the mountain, specifically, the circumstances under which they each were forced to give up their son five years earlier.

Phyllis' flashback takes the viewer back to the moment when she returns home from her job as a war correspondent. Her husband, Duffy, informs her that he wants a divorce. Kaus, who wrote the dialogues, has Duffy speak the following words: "I happen to be a sentimental guy that comes from a big family of twelve kids. I get lonely when the other eleven are not around—or even one." Phyllis reacts quickly and rather harshly: "What do you want me to do? Stay home and cook for you? Wash the dishes? No, Duffy. I am not that type. You knew that from the beginning."

The post–World War II idea of the working woman as undesirable plays out in this scene. The interaction of the characters brings the ideological contradictions to the foreground. The dialogue reveals Kaus' discontent with the discourses that position women as "natural" caretakers. This also reflects Kaus' encounters with various ideas about gender, nationally as well as transnationally. Kaus came of age during the Constitution of Austria[11] and the Weimar Republic, both of which were extremely progressive in comparison to gender discourses in the United States, and at that time in Hollywood in particular. However, even during her time in Vienna and Berlin, Kaus knew that she had to fight actively for equal rights and access to education. Hollywood's conservative outlook and heteronormative presentations of women provided a challenging work environment for the feminist Kaus.

In 1945, not only does Phyllis work in a male-dominated and dangerous work environment, she also uses her income to support her husband. As a "manly man," her husband resists such progressive and non-conformist behavior. He even feels betrayed by Phyllis and argues, "I don't understand you either. Seven years ago, you had me fooled for a while. Long enough to get a license and marry you." He concludes his speech by saying, "Just for a moment there, I thought you were a human being. Ever since then, in a hundred ways did you prove me differently. Well, it's all over." In this scene Kaus vividly demonstrates the consequences of the government's political agenda which convinced white middle-class women to work outside the home for the nation's sake. Phyllis and Duffy's marriage began before the war, prior to the time in which women were heavily recruited to take men's jobs while they were in the war. Duffy is unwilling to accept the social reality of shifting gender roles, longing for the traditional model.

Since Phyllis loves her husband and wants to make the marriage work, she decides to give up her job and become the housewife her husband wants her to be. When her boss offers her work as a war correspondent, however, she is torn between, on the one hand, her profession, career, and independence, and on the other hand, not wanting to lose her husband. Because of the war, she had been able to break out of the socially enforced binary opposition while being married, but after seven years, her husband is no longer willing to accept and support her desire, threatening her with an ultimatum.

As Judith Butler points out, "those who fail to do their gender right are regularly punished" (Butler 191).

When Phyllis asks her husband to at least try and understand her inner conflict between wanting to please him and also wanting a career, he calmly answers, "I do understand. I am sorry for you, Phyllis. You tried very hard to be a woman. You just couldn't make it." Phyllis is not only challenged in terms of her femininity but also in terms of her humanity. The scene exposes the psychological abuse involved in the reinforcement of traditional gender roles. Duffy is unwilling to remain married to Phyllis if she returns to her position as a reporter. The conversations with her husband illustrate how ideas of normative "ethical justification, how it is established, and what concrete consequences proceed therefrom" are constantly reinforced at home (Butler 98).

The severity of Duffy's behavior and the struggle a working woman faces is presented even more starkly in the subsequent scene. Phyllis is at a doctor's hut at a war camp and finds out that she is pregnant. When the doctor enquires about the father, she sarcastically states, "He divorced me two weeks ago.... Is he going to be surprised.... You know what his grounds were? He said I wasn't a woman." The scene reveals that ideas of "femininity" or "masculinity" are discursive constructions and exposes them as part of a patriarchal ideology. Moreover, it exposes the uneven power structures present at this particular time. Phyllis gives up her child to return to her career and to support herself.

The third woman the audience encounters after the plane crash is Ann Lawrence. Her introductory shot stages her as a drunken and rather aggressive woman. She is fighting loudly with a reporter about one of the last available bottles of hard liquor. Phyllis, who fears too much attention and who does not want the three of them to become the center of a potential news report, secures a room in the cabin at the bottom of the mountain where Johnny is trapped. Away from the chaos of the rescue team, reporters, and spectators, the three women can celebrate a moment of female solidarity and enjoy their autonomy. It is also within this space that Ann discloses her story to Phyllis and Susan. Just as with the two previous women, Ann's recollections are also presented to the viewer in the form of a flashback.

At first, the audience receives a glimpse at Ann's earlier glamorous lifestyle when she is a successful dancer in New York. A detailed shot of the dance company's poster features the name "Gordon Crossley" as the producer. Crossley is Ann's boyfriend and a wealthy and influential businessman. Ann's voiceover informs the viewer that he is everything she ever wanted in a man; therefore, it comes as quite a surprise to her when she finds out that he is getting ready to leave the city without even informing her personally. Ann suspects Crossley's assistant resents her relationship with Crossley and is sabotaging it. Unbeknownst to Ann, the assistant merely follows his boss' orders and tries his best to dissuade Ann from further pursuing a relationship with Crossley. Once Ann figures out where Crossley is, she follows him across the country. She will not believe that Crossley does not consider their relationship serious, as the assistant informs her. Once again Ann is greeted by the assistant who tells her to return to New York and to forget about Crossley. When he tells her that she was nothing but fling for Crossley, just like any of the other girls that fall in love with his boss, Ann says it is different with them. She then informs the assistant that she is pregnant with his boss' child.

During a last desperate attempt to speak directly to her boyfriend, Ann is ridiculed to a point where she loses control over her actions. When she arrives at Crossley's apartment, the personal assistant tells her that her boyfriend refuses to see her, due to her infidelity. Ann is outraged, swearing that she never did such a thing. Then a man who had been sitting quietly in the apartment gets up. He was hired by Ann's boyfriend to pretend that they had an affair; he even comes up with exact dates and a hotel room in which they supposedly met. According to the assistant, Crossley has many more men who would testify to the same thing, as he believes that Ann "wants to shake him down with all this talk about a kid." Ann is desperate and helpless in this charade but is still convinced that the assistant invented all of this. However, when the assistant offers her a check for more than $10,000 "to take care of everything and cover a lot of heartbreak" Ann sees that it is indeed signed by Crossley himself. She finally realizes that her boyfriend took advantage of her without ever considering marriage. Ann runs into the room where her boyfriend is, and beats him to death with a lamp.

A short scene at court informs the audience that Ann is convicted of manslaughter and sentenced to ten years in prison. A longer scene follows in which Ann is taken to the warden's office. In a caring voice the superintendent informs her: "The state has no quarrel with your child. It is the right of every citizen to be born without prejudice and stain. So we made arrangements for you to have your baby outside these prison walls." The warden's words echo clearly the 1940s and 50s ideas that "adoption protected children from troubled mothers and doomed lives, offering a positive solution for everyone involved" (Herman 97).

Since Ann does not have relatives or friends to whom she would entrust her child, the warden informs her that her baby will be turned over "to an accredited agency, which will care for it and plan its future." Ann cries uncontrollably when hearing about her child's fate. This interaction exposes a recurring theme in Kaus' work: the power of the state apparatus and dominant discourses. It becomes clear that individuals are helpless when institutions preside over their lives or those of their children. Not even the individual's body is owned by him or herself. The flashback scene ends and Ann explains that the forced adoption of her child and the fact that she knew nothing about his whereabouts led her to become an alcoholic.

"Cut out to be a mother": Women Resisting State Authority Over Motherhood

Toward the end of the film, Phyllis uses her connections as a reporter to make the necessary inquiries, resulting in the finding that Johnny is actually Ann's child. Phyllis shares the information with Ann. When the boy is finally rescued, the three of them watch him being carried to an ambulance. Susan is visibly worried to which Ann responds by saying: "You were really cut out to be a mother, weren't you?" This representation of Susan fits the expectation of the Hollywood audience perfectly. As Carolyn Galerstein points out in her filmography of *Working Women on the Hollywood Screen*: "In the world created by Hollywood, a real woman is caring and nurturing, concerned with affairs of the heart rather than matters of the mind" (16). In the dominant societal discourse and in the Hollywood logic of the 1950s, neither Phyllis nor Ann could take on the role of the mother for Johnny. Susan, however, complies perfectly with the agenda for women at the time: she plays her "proper role," has a successful husband, and thus represents a desirable role model as a mother for the audience. However, Kaus gives more agency to the women who tend to be outside Hollywood's prescribed gender roles. Whereas Galerstein observed that female characters "who step outside of prescribed sex-defined boundaries … are punished for their transgressions" (16), Ann and Phyllis take matters into their own hands as soon as they can. Even though they might initially fail, they recover, and then also manage to find ways to undermine and fight the structures and expectations with which they are presented.

When Susan wants to know whether the two had found out which of them is the mother, Ann answers immediately. She lies and tells Susan that Phyllis and she decided to cancel the call. The transformation of Ann's character is very obvious. She is no longer drunk, but staged as rational and determined. Ann does all the talking and explains: "We thought it was better if we never find out. And in a way he belongs to all three of us. And since all of us can't have him, we decided that you are the one who should try and adopt him." Phyllis agrees. When Susan argues that Phyllis and Ann are not being fair to themselves in making such a decision, Ann responds that "no court would turn you two down," referring to Susan and her husband, to whom Susan had revealed her adoption. Once again, Kaus' dialogue alludes to class and social conditions here. Ann is portrayed as cognizant of the role of the state and its institutions, and their power over her. She recognizes that the three women will need a backup plan in case the state interferes with what she understands to be her decision.

With *Three Secrets*, Kaus illustrates a resistance to the cruelty of the state apparatus and the institutions associated with it. Moreover, she creates an awareness of the social prejudices and behavior toward children of unwed and criminal mothers. Instead of letting the bureaucracy decide the fate of the boy, the women become active and make a decision, creating yet another "secret," but a secret which they control.

A 1950 *New York Times* review is dismissive of these female characters' predicaments, and is likely representative of the white male middle class perceptions of the plight of women who gave their children up for adoption. The journalist Bosley Crowther refers to the stories of Ann, Susan, and Phyllis as "mawkish" and calls them "'true story romances' [that] are foreign to the genuine nature of the film when it is briefly concerned with the rescue." He infers that Kaus' social commentary detracts from what would otherwise be a compelling story.

Conclusion

As this examination of select works by Kaus has shown, the response of state institutions to unwanted pregnancies differed considerably from post–World War I Vienna to post–World War II America. From the magazine *Die Mutter*, to Toni's coming-of-age New Woman, to the choice of Susan Connors as the "best mother" for Johnny Peterson, the limitations imposed on women by dominant gender discourses appear at every turn. Thanks to Kaus' international experience and her concern with adoption and motherhood, we are able to trace discourses about reproductive rights and social attitudes over decades in Austria and also the United States. Insight into different perceptions at different times in different geographical spaces makes the social reality and constraints on women apparent, and it sheds light on the connection between women's oppression and the socio-political climate of the 1920s, 1930s, and 1940s in Austria and Germany as well as the 1940s and 1950s in the United States.

NOTES

1. *Die Mutter* was created by Gina Kaus and was published from 1924 to 1926.
2. This 1990 reprint of Kaus's memoirs, *Von Wien nach Hollywood. Erinnerungen* is based on the 1979 first edition *Und was für ein Leben. Mit Liebe und Literatur, Theater und Film*.
3. In the original: "So etwas gab es damals weder in Wien noch in Deutschland." All translations are my own, unless otherwise noted.
4. The letter stems from a woman referred to as Frida P. which was not only approved but also supported by the editor. It directly addresses the readership and refers to the readers as "unsere Leserinnen" ("our female readers").

5. As of 1927 the baby linen package (*Wäschepaket*), a form of care package for infants, was reintroduced in Vienna. This allowed for official social workers to at least get a glimpse at each baby that was born and prevent abandonment or infanticide.

6. Although Kaus was a citizen of Austria and not Germany, she, like so many other intellectuals, constantly traveled back and forth between Vienna and Berlin, the latter which was considered the vibrant center of Weimar culture. Gina Kaus must be regarded as an integral and vital part of the wider German culture centered in Berlin as she interacted and wrote with and for German intellectuals. Kaus' work, as I have argued in my dissertation, *Positioning Gina Kaus: A Transnational Career from Vienna Novelist and Playwright to Hollywood Scriptwriter*, thus needs to be contextualized in a larger transnational context, including the very beginning of her career as a novelist and playwright in Vienna and her later profession as a scriptwriter and autobiographer in the United States, as well as Austria and Germany.

7. His book *Geschlecht und Charakter* (*Sex and Character*), first published in Vienna in 1903, "immediately goes into a second edition, becoming a best-seller in Austria and Germany.… Misogynist, anti-semitic, anti-sexual, the book's themes highlight the anxieties of the age" (Bland 27).

8. This script is located in the Special Collections at the University of Iowa Library among the Robert Blees Production Papers. A more detailed discussion of this script version is provided in *Positioning Gina Kaus* (Range 106–110).

9. The scripts in the Margaret Herrick Library in Los Angeles are dated April 15, 1949, and November 14, 1949.

10. Martin Rackin (1918–1976) was head of production at Paramount from 1960 to 1964. He left Paramount in order to set up his own production company, Mart Rackin Productions.

11. In 1918 when Austria became a republic after World War I, the elections resulted in a coalition of left-wing and right-wing parties. A variety of very progressive socioeconomic and labor legislation were passed.

Works Cited

The Adoption History Project. Ed. Ellen Herman. Dept. of History, University of Oregon, Eugene, 24 Feb. 2012. Web. 6 Aug. 2016.

Bland, Lucy. *Sexology in Culture: Labelling Bodies and Desire*. Chicago: University of Chicago Press, 1998. Print.

Crowther, Bosley. "*Three Secrets*, Containing Some Absorbing, Dramatic Parts, Makes Bow at Strand." *New York Times*. New York Times, 21 Oct. 1950. Web. 10 Oct. 2016.

Bridenthal, Renate, Atina Grossmann, and Marion A. Kaplan. *When Biology Became Destiny: Women in Weimar and Nazi Germany*. New York: Monthly Review, 1984. Print.

Butler, Judith. *Gender Trouble: Feminism and the Subversion of Identity*. New York: Routledge, 2008. Print.

Carp, E. Wayne. *Adoption in America: Historical Perspectives*. Ann Arbor: University of Michigan Press, 2002. Print.

Fessler, Ann. *The Girls Who Went Away: The Hidden History of Women Who Surrendered Children for Adoption in the Decades Before Roe v. Wade*. New York: Penguin, 2006. Print.

Galerstein, Carolyn L. *Working Women on the Hollywood Screen: A Filmography*. New York: Garland, 1989. Print.

Gruber, Helmut, and Pamela M. Graves. *Women and Socialism, Socialism and Women: Europe between the Two World Wars*. New York: Berghahn, 1998. Print.

Herman, Ellen. *Kinship by Design: A History of Adoption in the Modern United States*. Chicago: University of Chicago Press, 2008. Print.

Kaus, Gina. *All Children*. Screenplay. 1949. TS Special Collections, University of Iowa Library, Iowa City.

_____. *Three Secrets*. Screenplay and story by Gina Kaus [uncredited] and Martin Rackin. Dir. Robert Wise. Perf. Eleanor Parker, Patricia Neal, and Ruth Roman. 1950. Olive Films, 2012. DVD.

———. *Toni. Eine Schulmädchen-Komödie in zehn Bildern.* Berlin: Propyläen, 1927. Print.
———. *Und was für ein Leben. Mit Liebe und Literatur, Theater und Film.* Hamburg: Knaus, 1979. Print.
———. *Von Wien nach Hollywood. Erinnerungen.* Frankfurt a. M.: Suhrkamp, 1990. Print.
———, ed. *Die Mutter. Halbmonatsschrift für alle Fragen der Schwangerschaft, Säuglingshygiene und Kindererziehung. Offizielles Organ des Bundes für Mutterschutz.* 41 issues. Wien: Ignaz Tenger, Stefan Popper, 1924–26.
McCormick, Richard W. *Gender and Sexuality in Weimar Modernity: Film, Literature, and "New Objectivity."* New York: Palgrave, 2001. Print.
Potter, Sarah. *Everybody Else: Adoption and the Politics of Domestic Diversity in Postwar America.* Athens: University of Georgia Press, 2014. Print.
Range, Regina C. *Positioning Gina Kaus: A Transnational Career from Vienna Novelist and Playwright to Hollywood Scriptwriter.* Diss., University of Iowa, 2012. *Iowa Research Online.* Web. 6 Nov. 2016.
Weininger, Otto. *Geschlecht und Charakter. Eine prinzipielle Untersuchung.* Wien: W. Braumüller, 1903. Print.

Pregnant Girls in the Attic—No Choices
An Analysis of Patrice Toye's Little Black Spiders

KIRSTEN E. KUMPF BAELE
and SOFIE DECOCK

Context

Since the 1950s approximately 30,000 Flemish girls and women gave birth anonymously in northeastern France. Because these were unwanted pregnancies, parents would first hide their daughters in facilities for unwed mothers, which were scattered throughout the region of Flanders. However, because in Belgium it is not allowed to give birth anonymously—the name of the mother is always registered—France proved to be an ideal place to carry out the actual birth. Formerly known as "accouchement sous X" (anonymous childbirth), French legal practice allowed a woman in France to simply sign an X on the birth certificate of her child in lieu of her name (the child was then referred to as "nés sous X" [born under X]). This pro-natalist policy dates back in one form or another to 1793 when, under the National Convention of the French Revolution, pregnancies and births were defended by law.[1] With the legalization of contraception and abortion as stated in the Neuwirth and Veil Law, respectively,[2] however, the number of babies considered "nés sous X" dwindled significantly,[3] thus creating a lack of adoptable babies in France—an increasingly attractive situation for the neighboring country of Belgium.[4] Unlike in France where access to abortion and anonymity were possible, Belgium provided no choices to women with unwanted pregnancies.[5] Prior to April 4, 1990, Belgium and Ireland remained the only countries in Europe in which abortion was deemed illegal.⁶ In fact, the 1990 ruling finally allowing abortion, submitted by Roger Lallemand and Lucienne Herman-Michielsens, replaced a ban that had been in effect in Belgium since 1867.⁷ A long historical tradition as well as the incumbent monarch's religious opposition resulted in complicated politics surrounding the implementation of this new law. Because King Baudouin I could not in good conscience as a practicing Roman Catholic sign the decree on April 4, 1990, the federal government declared the King "unable to govern" which allowed the Cabinet to enact the abortion law; Baudouin I was reinstated the following day.⁸

As history unfolds and stories of forced adoption are finally being disclosed, the magnitude of similar cases is astounding. In Europe alone one must consider the stories of involuntary adoption as carried out in Britain, Ireland, and Germany. Studies such as Mike Milotte's *Banished Babies*, the recent PBS documentary *Ireland's Lost Babies,* and Ann O'Loughlin's 2015 novel *The Ballroom Café* reveal how the Irish state colluded with the Catholic Church into coercing single mothers to surrender their infants to adoptive parents, many in the United States, who, if "Catholic" and "moneyed," could conveniently "take [their] pick."⁹ Initially the argument to "save a life" (one could argue both for the mother out of wedlock and for the child not aborted) seemed morally compelling to individuals and families from a deeply-rooted, pro-life Catholic tradition.¹⁰ However, as accounts surface, ultimately both countries' state and religious institutions encouraged an elaborate, illegal black market exchange and placed the concealment of scandal above the interest of the children. Today Britain is the only country in Europe that allows social workers to place children into new families without proper justification.¹¹ A heyday for the media, stories abound that document the unjust conditions of these arrangements including how targeted families are pursuing means to escape Britain (Booker). For example, according to the *Irish Post*, around 270 women fearing their children may be seized by social services in Britain have fled to Ireland to seek refuge (Balasundaram). Comparably during the Cold War, children were taken in similar fashion from their families in the former German Democratic Republic. Politically motivated, socialist authorities removed the children of dissidents and those trying to escape the Communist country without consent. Memoirs such as Katrin Behr's (2011) and Heidrun Groth's (2013) exemplarily tell the stories of children, presumably in the thousands, who experienced separation from their parents.

Beyond European borders, there also exists a long history of child removal policies in Australia. From the beginning of the 20th century until approximately the 1960s, children of Aboriginal and Torres Strait Islander descent were taken away from their families by authorities as a means to end

Aboriginal culture. These mixed-race children collectively referred to as the "Stolen Generations" were forced to leave their families and to integrate into a Euro-Australian environment where they were expected to work and marry white.[12] Furthermore, between the 1950s and 1980s, government intervention denied many unwed, pregnant Australian women motherhood. Figures were not recorded, but it is estimated that between 210,000 to 250,000 babies were taken from their mothers by doctors, nurses, social workers, and religious officials with the support of government agencies.[13] Often under the influence of drugs or by means of verbal trickery, women were uninformed about their right to revoke adoption consent and compelled illegally to relinquish their little ones. After lengthy and generally unsupported, physically-restrained births, midwives held pillows and sheets in front of birthing mothers' faces as to prevent any sight of the child and followed up with anti-lactation medication.[14] These dire conditions inspired Australian women to fight. Societies such as the Association Representing Mothers Separated from their Children by Adoption (ARMS) in South Australia and Post Adoption Support Services (PASS) provided counseling, education, political activism and reunion services to those impacted by adoption. Due to the efforts of ARMS in particular, South Australia passed the first laws in the English-speaking world which provided mothers with the same rights as adopted individuals: information about one another.[15]

Little Black Spiders: *The Film*

"Ondertussen zijn de tijden veranderd, maar pas op. Toen ik vijftien was, was zwanger zijn een grote schande" ("In the meantime the times have changed, but mind you, when I was 15, being pregnant was a huge disgrace"[16]; Sartor). These are the words of Belgian (born in Ghent, 1967) film director and screenwriter Patrice Toye, whose newest movie *Little Black Spiders* (2012) sheds light on Belgium's recent yet shockingly and relatively unknown handling of unwanted teenage pregnancy. In 2003 in a local Flanders newspaper, Toye read a short article about a group of expectant teenage girls who were made to live out their pregnancies hidden away in a hospital attic run by Catholic nuns. Much to Toye's surprise this dark reality took place in her home country—more specifically in the town of Lommel, where from 1970 until 1982 an institution known as "Tamar" housed young girls until they were about to give birth to their babies. Control did not stop here; once a girl started contractions, the nuns placed her in a car and drove her over the border to northern France. Following the birth, she was forced to give up her child for adoption, which the nuns had already prearranged. Once all was said and done, the girls were brought back to Belgium and they had to pretend that nothing had ever happened. The nuns purposefully broke the bond between mother and child. The files were burned which is why dozens of women still today are searching for their own offspring. These traumatic, local events on the one hand troubled Toye but on the other hand they fascinated her. She recognized that this was a story that needed to be told.

Together with Ina Vandewijer, Patrice Toye spent roughly seven years writing the screenplay *Little Black Spiders*. During this process, Vandewijer and Toye not only met "victims" who had had their babies taken from them, but they also researched the story of the Catholic sister who had turned the facility in Lommel into a profitable business, selling the teenage girls' babies for adoption. The film was presented at the Opening International Film Festival in Ostend (Belgium) in 2012; it received the award for Best Director at the film festival of Arras (France); it was chosen for SEMINCI in Valladolid (Spain); it was selected for the International Film Festival of Montreal (Canada); and it was designated as Best Feature Film, Best Directing, and Best Screenwriting at the Vancouver (Canada) Women in Film Festival.

Beginning with the first scene, viewers will notice that *Little Black Spiders* documents a journey, and a shared one for that matter. As the opening credits are displayed, we see Katharina's suitcase in her room at the Catholic orphanage—packed and locked. A few moments later, Katharina is sitting in a car together with the driver, Cecilia, an assistant to the nuns who oversee the Tamar facility. Having learned that Katharina is 28 weeks pregnant with a child by her teacher of ancient Greek, Guy Vriendts, the sisters at her school decide that it is best for her to leave. Thus, they ask for Cecilia to take her to the attic of a hospital where ten other girls who are "just like her" live together. En route, Cecilia tells Katharina that there is no need to worry: "Bekijk het als een grote vakantie" ("consider it as a big vacation"). The film later discloses that Cecilia herself was pregnant as well seven years earlier and had stayed in the very same attic run by Simone, sister of the order *Zusters Kindsheid Jesus*.[17] Simone arranged for her own brother and his wife to adopt Cecilia's baby boy. Cecilia was permitted to see him under the provision that she would stay at the attic and assist in taking care of prospective pregnant girls.

Upon arrival in Lommel, Katharina meets Simone. Without obtaining consent, Simone calls Katharina "Katja"; Cecilia follows Simone's lead and quickly communicates to Katharina that autonomy and individuality are not significant in this place. She tells her, "Hier op zolder heeft iedereen een andere naam. Hier ben je iemand anders" ("Here in the attic everyone has a different name. Here you are somebody different"). Katharina is led up a long exterior staircase to her room, number six, and is told to make herself feel at home. The next morning Simone calls Katharina into her office to finalize her paperwork. First, she confirms details about Katharina's age, her deceased parents, and her illegitimate pregnancy. Then she lays out the rules of the attic and reassures her that she is in a location ideal for girls in her condition. Katharina listens and agrees to sign the correlating paperwork not realizing that she is, in fact, signing up her baby for adoption. Toye's viewers recognize early on that the young couples who come to visit the hospital's attic are the intended parents of the girls' infants. Only later in the film does Katharina learn what she had actually signed. Horrified by her naiveté, she takes matters into her own hands by sneaking into the office and secretly burning her file, thus erasing all documentation.

It is through Katharina that we are introduced to Roxanne, Mia, Clara, Liesbeth, Sabine, and other high-spirited girls who are almost mothers. Although the nuns view these teenagers as a homogenous group of hormone-dominated wrongdoers, the film accentuates and reveres their differences. For example, each girl has a slightly different vision of life after the birth. Roxanne ponders, "Dat stinkt. Dat bleit 's nachts. Je moet daarvoor opstaan" ("That thing stinks. It screams during the night. You have to get up for it."). Roxanne is convinced that she wants to give up her baby whereas Katharina is adamant about raising her child herself; she already has decided on a name (Helena) and devises ways to care for it. Mia, who was raped, chooses for neither alternative; after numerous hallucinations that the devil is inside her, she chooses to kill her baby with a crochet needle. Despite their contrasting motivations, the girls are woven together by sorrow and love and form a cohesive web of friendship.

Most intimate is the relationship between Katharina and Roxanne whose personalities and sentiments concerning their babies are polar opposites at the film's beginning but ironically reverse at its conclusion. When Roxanne starts having contractions, Simone and Cecilia inform her that she will need to be transferred to another nearby hospital, since the obstetrician at the clinic below them does not work on Sundays. Katharina, who had vowed to stay by Roxanne's side, begins faking contractions so that Simone and Cecile will let her accompany Roxie with them in the car. Unbeknownst to the girls, however, Simone and Cecilia drive Roxanne and Katharina from Lommel, Belgium over the border and into France to Malo-les-Baines (approximately two and a half hours by car). Roxanne is immediately admitted for delivery. Since Katharina was not actually showing signs of labor, Simone summons the nurses to induce her. Both girls give birth in separate rooms. Roxanne's baby dies in childbirth, and she is not granted any chance of seeing or holding her child. Katharina, on the other hand, thwarts Simone's financial plans. Her file has been burned, and the couple who had previously visited the attic does not receive her child. She and Roxanne flee the hospital in order to return to Belgium so that Katharina can register her baby. Unfortunately, matters take a turn for the worse. While hiking along the shores of the North Sea, Katharina becomes so weak that she can no longer walk. Blood trickles down Katharina's legs and she dies from postpartum hemorrhage. Roxanne takes Katharina's baby, returns to Belgium and registers the baby as her own daughter. She names her Katharina.

Little Black Spiders *through the Eyes of Writer-Director Patrice Toye and Reviewers*

In several interviews (e.g., Sartor, "Patrice Toye: Een Interview"), writer-director Patrice Toye explained what kind of film she wanted *Little Black Spiders* to be. She emphasized that, although the movie deals with a very sad and tragic chapter in the history of the Catholic Church of Flanders, she did not want to make the film into an indictment of the church. Nor did she intend to focus on the sensation of this past scandal. Instead, she chose rather to create a nuanced movie about girls who were vulnerable and brave at the same time and who tried to cope with the injustice which had been inflicted upon them by supporting each other and by fostering bonds of friendship. In other words, she refused to portray the girls as mere victims.

She also explained the narrative technique, which she used in order to be able to tell a story that was not purely negative but more importantly also hopeful. She tried to do this by telling the story through the eyes of the girls, who, in their ignorant youthfulness, do not yet fully comprehend all the tragic implications of their predicament (Sartor). These girls are brought together in the same secluded space for a period of time, and they are encouraged to see it as a holiday. This narrative perspective made it possible for Toye to "lighten up" the film by including scenes of joy and humor in which the girls are having fun together. In this way, the viewer is confronted with the sadness and seriousness of their situation only in dribs and drabs. It is not until the final scenes of the movie that the two girls Katharina and Roxanne are confronted with the harsh reality of their fate. Patrice Toye does admit, however, that, though the movie is based on true events and adapted according to the writer-director's preferences, the lives of these girls might have been much harder in reality. Toye asserts that the film's artistry takes precedence over but certainly does not exclude its social message (Sartor).

Interestingly, it is exactly this approach, this compensation of the heavy topic with scenes of lightness and signs of hope, that some reviewers see as one of the movie's weaknesses. To quote one reviewer: "Toye is absolutely right when she states that Katharina and her companions in misfortune did not only experience trouble and affliction, but it is also definitely true that they must have strongly depended on each other. These sides of the story deserve to be told. But by giving the girls the leading part, the movie overreaches the essential elements" (Nollet). Another critic defends Toye by acknowledging that this approach is typical of her work: "This kind of topic could give cause to a harsh indictment of Catholic hypocrisy and societal sanctimoniousness.... But choosing that angle would be nothing for Toye" (Temmerman). Indeed, Patrice Toye's films, most notably *Rosie* (1998) and *(N)iemand/Nowhere Man* (2008), illuminate first and foremost the existential search for an individual's own identity. Her characters are known to lock themselves up in their own, often quite surreal, "soul space" in order to arm themselves against reality.

This particular approach is also what distinguishes *Little Black Spiders* from films dealing with similar topics such as the 2002 British-Irish production *The Magdalene Sisters*, written and directed by Peter Mullan, and the 2013 British-French-American production *Philomena*, directed by Stephen Frears. *The Magdalene Sisters* tells the story of four teenage girls who were sent to Magdalene Asylums, homes in Ireland for women who were labeled as "fallen" by their families and society, while *Philomena* tells the true story of Philomena Lee's 50-year-long search for her son. She had been brought to a Catholic convent in Ireland by her father when she was pregnant, and the nuns at this convent had arranged an adoption of her son to a wealthy American couple. The story lines of both productions focus much more than Toye's *Little Black Spiders* on the grave injustice that had been done to these young women. Movies which Patrice Toye does refer to as sources of inspiration are the 1999 American production *The Virgin Suicides*, written and directed by Sofia Coppola, and the 1975 Australian production *Picnic at Hanging Rock*, directed by Peter Weir.

In Patrice Toye's film, it is the nuns who control the birth and the fate of the babies, and the girls' rights are denied in the name of a Christian moral code in which (teenage) sexuality and unwed pregnancy are taboo. Although not technically a form of contraception since pregnancy is in no way prevented, this practice of forcing young, unwed expectant mothers to carry their babies to term only to give up their newborns immediately after delivery is undeniably a form of "birth control." Quite literally, the birth of their babies is "controlled" in that, when the time comes, the girls are transported across the border to France (where, unlike in Belgium, the name of the mother is not required to be on the birth certificate), drugged and masked in an effort to minimize their memory of the actual birth, and never allowed to see their baby. This interpretation of "birth control" is not the traditional definition and yet it deepens the concept of what it encompasses and thereby increases the challenges with it.

Movie Analysis: The Paradox as Guiding Principle

The pregnant teenagers are temporarily "excommunicated" on moral grounds and brought by their families or by the fathers of their babies to an isolated hospital where they are practically invisible to the outside world. The girls sleep in the attic of the hospital, which they reach by using stairs (a fire escape route), an entrance not accessible to the regular hospital patients, and they are allowed to keep themselves busy in a "workshop" and to take walks in the forest on hospital territory. Over the course of the film, the space of the hospital reveals itself as a highly paradoxical space, one which escapes simplistic qualifications and clear typification. Through spatial and also cinematographic and psychoanalytic analysis, we show how the film works visually as well as narratologically with oppositions such as life versus death, tradition versus modern popular culture, freedom versus imprisonment, homosexuality versus heterosexuality, and dream versus reality, and how the film then subverts these oppositions by blurring the lines between them and in doing so reveals their paradoxical nature. We also discuss scenes from the film relevant to these paradoxes.

Life vs. Death

Contraception and unwanted pregnancy inevitably confront questions of life versus death. Does human life begin at conception, at implantation, or somewhere thereafter? How do we perceive old life, new life, entrances and exits? *Little Black Spiders* is unique in that it does not offer a straightforward answer regarding these antithetical positions but chooses instead to focus on their powerful interplay. In the following select scenes, we attempt to identify how life and death merge, converge, and also diverge not only in the film's storyline but also in its cinematic portrayal.

Near the beginning of the film, Katharina spends some time in the forest that surrounds the hospital in Lommel. In the midst of red and purple rhododendrons she meets Hendrik, the hospital's groundskeeper. The excitement in Hendrik's eyes upon seeing Katharina slightly alarms her. Hendrik steps closer, and the viewer wonders: will he hurt her? Instead Hendrik reaches into the pocket of his overalls; he has something to show Katharina. He opens his hand and reveals a baby chick whose eyes have not yet opened: "Uit het nest gevallen. Hij overleeft het niet. Niet zonder zijn moeder" ("It fell out of its nest. It won't survive. Not without its mother"). Coincidentally, Hendrik is speaking to a girl who, like the chick, has herself no mother and soon will have a baby who too will be motherless. In many ways, this brief encounter foreshadows the end of the movie but it also subverts it. Katharina, the girl who wants nothing more than to have and raise her own baby, dies at the end of the film, and yet her daughter will neither perish nor be deserted because her friend Roxanne, who initially had no desire to keep her child, takes Katharina's as her own.

Because Katharina's baby lives and takes her mother's name, one can argue that Katharina's life does not end. One's life does not end with death if there are children that will tell your story. For Roxanne, taking on Katharina's baby is a life-altering decision, one that will never allow her to forget her own experience with her pregnancy. The memory of being a teenage mother will never die if she is reminded daily by Katharina's baby who depends on her to live. The starkest juxtaposition of life and death occur in the penultimate scene. Katharina, dressed in a bright red sweater and carrying her baby, falls to the ground. In her final moments, she places her baby wrapped in a white blanket next to her in the sand and dies. Through the choice of these stark colors Toye reinforces the film's themes of passion, pain, and purity.

Tradition vs. Modern Popular Culture

The film's title *Little Black Spiders* refers to the web-like intertextuality which constitutes the film and which also lends it its universal quality. The movie is interspersed with references to past as well as present culture, and its cinematographic and spatial organization seems to be oriented toward blurring the lines between the two by establishing intertextual connections. In doing so, the movie shows, on the one hand, that social control and punishment oppress people both in the remote and recent past, and on the other hand that people have the power to overcome these oppressions. In this universal constellation, the spider with its ability to create a web, a beautiful and ornate construction, symbolizes not only the connections between the female pregnant characters but also serves as an image of hope. We now discuss the intertextual references to traditional and modern culture in greater detail, and we will demonstrate how they contribute to highlighting the tragic and at the same time hopeful experience of the young protagonists.

The film is full of citations of ancient Greek mythology as well as of Catholic tradition. Most prominent are references to the Greek myth of the Minotaur and to the Catholic figures Maria, Jesus, and Catherine of Alexandria. The myth of the Minotaur is recounted in one of the books Katharina brought along and which belongs to the father of her unborn child, a high school teacher of Classical Greek. One of the girls, who reads a passage of the book, calls it a "sex book." To fight the boredom of life in a hospital attic, the girls decide to practice and perform the myth as a theatre play. They are so enthusiastic about the play that in their imagination they start seeing the forest outside the hospital walls as the labyrinth, and the hospital's gardener, who is the only male person around, as the Minotaur, a creature with the head of a bull and the body of a man, born from illicit sex between Pasiphae and her husband's bull. The girls' modern reenactments of the play can be interpreted as a hopeful sign of their hormonal rebellion and human power, especially when one takes into consideration the psychoanalytic dimension of the myth of the Minotaur. King Minos, husband of Pasiphae, the Minotaur's mother, imprisoned this product of illicit and perverse love in a labyrinth and fed it periodically with seven young boys and girls. Theseus, the son of the king of Athens, entered the labyrinth in order to save these young sacrificial victims and was able to kill the Minotaur thanks to Ariadne's thread, which helped him find his way out of the dark subconscious space of the labyrinth and back to the light. The myth in its totality symbolizes the spiritual battle against repression of the socially unacceptable, and Ariadne as the "spider goddess" is the one giving Theseus the spiritual force to succeed. In the film, the girls perform a part of the myth featuring the Minotaur. Prior to their dance, viewers receive a close-up of a little black spider making its web in the forest. Shortly after, one sees—against the acoustic background of Armand Van Helden's song "Little Black Spiders" (composed for the film)— how the girls through a mysterious kind of performance help Katharina to escape from the hospital and visit her former boyfriend, which results in disappointment about his cold reaction. These scenes exhibit the different intertextual layers of the film title *Little Black Spiders*.

As mentioned above, the movie also offers numerous references to Catholic tradition. It accentuates cinematographic images of Mother Mary, of Jesus, and of the cross—typical decorations in Catholic hospital rooms or on nuns' cloaks that serve as watchdogs of Catholic moral dogma. Simultaneously, the film subtly weaves in modern, subversive reenactments of parts of the symbolism which is traditionally associated with these figures. We will offer some examples of such modern and subversive reenactments of Catholic principles: Our first example deals with Mother Mary as the Virgin Mother, who is believed to be the ideal mother and a symbol of purity. These characterizations do not seem to apply to teenage mothers who listen to and are fond of songs titled "Adolescent Sex" (of the band Japan). At some point, however, Roxanne's breasts start to leak with milk, and shortly thereafter she starts feeling contractions. In this scene, Roxanne's posture and dress remind us of depictions of Mother Mary. Thus, Roxanne's supposed moral guilt is called into question. The same holds true for Katharina, whose name refers to purity and to Catherine of Alexandria, a Catholic Saint known to be a symbol of chastity. By naming the surviving baby Katharina, Roxanne rejects the moral stigma of impurity which society had wanted to bestow upon them as teenage mothers. Our second example deals with the principle of resurrection as embodied by the figure of Jesus. According to Catholic doctrine, resurrection from the dead is only reserved for those who are without sin or who repent. Roxanne subverts this teaching by making Katharina, who died shortly after giving birth, "resurrect" in the name of her baby daughter.

Heterosexuality vs. Homosexuality

Toye's film also explores the girls' instability concerning their sexuality, which not only challenges normative definitions of sexual orientation but also further complicates their identity formation. Clearly, each of the girls in Lommel has taken part in a heterosexual relationship which has resulted in pregnancy. Even at the hospital, they manage to find ways to express their interests in the male sex. For example, while they are passing their time in nature, Toye privileges the female gaze. Hendrik, the gardener and only man with whom the girls have any contact, is shown center-screen, full-body, and wearing an undershirt with his eyes fixed on the chainsaw that he is using. Meanwhile, we see Liesbeth smiling to herself with a shy look on her face. Viewers could not be more privy to a moment of male objectification; for Liesbeth, Hendrik directly corresponds to the chainsaw—man as a machine and the body as a mechanism.

The film is pregnant with other moments of heterosexual yearning such as Katharina's many love letters that she writes to Guy. Viewers also gain access to her inner monologue while she talks to and dreams of him while taking a shower. At another point in the film, the girls create scenarios about men who supposedly are looking at them and wanting to get to know them. When Roxanne asks Katharina what this man looks like and what he wants, Katharina gives a long answer which translates to "He's very cute, tall, he has dark blond curls and he's nicely built and has chest hair, quite a lot of chest hair. Lots of chest hair. He's got a car. He's a real gentleman and he wants to dance with you. He thinks you're the prettiest girl at the party. He wanted you. He's wondering what he thinks is more beautiful your eyes or your mouth or your hair. He can't choose. He thinks you are beautiful."

Within her film Toye, however, also deconstructs this hegemonic situation, one that only reduces the girls' identities to heteronormativity—gender roles conformed to cultural norms of all-male or all-female and heterosexuality as the normal sexual orientation—by including an intimate connection between Roxanne and Katharina. In doing this she subverts the incident between Liesbeth and Hendrik by now making Roxanne the peeping tom. A powerful scene shows Roxanne looking at Katharina who is half naked and washing her pregnant belly. By peeping through a small opening in the wall which the nuns had covered with a picture of Jesus, Roxanne is able to view the semi-nudity of Katharina through the holes, the eyes of Jesus. Complementing this scene are other shared moments between these two girls that suggest homosexual tendencies. For example, in Katharina's room, the girls recite love poetry together. They sit next to each other each one reading her lines (both female and male parts). They look at each other longingly. Since the lines indicate that the couple is kissing, Katharina and Roxy take a moment to reflect on what a good kiss would entail. Their creative imaginations as well as their loneliness and hunger for a passionate kiss result in them kissing each other. This scene undoubtedly deepens their relationship and additional acts of intimacy occur. The film shows them sleeping together in the same bed. Often they hug and touch each other's faces and hair lovingly. Katharina even tastes Roxanne's breast milk, which leaks milk (colostrum) right before she begins having contractions.

In line with theories by Michel Foucault and Judith Butler, Toye proposes ways to counter the normative discourses of identity. She offers a queer reading that deconstructs a hegemonic heteronormative discourse and thereby presents sex, gender and sexuality as fluid constructs. In the attic, the girls' identities are in continuous flux—as Toye illustrates through the blending of both heterosexual and homosexual impulses, their relationships and sexuality too cannot be demarcated with clear boundaries.

Freedom vs. Imprisonment

In view of the societal discourses controlling women and adolescents in their decisions and self-development, one can interpret the hospital in Belgium as the spatial epitome of the girls' confinement, and therefore as a negative type of space. This hospital has certain characteristics in common with a prison, in that its attic serves as a space in which people are hidden away whose behavior is perceived by mainstream society as deviating from the norm and from moral codes. In this respect, the space of the hospital attic also resonates with cultural representations of the attic as a secret space housing the subconscious—we all know *The Madwoman in the Attic*.[18] In *Little Black Spiders*, the hospital attic could be seen as housing the collective subconscious of Catholic sexual ethics. It is, however, not a legal prison, in the sense that the girls have not been legally convicted to live there. It is societal oppression which almost "forces" them to stay there and punishes whoever escapes and has contact with the outside world as Katharina does. But, at the same time, by establishing tight bonds of friendship and also by using their creativity and imagination, the girls are able to turn this initially negative space into a partly positive one. They find ways to express themselves more freely through games and through literature, dance, and modern music, and these joint projects and activities also stimulate their affection toward each other. When Katharina and Roxanne are at the French hospital, they take their claim to freedom one step further by escaping with Katharina's baby. In doing so, they challenge the societal norms and discourses which had tried to confine them and which did not deem them fit to be good mothers.

Dream vs. Reality

The final opposition addressed in this chapter is that of dream versus reality. Just as teenage girls are liminal people—neither adult nor child—similarly the lives they lead are also comprised of two colliding worlds: a playful, whimsical one and one filled with truth and consequences. The reality as displayed by Toye exists only outside the confines of the hospital in Lommel, and although a number of the girls choose to revisit it, their experiences are universally represented as negative. One injection of reality occurs when Liesbeth's parents come to the hospital to discuss her status with Simone. From the window of the attic, Liesbeth sees her parents below on the driveway. She runs downstairs screaming for them to wait for her, but by the time she makes it downstairs, they have already left. Additionally, Liesbeth's boyfriend visits the hospital in hopes of finding her. Simone confronts him and tells him that the attic has been vacant for years. Katharina too with the help of her friends escapes the hospital and hitches a ride on a motorcycle to the suburbs so that she can visit her high school Greek teacher and lover, Guy. She is crushed when Guy tells her that besides financially supporting her stay in Lommel, he is ashamed of his relationship, does not want the baby, but chooses instead to maintain his marriage. Katharina returns to the hospital the next morning, apologizes, and practically begs Simone to take her back into the world that will enable her to deny reality once again.

One could argue that once the girls enter the facility at Lommel, they close their eyes to the outside world and fall into a deep Cinderellian sleep. Their names are changed, they enter "vacation time," and they climb a fire escape so as not to disturb the hospital patients or even suggest that they are there. Fully isolated and tucked under a blanket of ignorance, they enter the land of nod. While going through their pregnancies in Lommel, Toye shoots the girls' story with soft-hued colors reminiscent of dreamlike recollections. By altering the light, more specifically by diffusing image-forming light, she blurs the reality of the girls for a dream-like effect. Toye produces a low-contrast haze that diminishes details, especially when viewing far-away objects. The purpose of these types of images is to expose the childlike elements integral to understanding the discrepancy between the childlike emotions of the girls and the grim actuality that awaits them. Pastel colors and ethereal sounds are combined with games, laughter, and make-believe and are then again juxtaposed with moments of uncomfortable truth. A scene which seems to encapsulate dream and reality perfectly into one shot occurs when Roxanne and Katharina enter Simone's office in order to snatch the bull's head off the wall for their play. In doing so, they hear Simone nearing her office and so they quickly hide behind the curtains. With one girl on each side of the window, they snicker and make faces at one another. Purely immersed in their immature game, they fail to absorb the reality that plays out in front of them. Simone is on the phone discussing the adoption process. The film continues to drift between these states of dream and reality and in doing so highlights how adolescence is supposed to move toward adulthood but feels a constant pull to digress.

Conclusion

What began as accusations of immorality against a group of young, pregnant women has ironically resulted in confessions of a new sort. Only in the past few years have penitent religious and political figureheads offered national apologies for the policies and practices that permanently severed mothers from their babies. In 2014 and 2015, more than 30 years after the scandal in the old Tamar Catholic hospital in Lommel, Belgium, Belgian bishops and the Flemish parliament publically acknowledged their wrongdoings to victims of forced adoption and proposed to mitigate these past hardships by means of the creation of a Flemish lineage center and a DNA database to help mothers and children identify one another. As a sign of responsibility, the official apology speech given by Flemish parliament president Jan Peumans is on permanent display in the parliament hall for all to see and never forget.

Although the words of clergymen and politicians cannot undo the harm that has been done, it is encouraging that public recognition of this scandal has come to light. Consequently, the media's reactions to these apologies have opened the floodgates for victims to feel confident and worthy in sharing their horrific experiences. What remains to be seen, however, is how the events that transpired in Belgium and other countries will impact future generations. Not all mothers and children have been fortunate enough to reunite. Many of these mothers, now in their 80s and 90s, may die before finding their sons and daughters. Since in most cases records were not kept or worse yet were destroyed, these deaths will eternally efface the genetic lineage.

In *Little Black Spiders* we see ten young girls in an unfortunate predicament, unintentionally pregnant and therefore publicly embarrassed and socially hidden away. Based on true events that unfolded in Flanders, Belgium during the 1970s and early 1980s, this film, like others that have been produced recently, deals with questions of sexual oppression, religious intolerance, and control of the female body. Although a very dark set of circumstances, Patrice

114 Part 2. Stories of Forced Adoption

Toye chooses to underline the naiveté, imagination, and self-discovery of adolescence. Even in the face of society's contemptuous judgment and disapproval, her characters are free to explore, to grow, to foster friendships, and ultimately to take control of their lives. Toye's story weaves multiple genres and a host of oppositions in the context of varied cultures and strict beliefs lending universality to *Little Black Spider*s.

Notes

1. Today records only mention "anonymous delivery" and refer to the mother as "X." For a thorough historical background regarding anonymous birth and family constructions in France see Fuchs and O'Halloran. Also consider Perreau who describes the evolution of adoption policies, the resulting political debates, as well as questions of French national identity.

2. Contraception was authorized via the Neuwirth Law in 1967. Simone Veil, French minister of health from 1974 to 1979, fought for and successfully passed the legalization of abortion in 1975.

3. O'Halloran's study points out that France's adoption of the abortion law reduced the number of "nés sous X" from approximately 10,000 babies a year to between 500 and 600 reaching 700 in 2010.

4. Contrary to France, in 1854 the Belgian court of cassation claimed that the mother had to be named in all birth registries and certificates, since it was crucial that the child knew his or her mother's identity.

5. Important to note is that the French monarchy was finally terminated in the mid–19th century at which time it became a republic. Belgium to this day is still governed by a king. Moreover, France has a long history of secularism with fewer religious constraints on decisions such as abortion. In Belgium, on the contrary, 75 percent of its population is Roman Catholic. These religious and governing disparities provide some answers to the two countries' historical reactions and proceedings to unwanted pregnancies.

6. For a discussion on the legalization of abortion in European countries and the separate policies that took place in Belgium and Ireland see McBride Stetson.

7. Attempts to liberalize the abortion law of Belgium began in 1971. From that time until the law was enacted on April 4, 1990, dozens of legislative proposals permitting abortions to be performed under various circumstances were introduced always to be rejected or allowed to expire. See the document for Belgium in the United Nations' "Population Policy Data Bank."

8. Since the 1990s, Belgium has advanced very quickly. Today Belgium has more progressive laws than France. For instance, in 2003, Belgium became the second country in the world to legalize same-sex marriage. It also has the world's most liberal law on physician-assisted suicide. This law does not only pertain to terminally ill adults and those suffering from psychological disorders but since 2014 Belgium became the first country to lift any age restrictions. Terminally ill children can request euthanasia (see Higgins).

9. Between 40,000 and 60,000 babies were involuntarily given up for adoption in the 1950s and 1960s by Roman Catholic Irishwomen. See Mangan.

10. For a comprehensive discussion on the effects of Roman Catholicism on attitudes toward abortion in Western Europe see Jelen.

11. Information on comparative systems for adoption without consent can be found in the European Parliament's study, "Adoption Without Consent."

12. For discourses, history and policies surrounding the "Stolen Generations," please consult Cole. Another example is the Australian film *Rabbit-Proof Fence* (2002).

13. The Australian report, "Commonwealth Contribution to Former Forced Adoption Policies and Practices" (2012), estimated that between 210,000 and 250,000 adoptions took place between 1940 and 2012. For an overview of forced adoption practices in Australia see the Forced Adoptions History Project.

14. For a study contextualizing the phenomena of forced adoption historically in Australia from the beginning of the 19th century to its decline at the beginning of the 21st century see Quartly, Swain and Cuthbert.

15. For details on the women who formed the Association Representing Mothers Separated from their Children by Adoption (ARMS), see Hale.

16. Translation provided by KKB and SD. The film is subtitled in English but for quotes we are also using our own translations.

17. This apostolic congregation *Child Jesus* was founded in 1835 by the priest Peter Joseph Triest. The congregation placed heavy emphasis on providing support to foundlings, orphans, and isolated youth.

18. See Federico.

Works Cited

"Abortion Legislation in Europe." Report. *The Law Library of Congress, Global Research Center.* Library of Congress, Jan. 2015. Web. 27 Apr. 2016.

Baert, Denny. "Vlaams Parlement Moet Zich Verontschuldigen Voor Gedwongen Adopties." *De Redactie.be*. VRT Nieuws, 4 May 2015. Web. 16 Oct. 2016.

Balasundaram, Nemesha. "British Families Flee to Ireland to Escape Threat of Social Services." *The Irish Post*. The Irish Post, 19 Aug. 2015. Web. 16 Oct. 2016.

Behr, Katrin, and Peter Hartl. *Entrissen: Der Tag, als die DDR mir meine Mutter nahm.* Munich: Droemer Knaur, 2014. Print.

Booker, Christopher. "Australia's Scandal of Forced Adoption Is Happening Here in Britain." *The Telegraph*. Telegraph Media Group, 23 Mar. 2013. Web. 16 Oct. 2016.

Buggenhout, Len. "Expertenpanel Onderzoekt Gedwongen Adopties." *De Standaard*. De Standaard, 15 Nov. 2014. Web. 16 Oct. 2016.

Butler, Judith. *Gender Trouble*. 1990. New York: Routledge, 2006. Print.

Cole, Christine. *Stolen Babies—Broken Hearts: Forced Adoption in Australia 1881-1987*. Saarbrücken: Lambert Academic, 2015. Print.

David, Henry P. "Abortion in Europe, 1920-91: A Public Health Perspective." *Studies in Family Planning* 23.1 (1992): 1-22. JSTOR. Web. 20 Oct. 2016.

European Parliament. Policy Department C: Citizens' Rights and Constitutional Affairs. "Adoption without Consent. Study for the Peti Committee." *European Parliament*. European Parliament, 2015. Web. 5 Nov. 2016. PDF.

Federico, Annette, ed. *Gilbert and Gubar's "The Madwoman in the Attic" After Thirty Years*. Columbia: University of Missouri Press, 2009. Print.

Forced Adoptions History Project. The National Archives of Australia, 2016. Web. 16 Oct. 2016.

Foucault, Michel. *The History of Sexuality: An Introduction*. Trans. Robert Hurley. New York: Vintage-Random House, 1990. Print.

Fuchs, Rachel G. *Contested Paternity: Constructing Families in Modern France*. Baltimore: John Hopkins University Press, 2008. Print.

Groth, Heidrun. *Zwangsadoption: Eine Spurensuche in Ostdeutschland*. Hamburg: Marta Press, 2013. Print.

Hale, Megan. *Mothers in ARMS: Forced Adoption—Mothers Find a Voice*. Kent Town, South Australia: Wakefield Press, 2014. Print.

Higgings, Andrew. "Belgian Senate Votes to Allow Euthanasia for Terminally Ill Children." *New York Times*. New York Times, 12 Dec. 2013. Web. 16 Oct. 2016.

Hope, Alan. "Flemish Parliament to Apologise for Forced Adoptions." *Flanders Today*. Flanders Today, 3 July 2015. Web. 16 Oct. 2016.

"Ireland's Lost Babies." *PBS.org*. PBS, 20 July 2016. Web. 16 Oct. 2016.

Jelen, Ted, et al. "A Contextual Analysis of Catholicism and Abortion Attitudes in Western Europe." *Sociology of Religion* 54.4 (1993): 375-83. JSTOR. Web. 20 Oct. 2016.

Lefaucheur, Nadine. "The French 'Tradition' of Anonymous Birth: The Lines of Argument." *International Journal of Law, Policy and the Family* 18 (2004): 319-42. Web. 20 Oct. 2016.

Little Black Spiders. Dir. Patrice Toye. Writ. Ina Vandewijer and Patrice Toye. Perf. Line Pillet,

Charlotte De Bruyne, and Dolores Bouckaert. Dutch with subtitles in French, Spanish, English. Prime Time, 2012. DVD.
The Magdalene Sisters. Dir. and writ. Peter Mullan. Perf. Nora-Jane Noone, Anne-Marie Duff, and Dorothy Duffy. Miramax Studio, 2003. Film.
Mangan, Lucy. "This World: Ireland's Lost Babies Review—An Appalling Story, Told with Admirable Restraint." *The Guardian*. Guardian News and Media, 18 Sept. 2014. Web. 16 Oct. 2016.
McBride Stetson, Dorothy, ed. *Abortion Politics, Women's Movements and the Democratic State. A Comparative Study of State Feminism*. Oxford: Oxford University Press, 2001. Print.
Milotte, Mike. *Banished Babies: The Secret History of Ireland's Baby Export Business*. 2nd ed. Dublin: New Island, 2012. Print.
(N)iemand. Dir. Patrice Toye. Writ. Bjørn Olaf Johannessen and Patrice Toye. Kinepolis, 2008. Film.
Nollet, Ruben. "Little Black Spiders. Patrice Toye." *Cobra.be*. Cobra, 18 Sept. 2012. Web. 16 Oct. 2016.
O'Halloran, Kerry. *The Politics of Adoption: International Perspectives on Law, Policy and Practice*. 3rd ed. Dordrecht: Springer, 2015. Print.
O'Loughlin, Ann. *The Ballroom Café*. Edinburgh: Black & White, 2015. Print.
Parliament of Australia. "Commonwealth Contribution to Former Forced Adoption Policies and Practices." *Parliament of Australia*. Commonwealth of Australia, 29 Feb. 2012. Web. 5 Nov. 2016.
"Patrice Toye: Een Interview." *Cinevox*. Cinevox, 20 Sept. 2012. Web. 16 Oct. 2016.
Perreau, Bruno. *The Politics of Adoption: Gender and the Making of French Citizenship*. Trans. Deke Dusinberre. Cambridge: MIT Press, 2014. Print.
Philomena. Dir. Stephen Frears. Writ. Steve Coogan and Jeff Pope. Perf. Judi Dench and Steve Coogan. The Weinstein Company, 2013. Film.
Picnic at Hanging Rock. Dir. Peter Weir. Writ. Cliff Green. Australian Film Commission, 1975. Film.
Quartly, Marian, et al. *The Market in Babies: Stories of Australian Adoption*. Clayton, Australia: Monash University Publishing, 2013. Print.
Rabbit Proof Fence. Dir. Phillip Noyce. Writ. Christine Olsen. Perf. Everlyn Sampi, Kenneth Branagh, and David Gulpilil. HanWay Films, 2002. Film.
Rosie. Dir. and writ. Patrice Toye. Perf. Sara de Roo, Dirk Roofthooft, and Aranka Coppens. Prime Time, 1998. Film.
Sartor, Freddy. "Patrice Toye, Line Pillet & Charlotte De Bruyne over *Little Black Spiders*." *Filmmagie* 627 (2012): 12–15. Web. 20 Oct. 2016.
Temmerman, Jan. "Recht uit het hart." *De Morgen.be*. De Persgroep Digital, 20 Sept. 2012. Web. 16 Oct. 2016.
United Nations. Dept. of Economic and Social Affairs. Population Division. "Belgium. The Population Policy Data Bank." *United Nations*. United Nations, n. d. Web. 5 Nov. 2016. Doc.
The Virgin Suicides. Dir. and writ. Sofia Coppola. Perf. Kirsten Dunst and Josh Hartnett, Paramount, 1999. Film.
"Vlaams Parlement Biedt Publieke Verontschuldigingen aan voor Gedwongen Adopties." *Nieuwsblad*. Nieuwsblad, 17 Nov. 2015. Web. 16 Oct. 2016.

PART 3. FROM UNPLANNED TO PLANNED PREGNANCIES

From Unwanted to Wanted Pregnancy
Pregnancy, Abortion and the End of the GDR in the Film Jana and Jan *(1992)*

BELINDA CARSTENS-WICKHAM

The government of the German Democratic Republic (GDR) generally advocated a pro-family policy marked by encouraging married couples to have children and rewarding them with special benefits such as free daycare, shorter work weeks, and access to improved housing. Yet open access to abortion in the first trimester was legalized in 1972. In the film directed by Helmut Dziuba, *Jana und Jan* (*Jana and Jan*, 1992), which takes place during the final months of the GDR or *Wende* (literally meaning "turn," 1989) in a youth detention center (*Werkhof*), it seems that these pro-family policies bypassed youth detention centers. In fact, the matrons actively pushed pregnant teens toward choosing abortion. Nonetheless, in this film, after much conflict the unmarried couple at the center of the action rejects abortion and chooses to have the baby which forms the central metaphor of the film. The "unaborted" child and the circumstances of its birth function as a symbol and a commentary on the future of the German Democratic Republic.

Background

The film director, Helmut Dziuba (1933–2012), studied filmmaking in Moscow beginning in 1953 after studying to become a high voltage installation technician in the GDR. He began working for the GDR Film Academy (DEFA) in 1962 as a director's assistant. He is well known for producing youth films with young lay actors. His later films present topical themes which engage with problematic issues relating to GDR society. Dziuba won several important prizes in the GDR and won the Bavarian film prize in 1993 for *Jana und Jan,* which was his last film. It was a co-production between the privatized DEFA and ZDF television. The director found the actors, apart from Jana, in juvenile detention centers and filmed it in 33 days (Richter). In this film Dziuba portrays GDR society's throwaway children.

The Original Screenplay

The initial impetus for the film *Jana und Jan* came from a screenplay, *Friedlose Herzen (Restless Hearts),* by the GDR author Manfred Haertel.[1] Mr. Haertel, a GDR citizen, worked for 15 years as a teacher in a youth detention center. During this time, he wrote three novels about youth detention centers which were not allowed to be published in the GDR. In 1987 he received an invitation from the *Styria-Verlag Österreich* (Styria Publishing Company Austria) to participate in a screenplay competition. With permission of the GDR authorities he took part, did not win, but was encouraged to send the manuscript to the GDR director Lothar Warnecke. He passed on the manuscript to Helmut Dziuba, and it was retained under contract. In the meanwhile, Manfred Haertel moved to the Federal Republic of Germany (FRG) after submitting an application to leave the GDR (*Ausreiseantrag*). After German reunification, Haertel found out by chance through the news in 1991 that his screenplay had been filmed. However, Dziuba had changed much of the content, while still taking over passages and dialogues from Haertel's manuscript. Subsequently, Haertel wrote a novel, *Flucht ohne Wiederkehr (Flight Without Return,* 2009), about the same subject, as he would have liked to have written it during GDR times but could not due to censorship. In the original screenplay, Haertel focuses mainly on life in the detention center, the relationship between Jana and Jan, the impact of the pregnancy on their lives, and interactions with a wise, elderly man, a church youth group and a pastor. Dana and André, the original names of the characters, discuss the possibility of an abortion but it is too late for she is in the fourth month. The final part of the screenplay focuses on their flight from the detention center and the efforts of the authorities to catch them. After the couple is recaptured and returned to separate detention centers, the reader discovers that the baby was stillborn. In the screenplay there is no indication of the political changes to come or any depiction of social unrest. Dziuba, on the other hand, in his adaption of the screenplay places the action squarely in the time period of the *Wende* and enriches the story and film by intertwining the politics and social changes of the era with the fate of Jana and Jan and their pregnancy. Whether or not this embryo will survive an abortion attempt and evolve into and enter the world as a healthy baby becomes the central metaphor of the Dziuba film.

Youth Detention Centers in the GDR

In the GDR it was important that its citizens conformed to and accepted the state's vision of the ideal socialist citizen. Therefore, from birth on the GDR citizen was educated to accept the primacy of the collective needs of the state as determined by its leaders, in particular by Margot Honecker, Eric Honecker's wife, who led the *Bildungspolitik* (educational and training policies) of the country. For the most part, one's accomplishments as part of the collective were valued and individualism, in terms of questioning the values of the state, was viewed as a threat. In particular, nonconforming behavior on the part of children could lead to placement in one of the GDR's juvenile detention centers. Juveniles had not necessarily committed any crimes in order to be sent to a detention center. They had generally called attention to themselves by not following rules in school and/or came from troubled homes. Girls particularly came to the attention of authorities due to "sexuelle Auffälligkeit" (sexual conspicuousness) or "sexuelle Interessiertheit" (sexual acquisitiveness) (Tesch).

Jana und Jan takes place in an East German detention center for so-called difficult to raise (*schwer erziehbar*) children who would not submit to the ideological and accompanying behavioral expectations of socialist society, in which Jana and Jan, the main characters, are confined. Between 1964 and 1989 the GDR contained approximately 474 state orphanages, 38 of which were *Spezialkinderheime* (literally "special children's institutions"; for misbehaving juveniles) and 32 *Jugendwerkhöfe* ("youth work depots"; for extremely misbehaving juveniles) (Posener). It is believed that 135,000 children were housed in the *Spezialkinderheimen*. Over 4000 so-called "renitente" (disobedient, stubborn, recalcitrant) youths, who would not cooperate with the SED expectations of group conformity and absolute obedience, were imprisoned in Torgau, a high security juvenile prison and the most infamous of these *Jugendwerkhöfe*. Many more were retained in similar "reform" or "corrective" institutions with little hope of release until the age of 18 and were shuttled back and forth to Torgau, depending on their behavior. Jan was confined in Torgau for attempting to flee to the West and was being moved to a less restrictive detention center at the beginning of the film. He is then returned to Torgau after beating up the pregnant Jana. The conditions in the detention centers such as Torgau were brutal. The wardens behaved as repressive criminal guards rather than educators or social workers.

Torgau is today a memorial site. It was viewed as the final station for youth who would not conform to the rules of the state. The goal was to break down juveniles who had developed a "falsche Persönlichkeit" (a false personality not in accordance with socialist expectations) and then reconstruct the juvenile with "Mithilfe des Kollektivs auf gesunde Weise" (the help of the collective in a healthy manner) (Posener). Juveniles were cured through "shock therapy" which included brutal exposure to extreme conditions, to iron discipline, strict punishments for the smallest offenses, isolation, physical punishment, and sadistic checking. Discipline was administered collectively in order to place extreme pressure on the misbehaving individual which then often manifested itself in the juveniles punishing the individuals in sadistic group administrations of justice. Many juveniles were subjected to physical and sexual abuse which was part of daily life. Some committed suicide although no records were kept in this regard.

On November 2, 1989, just a week before the fall of the wall, the GDR government began to dismantle Torgau. Within two weeks all the "residents" were released and the supervisors began to renovate the building in order to hide its purpose, as well as destroying as many files as possible. In 1993 the Torgau detention center was declared a symbol of "die Bankrotterklärung des Systems" (the declaration of bankruptcy of the system) in the GDR (Kleikamp).

In revisiting the damage done to juveniles in these detention centers, administrative agencies have been set up to receive accounts from those detained and to offer some kind of compensation for damages. The deadline was September 30, 2014. More than 25 million Euros were made available to survivors by 2017 (Tesch). The response has been so large that in Thüringen alone 3,000 former residents have applied, in Saxony 3,500, and in Saxony-Anhalt almost 2,400. Many were victims of widespread sexual abuse, and, today, many prefer not to speak about their past abuse and feel stigmatized. Some are still viewed by parts of the population as *Asoziale* (Tesch). There currently seems to be widespread interest in the abuses in these juvenile detention centers given the number of recent publications regarding this topic.[2]

Family and Birth Control

The GDR constitution of 1949 stated that marriage and family were the "foundation of communal life" and emphasized that traditional family life was essential to personal well-being and happy children (McClellan 53). In 1958 the Ulbricht regime offered the "Ten Commandments of Socialist Ethics and Morals" to its people in which it stated that citizens should live cleanly and decently and respect their families (McLellan 7). Family Law in 1965 decreed that "socialist society expects all its citizens to act responsibly with regard to marriage and the family" (McLellan 60). Policies focused on maintaining solid family units which would produce an abundance of children in order to provide workers for the state. It was essential to maintain and increase birth rates while retaining women and mothers in the workforce. This was a cornerstone of labor policy.

Many of the East German leaders spent World War II in the Soviet Union and returned in 1945, bringing back with them conservative views toward abortion, homosexuality, and alternative family units. However, initially, abortion was permitted because so many German women became pregnant due to rapes by the Soviet forces (McLellan 6). In 1950 the law for the Protection of Mother and Child was tightened to only allow abortion to save a mother's life or if the baby had genetic defects. After the fifties, the government attitudes toward sex and family became more liberal and less morally proscriptive, perhaps due to a desire on the part of the GDR to appear more forward looking to the rest of world. With the leadership transition from Ulbricht to Honecker in 1971, abortion was decriminalized and became widely available on demand in 1972 as long as it occurred during the first three months (McLellan 53). In fact, abortion came to be regarded as an alternate form of birth control (Clements 39). Likewise, in the film, the female boss, Lady, states that she has had three abortions. Because she has had three abortions, she thinks that Jana should conform and have an abortion as well and proceeds to try and intimidate Jana into terminating the pregnancy.

In 1965 East German women gained access to the pill and by 1990, 90 percent had used or were currently using the pill. This, combined with the 1972 law making abortion available up to 12 weeks and paid for by the state, led to a sharp fall in the birth rate during the 1970s (McLellan 55). Within one year of its legalization, 38 percent of pregnancies were aborted. In 1987 the abortion rate decreased to 27 percent, probably a result of fewer pregnancies due to the use of the pill. However, in *Jana und Jan*, there is no indication that the teens in the detention center had any education about or access to birth control, and abortion was considered by the supervisors to be the only option. Because of the drop in the birthrate, the government then offered incentives to women to procreate by introducing the baby year and other benefits which were well received by women.

The 1970s and 1980s were marked by further relaxation of tight state control over the individual and the family. Family planning became more the decision of the individuals involved and less the providence of the state. Startling trends arose including the increase in single parent households. Marriage became less popular, divorce increased, and most surprising the number of children born outside of marriage increased dramatically. Unlike in West Germany, where about 10 percent of births were outside of marriage, by the mid–1980s a third of children in East Germany were born out of wedlock, the highest percentage in the Eastern bloc (McLellan 53). In fact, the married birth rate dropped and the unmarried birth rate rose, which indicates that the primacy of the nuclear family in the GDR had declined in everyday life and alternative lifestyles became more acceptable. One East German teenager in McLellan's book states, "I can imagine having a baby without a man.... I don't know why some girls are so keen on getting married" (McLellan 68). In the film at hand, such a pregnancy was simply regarded as a disaster, clearly indicating that this liberal point of view had not reached the administrators in the detention center.[3] Despite apparent progress toward equality regarding women's roles in the GDR, a study in 1974 showed that only 28 percent of men did housework and it continued to be regarded as women's work. In contrast, "expectations of women were extremely high: education, training, work, childcare, housework, shopping, not to mention voluntary work in one of the GDR's mass organizations" (McLellan 72). While on the surface it appeared that GDR women had obtained equality with men, traditional gender relations still governed family life with women carrying the double burden of working both in the labor market and at home (Boa and Wharton v). According to Dinah Dodds in her article about women in East Germany, it was only a "Scheinemanzipation" (the illusion of emancipation) that never changed traditional attitudes toward men's and women's roles in GDR society (Dodds 106). Likewise, in the film, Jana has to do the hard-lifting with her decision to carry on with the pregnancy, while Jan remains relatively unaffected.

Sexuality

Although the state continued to propagate the view that sex should only occur in the context of a loving, monogamous relationship culminating in marriage and leading to procreation, it used sex to pull in the younger generation. McLellan offers as an example the film *Sieben Sommersprossen* (*Seven Freckles*, 1978) in which a young couple, aged 15 and 14, both from unhappy families, address the issues of adolescent sexuality. There are scenes where the two swim naked together, chase each other naked, and discuss whether or not to have sex (McLellan 30). In the film the older generation must recognize the young lovers' legitimacy and right to make their own relational and sexual decisions. In so advocating, the regime hoped to draw in youth ultimately bending them in service of the state need for offspring to support labor policy. The state may have also hoped to appear more progressive and liberal to the younger generations (McLellan 51). However, as will be seen in the film, this progressive route was not advocated in the detention centers.

Finally, however, although the East German state publically maintained that an essential characteristic of socialist sexuality was the linkage of sex and love, this was not consistently the case during the declining years of the GDR. East German citizens engaged in sex outside of relationships and in non-reproductive sex. Later years were characterized by hypocrisy on the part of the state which preached a "romantic view" of sexuality (McLellan 113), but compromised these principles if "political necessity or expediency willed it" (McLellan 113).

The film *Jana und Jan* engages in a dialogue with many of the issues pertaining to the incarceration of non-conforming youth in the juvenile detention centers and uses familial and sexual mores in the GDR as an opportunity to comment on the present and future of the disintegrating country. The film depicts the everyday life of teenagers incarcerated in detention centers, with a focus on Jan and Jana, the main characters who are part of the ranks of the "asocial" youth detained therein. As Jana watches Jan's transfer from the infamous Torgau center to the detention center where Jana is housed at the film's beginning, Jana bets with the other female teens that she can seduce Jan immediately. This sexual act evolves into an apparently somewhat loving relationship between the two and ultimately results in Jana's pregnancy. The two argue about Jana's decision to abort the baby which Jan wants to keep. Jan attempts to beat Jana into agreeing to keep the baby. At the last minute Jana decides not to undergo an abortion. In response to her decision to keep the baby, she must endure acts of cruelty meted out by her peers. Finally, she and Jan run away. The authorities do not chase them. At the close of the film, Jana is seen giving birth alone in an indeterminate location. The events in Jana and Jan's lives are interpolated with scenes on East German TV showing actual TV footage of demonstrations in the GDR leading up to and during the fall of the Berlin wall and end of the GDR.

Jana und Jan focuses on severely alienated teenagers as mirrored by their incarceration in a detention center with little or no hope for their future. These centers represent a microcosm of GDR society at its most repressive, with little to no evidence of an easing of restrictions on the residents as the "Volk" (people) protests against the regime in the waning years of the GDR. In its propaganda the GDR views itself as a large collective family which represents the bedrock of society. Marriages based on mutual support and sharing of duties, loving sex, and state-regulated childcare and education for the children of such marriages were to ensure the future of the GDR. Yet, the film undermines the concept of society as a happy family by showing the collective family in the detention center as a brutal place in which out-of-control youth, defying the efforts of ineffectual supervisors, seek to terrorize those teenagers seeking kindness and love. Both teenagers and supervisors ignore external society's liberalizing trends in social mores and politics. In the detention center the more life changes on the outside, the more it remains the same on the inside.

Jana and Jan in the Youth Detention Centers

In the film, traditional families reflecting GDR governmental policy do not exist nor do healthy interpersonal relationships. Such relationships could have been made visible by showing the families of the administrators and workers or by showing teens in smaller groups of friendly cohorts. Instead, the majority of the teens are depicted as abusive bullies. In fact, ironically, the wardens, representing those in charge, embody perhaps the manner in which the GDR leaders hoped to be viewed, as strict but kind parental figures, and are more humane than the teens. In contrast to Torgau, where Jan has been brutally incarcerated for trying to flee to the West, the director of the second detention center is more sympathetic toward Jan. After having served his time with good behavior, Jan is transferred to a less repressive detention center where the director offers to shake his hand. Jan rejects the gesture but then states that no-one has ever offered to shake his hand. Likewise, the matron attempts to help the girls and influence them to make decisions that she thinks will positively affect their lives. Beyond these authority figures, the film contains no helping adults, no social workers, psychiatrists, or any other kind of professionals who could facilitate in "re-socializing" the young people.

In fact, there is no indication of any efforts on the part of the detention center supervisor to educate the residents socially or intellectually. The residents go to work every day, rising very early. The females work in a repulsive slaughterhouse on a conveyer belt where they clean and package chickens. The work is mechanical, exhausting, and dehumanizing. What the boys do is not shown. The rest of residents' time is spent in their dormitories tormenting each other, in the cafeteria eating, and in the evening, watching TV in a common room. There are no indications of any attempts to educate the residents about contraception or to make contraception available to them, although the boys and girls, all teenagers, live in close proximity to each other. What is available to the general population is not available to them.

In separate gender-specific groups the residents have banded together in hierarchal, repressive, abusive units in which any attempts at humanity are quickly eliminated and forgotten. As victims themselves of abandonment by their parents and the state, as the anti-poster children of the so-called family friendly GDR, these teens abandon and abuse each other at will. As their lives have been aborted so they abort the lives of those around them. Jan's only connection with his past is a newspaper article scrap relating how he was abandoned by his mother who left for the West, as was another of the girls, named Julia. Jan only remembers that his mother was beautiful. Jana tells how at the age of 12 she was sexually molested by her stepfather who was a party activist who wore a uniform and gave her rewards in return.

Julia Abandoned

In some ways the most pathetic and tragic figure in the film is Julia, who is shown as a loving and sensitive character. Abandoned by her mother, she dreams of the day when they will be united. It is not clear if she is a lesbian or simply seeking affection, as she seeks love from the dominant and cruel leader of the female group, Lady, by asking her permission to fondle her breasts. Lady allows and then rejects arbitrarily occasional affectionate moments with her. According to Haertel who worked for many years in such a center, any discussion of or engaging in same-sex relationships was totally taboo. In its ambivalent portrayal either the film is reflecting the liberalization in GDR society toward such relationships or the opposite by not revealing clearly the nature of the relationship. It remains murky just as does the film's conclusion. In contrast to the other girls, Julia also sensitively relates to Jana as they discuss Jana's photo of Jan and Julia's photo of her mother, and as she asks Jana about her pregnancy. However, her lack of toughness, her sensitivity and need for love lead to her suicide. Her hope to join her mother in the West is dashed when she receives a letter from her mother saying it is not possible. Friendless and unloved, Julia commits suicide in a toilet cubicle, reduced to the least of the least. While her suicide seems motivated by her mother's rejection, her confusion about her sexuality may have also been a contributing factor. Access to the West and to happiness and acceptance as symbolized by returning to her mother is denied to Julia. A future in the West eludes her and none of the administrators shows any awareness of her despair. In fact, attitudes toward same-sex relationships had liberalized in the GDR and the FRG and Julia most likely could have found her way in the future, thus intensifying the tragedy of her suicide.

Alternative Family Structures

In the center the juveniles have created a brutal alternative family structure which complements the quasi-military drills that occur on a regular basis. The structure for both genders is based on absolute obedience and control. The main information about the male group is offered in the first scene where Jan meets his new fellow "inmates." Because he does not show enough obedience and respect to Sir, the "boss," his chair is pulled out from under him and he lands on the floor. Jan reacts immediately and humiliates the leader by pressing his face in food, at least insuring that he will be left in peace. The boys work outside the center but it is not shown at what, they clean bathrooms, and they exercise. The female group is presented in much more extensive detail, mainly in their cruelty, even though the matron, Natter, tries her ineffectual best to help the girls. Representing past repressive societal structures, as do the boys, the girls treat Jana with unbearable cruelty once Jana decides not to abort and thereafter. They draw an obscene picture of a penis and a baby doll in her locker, they group "assault" her by encircling her and shaving her pubic hair, and mock and marginalize her at work. As the dehumanizing work in the chicken factory gradually overwhelms the pregnant Jana, they show no sympathy and on the way back to the detention center, with not enough seats on the bus, they force the fainting Jana to stand. Julia is not allowed to share her seat, and, finally, Jana jumps out and starts to walk on her own, taking fledgling steps as an independent woman. It is as if the girls have aligned themselves with their captors, the brutal leaders of their groups, who behave like the deteriorating repressive Honecker government attempting to retard or deny the progress of the *Wende*'s liberal political developments. The film's viewer sees the teens' lack of interest in the political developments of the *Wende* shown on TV news as they seem totally bored, yet happily relax and show enjoyment when the TV shows their favorite childhood program *Sandmännchen* (Little Sandman), short good-night episodes. Confronted by positive social change, they retreat into the past.

Jana and Jan

The relationship between Jana and Jan, who are depicted at the film's beginning as tough characters, mirrors the contradictions between government's social policies regarding the happy family which reproduces future workers in abundance with the state allowing the citizens liberal access to birth control and abortion as well as the documented radical increase in births among single parents. At the film's beginning, Jana, who is portrayed as quite sophisticated and experienced with sexual matters, seduces Jan. During the seduction, the result of a bet Jana makes with the other girls, Jana is shown to be capable of being gentle and caring. Her gentleness is ruined by the derisive voyeurism of her fellow teens, who watch through a window and then fall noisily from a stool. Subsequently, a relationship of sorts develops between the two—where they meet secretly in an attic, not just for sex but also talking, for human connection, a touch of humanity through soft candlelight lighting. Jan even asks about the nature of their relationship, inquiring if it is still a bet, to which Jana responds she does not know. Yet, as he caresses her cheek, she closes her eyes to take in the moment and the camera lingers on them for a few seconds before moving to a new scene. They seem to be developing a capacity for love and a relationship which the pregnancy puts to a test.

Birth Control, Pregnancy and Abortion in Youth Detention Centers

Despite the goal of the socialist government to encourage women to bear and raise children and participate in the workforce, as mentioned earlier, access to birth control and abortion were widely and freely available. However, according to Haertel (personal message), the subjects of sexuality, birth control, and pregnancy were taboo in the detention center. Ninety-six percent of boys and 95 percent of girls responded in a study that they had not received information for their personal study about sexual problems. To the question as to whether sexual education should be part of their routine, boys answered 90.8 percent yes and girls 90.2 percent yes. Likewise, in the film, access to information about contraception has not been granted to the residents. Jana and Jan indicate no awareness of contraceptive methods, including the rhythm method or withdrawal, nor do they show any concern about the possibility of becoming pregnant. Again, according to Haertel, these subjects were forbidden and no records were kept regarding pregnancies in the centers. Teens were forced to have abortions. Likewise, the matron immediately advocates abortion as a resolution to Jana's pregnancy. That Jana could give birth to the child and raise it is never presented as an option by the matron, the representation of authority.

Jan and Jana have opposite reactions to the pregnancy. Jan's immediate reaction is positive but selfish and immature, for he does not think of Jana or the baby's future, but only of himself. In so many words he declares that he is happy because he now understands why he is in this world with the baby offering a way for him to situate himself meaningfully in the societal structure and life cycle. Through this child he will form a connection between the past, present, and the future, with himself as the meaningful link, as the father and later as a grandpa. In contrast, Jana rejects the pregnancy immediately, accepting the prevailing institutional viewpoint that having a baby, especially as an institutionalized single teenager, is impossible. Despite the interpolation of GDR demonstrations into the daily life of the detention center, she, and the institution, as represented by the matron, do not seem to have noted that political change is afoot and that possibly having the baby might be an acceptable option.

The emotionally damaged residents only know how to solve their problems through violence and not discussion and communication. Jana's initial cold-hearted rejection of the pregnancy results in violence and damage. In an attempt to force Jana to have the baby, Jan brutally beats her which results in his return to Torgau and her hospitalization. Representing actually a retrogressive point of view, contrary to the liberal developments outside, the matron visits Jana in the hospital as she recovers from Jan's beating, and affirms Jana's decision, reinforcing Jana's initial understanding of societal expectations. The house matron, already stressed by the potential political liberalization, sees herself here as victimized and says, "How could you do this to me: I've been the house matron for 25 years. Such a disaster, *at such a time*" (my emphasis). In times of instability, the middle-aged Natter reacts conservatively by attempting to maintain the status quo, similar to how Honecker carried out traditional 40th birthday celebrations in a destabilized GDR. The matron advocates backing outdated norms rather than taking risks as the future unfolds. But Jana assures her that she is going to get rid of the child (using the dismissive word "wegmachen," to do away) when her condition is more stable. In the meantime though, Jan has sent her a picture of himself, reminding her of their relationship and a possible future together with the baby. At the same time, the woman in the neighboring bed offers Jana an emotional insight into maternal loss, for the woman has miscarried and gives the pregnant Jana the baby clothes in a gesture of kindness and hope which subsequently influences Jana to change her mind.

Although the abortion along with the question of whether or not the baby will ever enter the world constitutes the central metaphor of the film, the actual abortion scene occupies a remarkably short time in the course of events. The abortions are conducted in a totally business-like assembly line process, just as the chickens are processed in the slaughter house. Jana is shown in an antiseptic hospital environment, prepared for the procedure and lying on the bed awaiting her turn, the last patient of the day. Buckets by the operating table are impersonally emptied and a new plastic bag for the next aborted fetus is inserted. Only minimal communication occurs between the medical personnel and the patients. As Jana is wheeled through the door into the operating room, the camera dwells on the do not enter sign on the door as it closes behind her, emphasizing what the viewer already knows, that there is no help and no return from an abortion. Just as the procedure is about to start, Jana decides not to go through with it. The doctor asks her open-endedly if she is afraid. She responds that she is not, indicating that still ("aber trotzdem") there are issues, but not what they are. The doctor does not try to change her mind. She is the last patient of the day and he would rather finish early.

The question about fear is multilayered. It does not just relate to the immediate question of whether Jana is afraid of undergoing the procedure, but rather to whether Jana is fully committed to such an absolute decision and whether or not she is courageous enough to continue with the pregnancy despite the potential backlash from fellow girls and the institution. Two scenes immediately follow the abortion scene in which Jana is questioned, first by Julia and then by the matron, about her motives. First Jana sits with Julia and folds baby clothes. When Julia asks her if she is excited about the baby, Jana answers that she is getting used to it and when Julia asks if Jana kept the baby to please Jan, Jana answers that she kept the baby for her own (Jana's) sake, echoing Jan's comments almost word for word about how having a child places one in a significant way into the life cycle and being a meaningful member of society. They both speak to the question of living a life in isolation versus being part of a larger social constellation. Both Jana and Jan now interpret parenthood as a way of becoming grounded and integrated into society. Like Jan, Jana talks about how she could become a grandma or even a great grandma, a part of a larger context. Both alienated teens in a not surprisingly immature thought process think that having a child reintegrates them into the world—much as distressed couples think that having a baby will save their marriages. Likewise, much of the media during the *Wende* used patriarchal images of engagement, marriage, and childbearing, with the GDR almost always assigned the weaker role, in which a new happy symbiosis would create a new happy whole. Of course, as we know in retrospect, the use of these images helped contribute to a number of injustices with regard to the unification process after the fall of the wall, especially with regard to the status of the GDR.

In her conversation with the matron about the pregnancy, Jana tells her that in four months she can leave the detention center and she will be free. But Jana does not fully grasp the reality of the situation, for Jan is only 16 and will not be released until he is 18. Where will Jana go and how will she support herself? Endlessly practical, the matron reminds Jana that "Muttersein bedeutet etwas mehr, Kind" ("Being a mother means something more, child"). She also tells Jana that she (Natter), Jana's closest adult contact, will not be there much longer, anticipating the collapse of GDR governing structures and future unemployment. But Jana ignores this comment and responds by saying "Ich will mehr sein" ("I want to be more"). This scene is immediately followed by scenes on TV from ongoing political demonstrations in the GDR, clearly linking the situation in the detention center to political events occurring outside which are being watched by the residents in the common room. Demonstrators are repeatedly shouting "Helmut, Helmut" and "Einheit, Einheit" (unity, unity), as Helmut Kohl, the chancellor of the FRG, waves to the crowd. At the same time a disjuncture is occurring, because, as mentioned earlier, these teens are not paying attention to the political changes which will, none the less, radically impact their lives.

GDR Politics and Escape from the Detention Center

The question then remains: Can Jana indeed be more? Can the GDR be more? Will the youth of the GDR (outside the detention center) and other demonstrators, who are generating the impulse toward the fall of the wall, unification, and the birth of a "new" nation, be able to handle the loss of the known—the political system, to which they have adapted and by whose rules they have lived? Will they be able to transform this embryo, this growing new political embryo into a viable new unified state? The film's answer is not clear although initially the film takes an optimistic turn. After a period of time in Torgau for beating Jana, Jan returns to the original detention center housing Jana. As Jan is processed for readmission, it is indicated that he has become more confident and self-assertive for he, of his own initiative, shakes his supervisor's hand, in contrast to the film's opening, where he rejects a handshake. Jana wants to run away. He agrees saying that the world has gotten so large, indicating that the world has expanded for them both because their baby is beginning to kick and because of the political developments.

The escape from the detention center does not progress well, although Jana and Jan are not chased down and caught by the authorities as occurs in the original Haertel screenplay. The difficulty of their journey, their search for help, and the lack of clarity about the birth of the baby, reflects the uncertainty in the film regarding the GDR's future immediately during and after the fall of the wall. The couple first steal a Moped and hope to reach Jan's aunt who lives some 370 kilometers away. This option evaporates when they literally and figuratively run out of gas and have no money to buy more. There will be no aunt and no help to be found. Again linking their escape to the *Wende*, a siren sounds and at that moment Jana recites the date, June 27, 1990, immediately before economic unification, the introduction of the common currency in the former GDR states. However, at this point it seems unlikely she will participate in the better life anticipated as part of economic unification. The two then hike through a deserted landscape where they come upon a Russian soldier baking potatoes on a roadside fire and directing nonexistent traffic, no longer a figure of authority, but merely a human being. The soldier and his comrades who later pick him up show no political interest in Jan and Jana, only congratulating her on the pregnancy, revealing their human side. Nonetheless, they drive off leaving the couple stranded and without help, similar to the manner in which the Russians and Soviets withdrew support from the GDR, helping accelerate the country's collapse.

Jana and Jan then walk into town where political confrontations are occurring and the police are throwing squatters out of an occupied house, but their main concern is evading capture. They first obliviously stand under a Schwarzenegger film poster ironically titled "Running Man," and a few seconds later in front a GDR poster featuring the GDR slogan "Glück für die Familie" (happiness for the family), something neither of them have ever known but are hoping to experience in the future. In the final scenes the couple is seen toiling through destroyed landscapes which mirror their own losses and isolation. They seek refuge in a deserted border station, a location offering nothing to help the exhausted Jana on the verge of giving birth. There is absolutely nothing physical or human to comfort or to support her. It is difficult to imagine a worse circumstance. All the symbols of GDR power are gone, the strong Soviet presence, the powerful well-guarded border crossings, the signs of a functioning society. Their country as they knew it either from the perspective of the *Wende* or the detention center has disappeared and they are lost physically and symbolically. The decision to have the baby, which one would generally interpret as a sign of hope (indeed, "guter Hoffnung sein" or to be of good hope is an expression in German to describe being pregnant) has actually come close to destroying their lives. The viewer knows they realize this from their conversation about the GDR slogan advocating protecting unborn life. They comment that no one had ever protected them, remarking that children suffer from their parents' (the state's) actions. As her contractions begin, Jan leaves, one assumes to seek help, and assures Jana that he will not let anything bad happen to the baby. Left alone in her time of greatest need, the viewer does not know how Jana gets to the hospital as shown in the final scene where Jana is in labor and screams for Jan. He does not reappear and the last image shows Jana's face in repose, but there is no indication of a baby. Whether or not the baby was born or there was a stillbirth is left open. That Jana anticipates a tragic conclusion to their odyssey, both for herself and the GDR, is indicated by her earlier observation made as they trek through the border wasteland: cats return home to die.

Choosing Life

Jana's decision not to abort may indicate an affirmation of her and Jan's faith in a better future and concomitantly a changed and improved future for the GDR. That this future is fraught with danger, however, is made clear by the ironic juxtaposition of signage and the precarious position in which the couple finds itself. The image of the couple caught in front of the sign proclaiming the GDR's apartment house building plan promising happiness for families underscores that this happiness was only available for cooperative citizens, not lost youthful souls such as Jan and Jana.

In Jan and Jana one sees an attempt to reconstitute relationships and a sense of meaning in their destroyed lives—albeit with destructive detours—as ultimately represented here by rejecting abortion and giving birth. This is mirrored on TV in the detention center by breaking political events in the GDR as first the Honecker government celebrates its 40th anniversary and subsequently the country's citizens march for their own freedom and dignity and ultimately the downfall of the East German State. In contrast to what actually happened in the GDR protests, however, only Jana and Jan are shown to break away from the detention center. No significant changes occur among the remaining residents and those in charge. In fact, many residents who left the detention homes during the *Wende* later returned within two weeks (Röske 224). This leads to a highly ambivalent projection in the early 1990s of the future for the citizens of the GDR as reflected in the contradictory events of the film.

What actually seems extraordinary is the lack of excitement or even interest in the political developments in the late stages of the GDR on the part of all the detention center residents and administrators other than Jana and Jan. Each evening they sit in the same room and watch first the celebrations of the GDR's 40th anniversary and then the movement of demonstrators and demonstrations closer and closer to the fall of the wall. It is as if they are onlookers, incapable of absorbing the information about their potential liberation, both from the detention center and from the GDR, two parallel units. When one of the supervisors, as mentioned earlier, turns the TV show to the children's "good night" program, *Sandmännchen*, there is no protest, but rather smiles. The residents apparently fondly remember younger days and return to the past, almost resembling the *Ostalgie* (nostalgia for the GDR) trend after the unification of Germany, where some from the GDR longed for a return to certain aspects of their former lives in the GDR. It is as if they are totally detached from life outside the facility, and passively remain caught in the past, in what is almost a microcosm of an earlier, frozen in time, authoritarian GDR, as described by the filmmaker as a "abgeschlossene Welt DDR" (sealed off world of the GDR) (Röske 244).

Giving Birth as a Metaphor for the Future

One interpretation of the film may be that people like Jan and Jana, who choose to have a baby despite overwhelmingly negative circumstances, who decide to flee the detention center and defy authority, will shape the future. Both have refused to give in to the oppressive expectations of the repressive juvenile detention centers. Jan has been shuttled back and forth to Torgau, but he continues to fight back and reforms his violent ways, at least in regard to Jana. Jana remains unbowed in face of the cruelty released upon her by the female residents when she decides not to abort the baby. They are the ones who mature and become truly if not naively engaged in their humanity and who choose the future despite the risks.

By rejecting abortion, they attempt to place themselves in the cycle of life and affirm the future by bringing a baby into an evolving world. In so doing they affirm the possibility of a new more enlightened, more humane GDR or whatever the ensuing years might bring. Despite past tribulations, they, and possibly the baby, might well persevere just as the population hoped in the early 1990s. But the film, released in 1991, offers a mixed message. It is the first time that the filmmaker does not show the main characters reintegrated into society (Heiduschke). What will happen to all the residents in the detention centers when they are suddenly freed? How will they integrate into this changing society? This question remains unaddressed. What remains is that the future of the GDR is not secure, but quite open and unresolved. For Julia, the most human of them all, the seeker and giver of love, the future is tragic, abandoned during the *Wende* to suicide in the toilet cubicle, a miscarriage of the future. Jana is helpless and alone. Further undermining the hopeful outlook is the absence of Jan in the final scene. While it seems that his violent behavior has disappeared, the film presents him ultimately as a weak character, unable to find transportation, organize food, or find a safe place to rest. In portraying Jan as weak and absent, the film further participates in the emasculation imagery used to describe East German men during the unification process (Sharp 180). The two main characters, both symbolizing the drive to seek and create a more meaningful future by not having the abortion and choosing to keep the baby, have been deprived of their power, thus leaving both with little hope for the future. After all her efforts, Jana may be abandoned, left to struggle on her own, a single, uneducated, teen-aged parent. Further contributing to a negative outcome is the silence at the end of the film. There is no cry of a newborn, no joyous parents and onlookers, and the viewer has no idea whether there has been a live birth.

A reason for optimism might be found in the deviation from the original screenplay by Haertel, where the reader knows for sure that the pregnancy results in a stillborn child. In an interview Dziuba states that he purposely chose an open, ambivalent ending where the cry of a newborn is not heard, in spite of the fact that he had become very pessimistic and distrustful about the future of society (Röske 245). What society this is he does not specify. In hindsight we know that generally speaking unification has gone well. However, during the 1980s and the early 1990s, as mirrored by the decision to abort or not to abort, and by the film's ambivalent, only partially hopeful open ending, it was unclear to many, including the film's director, as to how the radical societal changes occurring during the fall of the GDR and German unification would be resolved.

134   Part 3. From Unplanned to Planned Pregnancies

Notes

1. I found Mr. Haertel through a Facebook search. We have been in touch since. He supplied me with the original copy of the screenplay used for the film as well as further information.
2. See, for example, Ministerium für Bildung; Zimmermann; Gatzemann, *Die Erziehung zum "neuen" Menschen*; Gatzemann, *Der Jugendwerkhof Torgau*; Krausz; Puls; Poppe; Glocke.
3. According to Manfred Haertel, after 1989 the detention center in which he worked became a home for troubled teens (*Jugendheim*) in which several teens lived with their babies. This was forbidden before the fall of the wall.

Works Cited

Boa, Elizabeth. Preface. *Women and the Wende: Social Effects and Cultural Reflections of the German Unifications Process. Proceedings of a Conference held by Women in German Studies, University of Nottingham, 9–11 September 1993*. Ed. Elizabeth Boa and Janet Wharton. Amsterdam: Rodopi, 1994. V-VII. Print.
Clements, Elizabeth. "The Abortion Debate in Unified Germany." *Women and the Wende: Social Effects and Cultural Reflections of the German Unifications Process. Proceedings of a Conference held by Women in German Studies, University of Notthingham, 9–11 September 199*. Ed. Elizabeth Boa and Janet Wharton. Amsterdam: Rodopi, 1994. 38–52. Print.
Dodds, Dina. "Women in East Germany: Emancipation or Exploitation?" *Women and the Wende: Social Effects and Cultural Reflections of the German Unification Process. Proceedings of a Conference Held by Women in German Studies, University of Nottingham, 9–11 September 1993*. Ed. Elizabeth Boa and Janet Wharton. Amsterdam: Rodopi, 1994. 107–14. Print.
Gatzemann, Andreas. *Die Erziehung zum "neuen" Menschen im Jugendwerkhof Torgau*. Münster: LIT, 2008. Print.
_____. *Der Jugendwerkhof Torgau. Das Ende der Erziehung*. Münster: LIT, 2009. Print.
Glocke, Nicole. *Erziehung hinter Gittern. Schicksale in Heimen und Jugendwerkhöfen der DDR*. Halle: Mitteldeutscher Verlag, 2011. Print.
Gries, Sabine. *Mißlungene Kindheiten: Zum unsozialistischen Aufwachsen von Kindern in der DDR*. Münster: Lit, 1994. Print.
Haertel, Manfred. *Friedlose Herzen*. 1987. TS Manfred Haertel, Lehnin, Germany.
Jana und Jan/Jana and Jan. Dir. Helmut Dziuba. Perf. Kristin Scheffer, Rene Guss. 1992. English subtitles. DEFA Film Library, 2009. DVD.
Kleikamp, Antonia von. "Sexueller Missbrauch war an der Tagesordnung." *Welt*. WeltN24, 25 Aug. 2014. Web. 6 Oct. 2016.
Krausz, Daniel. *Jugendwerkhöfe in der DDR. Der geschlossene Jugendwerkhof Torgau*. Hamburg: Diplomica, 2010. Print.
McLellan, Josie. *Love in the Time of Communism: Intimacy and Sexuality in the GDR*. New York: Cambridge University Press, 2011. Print.
Ministerium für Bildung, Jugend und Sport des Landes Brandenburg, ed. *Einweisung nach Torgau. Texte und Dokumente zur autoritären Jugendfürsorge in der DDR 4*. Berlin: BasisDruck, 1997.
Poppe, Grit. *Weggesperrt*. Hamburg: Oetinger Taschenbuch, 2011. Print.
Posener, Alan. *Der brutale Alltag in den DDR-Jugendwerkhöfen*. *Welt*. WeltN24, 1 Apr. 2010. Web. 6 Oct. 2016.
Puls, Heidemarie. *Schattenkinder hinter Torgauer Mauern*. Rostock: Rinck, 2009. Print.
Richter, Maxi. "Working with Lay Actors in *Jana and Jan*." Transcription of interview with director Helmut Dziuba. Included on *Jana und Jan*, DEFA Film Library, 2009. DVD.
Röske, Stefan. *Der Jugendliche Blick: Helmut Dziubas Spielfilme im letzten Jahrzehnt der DEFA*. Berlin: DEFA-Stiftung, 2006. Print.
Sharp, Ingrid. "To the Victor the Spoils: Sleeping Beauty's Sexual Awakening." *Women and the Wende: Social Effects and Cultural Reflections of the German Unification Process. Proceedings of a Conference Held by Women in German Studies, University of Nottingham,*

9–11 September 1993. Ed. Elizabeth Boa and Janet Wharton. Amsterdam: Rodopi, 1994. 177–88. Print.

Tesch, Angela. "Kinderheimfonds Ost: Antragsfrist für Hilfeleistungen läuft bald ab." *MDR*. Mitteldeutscher Rundfunk, 25 Aug. 2014. Web. 6 Oct. 2016.

Zimmermann, Verena. *"Den neuen Menschen schaffen." Die Umerziehung von schwererziehbaren und straffälligen Jugendlichen in der DDR (1945–1990)*. Köln: Böhlau, 2004. Print.

Finding Humor in Birth Control
Fiction and Film from Hugh Mills to Matthias Schweighöfer

WALTRAUD MAIERHOFER

Some of the best-known tragedies of German literature have an unintended pregnancy at their core: from Margarete in Goethe's *Faust* tragedy to several other tales and ballads of 18th century seduced bourgeois girls and young women who commit infanticide, from the untimely death of a teenage girl due to an unsafe abortion in Wedekind's *Frühlings Erwachen* (*Spring Awakening*, written 1890–1991) to the pregnancy and dead child in the youthful past of the protagonist in Dürrenmatt's grotesque drama *The Visit* (*Der Besuch der alten Dame*, 1956). Pregnancy is fraught with disaster and often ends the hopes and dreams of women, if not their lives. These stories reflect and raise great anxieties and fears; however, there are others that address and ease such complicated issues with humor.

Much research has been done regarding humorous approaches to sexuality and related issues including unintended pregnancies, for example by American cultural critic Gershon Legman. He emphasizes an "anxiety-reduction" component arguing that many people are scared by or uncomfortable about sex and use humor to reduce those anxious feelings (Bancroft 9). This essay investigates several works of 20th- and early 21st-century fiction and film which take a lighter, comical approach to birth control. It will examine select German, British, Croatian, and American works: the British novel *Prudence and the Pill* (1966),[1] the Croatian film *Svecenikova djeca* (*The Priest's Children*, 2013) based on the play by Mate Matisic (1990), the U.S.–American independent romantic comedy *The Pill* (2011) directed by J.C. Khoury, and the German novel *Frettsack* (*Ferret Balls*, 2012) and its film adaptation *Vater-*

freuden (*Joys of Fatherhood*, 2014). The first two works listed give a humorous twist to dealing with and sabotaging birth control pills, condoms, and the morning-after pill while the plot of *Joys of Fatherhood* revolves around fathering despite involuntary sterilization.

Humor is an adaptable narrative device often used in many cultures for otherwise embarrassing discussion of sensitive topics around sexuality because it "plays with the most deeply seated cultural assumptions, it makes visible areas of unacknowledged attitudes and behaviors in private realms" (Draitser cover). I analyze patterns of humor in these works and argue that the comedies of sabotaged contraception (*Prudence and the Pill*, *The Priest's Children*) return to and continue the pre-modern farcical treatment of pregnancy and shotgun marriages. This concept was common in pre-modern European culture[2] and appears to have been revived in lowbrow fiction and theater of the 1960s and in post–Communist Croatia. The two recent films *The Pill* and *Fatherhood*, both by male filmmakers, thematize today's Western men's ambivalences toward parenthood given the availability of birth control, but also of medically assisted reproduction.

In her important study *Textual Contraception: Birth Control and Modern American Fiction*, Beth Widmaier Capo has revealed the rich cross-influence of contraceptive and literary history between the 1910s and 1940s. She has shown how fiction played a significant role in shaping public consciousness of women's needs and the evolving discourse of reproductive rights. As other contributions in this book demonstrate, this was radicalized with the sexual revolution and its openness to discussion of all aspects of sexuality. At the beginning of the 21st century the use of contraception and family planning is uncontested in public consciousness in most countries. In 2012 the United Nations declared "Access to contraception is a universal human right" (Beadle 1; see "The Rights to Contraceptive Information and Services for Women and Adolescents"). In many countries there are still huge unmet needs. Access is available mostly in the Global North—in Europe more so than in the United States where up to the so-called "Affordable Care Act" of 2010 the public debate was in terms of privilege and not of right.

The women's movement of the 1970s used humor to address issues such as menstruation, pregnancy, contraception, and abortion in women's lives as well as gender equity and men's participation in child rearing. Since these ideas have been widely accepted, we seem to be able to find humor again in failed birth control, at least in novels and films. Is this part of a backlash movement or part of postmodern, lighter approaches to representing birth control and women's right to control their fertility? After generations of writers and filmmakers have explored new narrative possibilities for female characters beyond marriage and motherhood, the shotgun marriage may make people laugh again. Others may not find birth control sabotage funny at all,

138 Part 3. From Unplanned to Planned Pregnancies

on the contrary a violation of what we have come to see as women's and reproductive rights. In U.S. law, birth control sabotage (and thus exposure to STIs) can be legally considered fraud or a form of sexual violence or assault. According to the American Congress of Obstetricians and Gynecologists it is an under-recognized problem ("Reproductive and Sexual Coercion").

Men also express their desires about parenthood and thus participation in the dialogue about contraception not only in private but in novels and films that speak to a mass audience. This cultural expression is an important aspect in addition to the increasing attention fatherhood has seen in recent research, after decades of focusing on motherhood.[3] It has challenged and disproven the long and widely held assumption that men remain disinterested in matters of reproduction including contraception and parenthood.

Sabotaged Contraception in Prudence and the Pill *and* The Priest's Children

Shotgun weddings belong to the "staples of late seventeenth-century English comedy" (Price 192). The short novel, or rather novella, *Prudence and the Pill* (first published in England in 1965) by the British playwright and novelist Hugh Mills (1906–1971), takes a witty, ironic, and over the top perspective of the quick rise of hormonal contraception and sexual liberation in the 1960s. The cover text advertises the plot as a mystery: "Prudence is on the pill; so is her sister-in-law, but someone has been swapping aspirin for their pills. Is it the teen-age niece, the maid, the chauffeur, a lover, Prudence's husband, or all of the above?" This "delightfully bright drawing room comedy" was supposedly based on actual occurrences ("Prudence and the Pill" Kirkus Review). The novel, although set among elite and well-to-do circles, hit the nerve of the time, was translated into several languages, and made into a U.S.–British film with the same title (directed by Fielder Cook, 1968) for which Hugh Mills authored the script.[4]

Prudence and the Pill sketchily tells and focuses on the British elite's use or believed use of birth control. It follows two families, both related to each other, throughout the course of a year (in under 150 not very dense pages). The title character, Prudence Hardcastle, who, of course, will turn out to be less than prudent in her affairs, is married to Gerald, a bank chairman and "eminent tycoon" (7). They live near London (7) and lead a semi–Victorian life of luxury and boredom. The turbulent events start in the house of Gerald's brother Henry, who enjoys similar social standing. He is happily married to Grace with whom he has a 16-year-old daughter, Geraldine, who is allowed to do as she pleases and is everything but old-fashioned. One spring evening they find this daughter in bed "with a young man of exceptional beauty" (14) and "well-bred" manners who soon admits that "pretty well everything" happened (17) and that he is intent on marrying. Grace's outrage softens considerably when she learns that 20-year-old Tony Bates is the son and heir of a knighted "shipping magnate" (23). Still, the concerned mother has a talk with her daughter about sexually transmitted diseases and pregnancy. To the latter, Grace responds rather nonchalantly, "I'm not a fool, I take my precautions" (27). She reveals that she is taking the hormonal contraceptive pill, which in 1965 is already known simply as "the pill," here under the fictional brand name "Thenol tablets" (27). Grace had simply exchanged her mother's Thenol tablets with aspirin and taken the birth control herself, thus avoiding "disgrace" for herself and the whole family (28), a revelation which makes Grace faint. Indeed, Grace is soon confirmed to be pregnant, a fact which she secretly is "quite proud and pleased" about (28). Thus, any major conflict about the pregnancy is avoided. Grace could not get a prescription for herself, because the pill was until 1966 only to be prescribed to married women. However, the exchange of pills has, as the narrator remarks, more unforeseen and far-reaching consequences and causes "great upheavals in both branches of the Hardcastle family" (28).

The story gets Henry's grave and dignified brother Gerald, who envies his brother for his happy marriage, thinking. He had been living with his beautiful but difficult wife, Prudence, "on rather distant terms" (8) and enjoyed a pleasant and understanding mistress, Elizabeth Brett, a happily divorced woman with no intentions of marrying. He had, however, bought a house for her. He knew about the pill because it was "much discussed and moralized about in the press" (31) and had seen the very same brand in his wife's belongings. There had been no sex—or in the author's words, "no very tender demonstrations between himself and Prudence for some years now" (32)—so if she was taking birth control, there had to be a lover. Gerald is determined to find out who it is because he wants to divorce Prudence and needs proof of *her* affair. This reflects that the divorce law was also hotly debated at the time. The Law Commission was set up in 1965 for the purpose of promoting a reform of the law, and it took effect in 1969.

Consequently, Gerald Hardcastle secretly exchanges his wife's Thenol tablets with harmless pain medication. This is easily successful because both are described as coming in a simple vial and generic shape, unlike today's elaborate packaging and tamper-proof sealing of hormonal contraceptives. This is historically correct, although it was already changing when the novel first appeared. The pill first came in a bottle, like other medicine, and the amount was not limited to a one-month supply. Women were to take a pill each day for 20 days, then not take it for the next seven days. Though some companies issued a calendar with the pills, the standard packaging confused many consumers. In 1962, the American engineer David Wagner first designed and patented a pill dispenser for a month's supply. The "dialpac" compliance dispenser first came on the American market in 1963, and Ortho launched "Ortho Novin" in Britain also in 1963; consequently, all "oral contraceptives would be packaged in memory-aid dispensers" ("Gallery: The Pill," images 1–4).[5]

To Gerald's disappointment, several months go by and Prudence is not transfigured (the narrator loves such puns). Instead, in June her maid, Rose, introduced as "a pretty, very silly girl" (8), is found pregnant and in a relationship with the chauffeur, Ted, "a very bright young man" (8). In this case the employers immediately decide that the couple has to marry, followed by conversations about failure to use "precautions" (54). It turns out that Ted had in fact provided his girlfriend with the pill, secretly. However, this proved detrimental to his progressive intentions. He believed Rose, being Catholic, did not to want to take birth control pills (56). This is another aspect where the novel accurately reflects historical tendencies and controversies. Just like the overall population, many members of the Catholic Church were in favor of the new birth control in the early 1960s. In 1964, Pope Paul VI convened the Commission on Population, the Family and Natality, and only in 1968 did Paul VI release an encyclical titled *Humanae Vitae*. The doctrine reaffirmed the contraceptive ban that dated back to the Augustinian teaching of the "sinful flesh" and declared all artificial methods of birth control sinful for Catholics (Juette 189). Ted therefore disguises the birth control pills, which he obtained not quite legally through a pharmacist friend, as vitamins. It turns out that Ted was wrong about Rose's Catholic resistance to birth control and Rose is much more modern then he believed. Rose exchanges the "vitamins" with her employer's pills, unaware that these were not birth control pills but the aspirins Gerald had provided. So, not Rose but Prudence took the real Thenol tablets and Rose became pregnant.

The plot gets more turbulent as both Hardcastles plan to vacation together in August. Elizabeth breaks up with Gerald, Prudence gets sick, visits her doctor in London and is confirmed to be pregnant. Gerald finds out that it is Dr. Hewit she is having an affair with. Gerald, very angry about the affair—and the fact that his mistress left—is in no rush to grant Prudence a divorce until he coincidentally finds out that Elizabeth is also "in a spot of trouble" (130). Only fleetingly does Elizabeth consider the possibility of abortion. She had not taken the pill during her time with Gerald because he thought of himself as sterile. He is overjoyed, and having already proposed to Elizabeth, is now in a big rush to get the divorce settled. Even clever Geraldine has to get married earlier than planned because her mother had her stop taking the pill leading to a "trivial mishap" (136) on their vacation together. In the end everyone has babies. Grace and Prudence both have baby boys. Geraldine and Elizabeth both have baby girls, and Rose, the maid, has triplets. The narrator comments that "the final result of all these exceedingly reprehensible machinations was a formidable avalanche of almost unbelievably handsome children" (137). To make the comedy ending perfect, everybody is happy in her or his relationships and with parenthood. Even Prudence is magically transformed into "one of the happiest and kindest people" (137).

Prudence and the Pill can be viewed in connection with the British "satire boom" of the early 1960s in reaction to the end of the British empire. Stuart Ward states: "From the 1950s, changing tastes in popular British comedy had begun to generate an unprecedented appetite for mockery and ridicule of the manners, pretensions, and pomposity of Britain's ruling elite—the so-called British 'establishment'" (91). Such mockery of the upper class, who had to return from servicing the empire to matters of the immediate family, is here combined with the new issues of the popularity of the birth control pill, the discussion of the divorce law, and the greater acceptance of premarital sex in the middle class, all elements of what is now referred to as the sexual revolution of the 1960s. The pill became available to unmarried women in Britain in 1966, and no-fault divorce was introduced in 1969 (Cook 121).

The novel *Prudence and the Pill* captures this moment of changing attitudes toward sex, marriage, and reproduction and related laws combined with the very British satire of the upper class and their life style. It is remarkable that both the daughter and the maid and chauffeur get the "precautions" talk after the fact. This shows that the short novel, although not well known anymore, can be a modern-day warning for parents to talk to their teenagers about pregnancy and contraception, or else they will find their own creative solutions and the parents will have bigger problems on their hands.

The outcome of sabotaged contraception is not as smooth and lighthearted in the 2013 Croatian film *The Priest's Children*, directed by Vinko Brešan, although it is classified as a comedy.[6] It is based on a controversial stage play of the same title (1999) by the Croatian playwright, screenwriter, composer, and musician Mate Matisic (born 1965), adapted for the film by the author himself. It became a top-grossing domestic film in Croatia and was also popular at international film festivals. It takes place on a picturesque Croatian island, an environment well known to the director. Framed by scenes of a priest's confession, *The Priest's Children* reveals the story of why Father Fabijan (Kresimir Mikic) is now in a hospital bed. The birth rate on the island—as in Croatia overall after the fall of communism and since the war of independence—has been plummeting. The island's zealous young priest comes up with a plan to counter the population decline and, with the help of the harbor-side kiosk-vendor Petar (Niksa Butijer), pricks holes in the condoms sold to the villagers. They even convince the local pharmacist Marin (Drazen Kuhn), who turned nationalist by the war experience, to sell their manipulated condoms and also swap his birth control pills for vitamins.

Consequently, the number of pregnancies and births is astounding and an amazing number of pregnant brides want to get married in Fabijan's church. The hilarious exaggeration does not stop here, as the news spreads quickly: The bishop visits the blessed congregation, and fertility-seeking foreign tourists flood the little island. The priest, who thought he was helping God's will for humans to be fruitful, finds himself more and more out of control, faced, for example, with sexual abuse and pedophilia, a disturbed woman, a suicide attempt, and an abandoned baby on his doorstep. What begins as a grotesque plot with naïve yet likable central characters, colorful supporting cast, common film gags, and offensive jokes then takes some very serious and surreal turns as the "acerbic satire pokes fun at hot-button ethical issues" (Simon). In framing the events with the priest's confession, the film not only stays within the parameters of a satire of Catholicism but also avoids delving deeper into the developing dramas or addressing any legal consequences of the sabotage.

The director, Vinko Brešan, as critic Alissa Simon wrote, is "known (and loved) for using humor to approach sensitive historical and cultural topics. Here it's the Catholic Church, which currently opposes sexual education in Croatian schools, that comes in for an irreverent ribbing" (Simon). As Gordana P. Crnkovic, a scholar of post–Yugoslav film, has shown, Brešan in his previous films such as the war drama *Witnesses* (2003) and the love story *Will Not End Here* (2008) thematized the profound and rapid changes by which Croatia has been transformed since the early 1990s ("The Battle for Croatia"). According to Crnkovic, Vinko Brešan "has emerged in the last two decades as one of the most interesting new Croatian film directors, and the most popular contemporary filmmaker among domestic audiences" ("The Museum Spills Out" 175). In interviews, director Brešan stated that *The Priest's Children* is "not quite a comedy" but "a film about life" with its serious problems, and "life is comedy and tragedy and drama at the same time" (Brešan, Interview). In this case it is the Catholic church which he called "such an influential and leading institution" ("eine derart einflussreiche und tonangebende Institution") in Croatia that he felt compelled to address it. Especially after Pope Benedict XVI made concessions regarding condom use in exceptional cases, the local story he wanted to tell became a global one: how the church dogmas lead to conflicts between honesty and manipulation, celibacy and sexuality, brotherly love and pedophilia, religion and hypocrisy (*Gott verhüte*).[7] This discrepancy even widened when Croatia joined the EU in 2013. The population is 86.3 percent Roman Catholic ("Demographic Picture"), and attitudes toward birth control are similar only to two other countries within the European Union, Ireland and Poland, where the Catholic teaching on family planning still has a large following. After the fall of communism Croatia gained independence in 1991. Because of the War of Independence (1991–1995), emigration, and displacement, the population steadily decreased.[8] According to the Croatian Bureau of Statistics with latest numbers for 2013, since 1991 Croatia's death rate has continuously exceeded its birth rate ("Natural"). The total rate of 1.5 children per woman of fertile age "puts Croatia side by side with other European countries" such as Germany ("Demographic Picture") in terms of population trends. (Germany's population has recently grown again, though, due to immigration.)

The Priest's Children is Brešan's third comedy. The audience has responded enthusiastically to the "assertion of laughter and playfulness" in his previous works portraying the "immense social changes connected to transition from socialism to capitalism" and to "comedy that departed from realism into the realm of parody and caricature" (Crnkovic, "The Museum Spills Out" 176–77). The Priest's Children can also be described in these terms. The tongue-in-cheek pun of the title is typical, as the fatherhood of well-meaning "father" Fabijan is all spiritual and limited to his nasty prank on the couples relying on condoms, except for the surprising last shot of the film which suggests that he also physically fathered a child. The dialogue has a lot of sexual humor and aphoristic observations, and the visuals are not timid either in revealing the islanders' secrets. In a reversal of the castration joke, the poked condom plot falls in the category of sexual humor that reassures the audience that these things happen only to somebody else.[9] Otherwise, they could provoke outrage about violated rights and legal responsibility. The resulting pregnancies pressure both men and women into marriages they do not want. Some have some very serious and sad consequences such as a suicide attempt and the abandoned baby. In the end, Father Fabijan cannot be proud of the outcomes of his attempts to play God and push fecundity. The film succeeds in satirizing church dogma in an age that believes in individual responsibility in sexual actions and in family planning. This serious side situates the film The Priest's Children firmly in the Enlightenment tradition of thinking for oneself, valuing the individual, and also of instructing through entertaining.[10] In this view, identifying with the Catholic belief and practicing birth control are not exclusive but a matter of an individual's ethical stand and courage—and the film shows how such decisions and new freedoms come with growing pains.

Emergency Contraception Made Funny: The Romantic Comedy The Pill

With the 2011 film The Pill, the debut film of the American J. C. Koury, who previously directed commercials—and does not reveal his first name—issues of contraception have reached the genre of romantic comedy, a "generally highly populist, mainstream genre" (Jermyn 10). The film plot centers on one couple's need for and handling of the morning-after pill, or emergency contraception, which is used when contraception either was not used or was thought to be ineffective. *The Pill* opens with a shot of Manhattan at night seen from Central Park and takes place in Manhattan. Dating back to the 1960s and Helen Gurley Brown's bestseller *Sex and the Single Girl*, Manhattan is often touted as a mecca for singles. Sex happens at the beginning, not the end of this comedy. *The Pill* follows Mindy (Rachel Boston) and Fred (Noah Bean) over a 24-hour period after they have a one-night stand. It is important that the characters are not college-age but around 30 (played by Boston, born 1982, and Bean, born 1978). Their occupations are discussed briefly or not at all; Fred is a "freelance copy-editing writer" with novel writing aspirations, Mindy does not reveal her work at all. Before his first attempt at intercourse, Fred puts on a condom but Mindy, having had quite a lot to drink, falls asleep before anything more happens. However, later in the night, Mindy seduces the very sleepy man in her bed—or, more accurately, coerces him—and they have unprotected intercourse because Mindy prefers the closeness. Upon waking up in the morning, Fred is immediately concerned and questions Mindy whether she is on birth control to which Mindy reacts evasively, stating that she is Catholic and does not take the pill. Finding a used condom in the bathroom, Fred is also alarmed about her sexual history, but Mindy attributes it to her roommate. Fred proves quite knowledgeable about calendar-based contraception when he then questions Mindy about her last period and the probability of ovulation. Mindy's emotional, evasive—and supposedly funny?—response ("I know my body, and I am not ovulating") suggests that she is not worried about becoming pregnant, maybe even seeks the risk because she then admits to being in her fertile days. Fred insists on immediately going with her to the pharmacy to get her emergency contraception, explaining that it is not the same as abortion to which Mindy is opposed. Fred coerces Mindy to take the pill right there in the drugstore to make sure she does not become pregnant. By now a pattern in their conversations has become obvious: She is feeling him out for relationship potential but she is not honest herself. She is very suspicious of being a one-night encounter and tends to run off abruptly; on the one hand she insists on trust, on the other she is evasive about the truth. The audience has seen Fred texting another woman but he denies being in a relationship and insists he only wants to make sure there will be no pregnancy. However, when they relax, they appear to have a lot of genuine good times together. After Fred gives Mindy the first pill right away at the counter, she is suspicious of his behavior and runs off. Fred is again worried about the chance of pregnancy when the pharmacist informs him that she needs to eat something to keep the pill down and that there is a second pill that needs to be taken 12 hours after the first dosage. The rest of the movie involved Fred chasing Mindy down and getting in awkward social situations to make sure she is not throwing up and finally takes the second dose of the contraceptive. He even meets her former partner when he helps her pick up some belongings from the former apartment, and her family when she tricks him into accompanying her to a birthday party for her little brother. This scene is complete with questioning by her parents about plans for children and about planned vs. unplanned children. To calm Mindy's suspicion and rebellious reactions, he keeps insisting that he wants a serious relationship, while his initial goal was ironically only to avoid the ultimate seriousness, a pregnancy. To add to the plot and turbulence of the film, Fred has a partner, Nelly, and he has to run back and forth between the two women, hiding them from each other. Of course, he gets more and more annoyed with the controlling aspects of his girlfriend who supports him financially and is very negative about his writing ambition, and he is genuinely drawn toward the lively and spontaneous Mindy who shows a lot of interest in him as a person and also in his writing. He seems to end up alone, however; when Mindy finds out he is living with Nelly and he finally breaks it to Mindy that it is time for the second dose. She is very upset and accuses him of just staying around to make sure she takes the second pill. He promises Mindy to break up with Nelly that same evening but does not seem determined until at the end of a boring evening with Nelly a fight evolves over a missing condom and her control needs. Fred admits to having had sex with another woman and finds the courage to end their relationship. He runs to Mindy's apartment but does not find her at home. An intertitle informs the viewer that the following last scene takes place "five weeks later." In a coffee shop, Fred types the last words of his novel. He then runs into Mindy on the street. At first Mindy sends Fred off with the words "You have really hurt me, and I am at a different place in my life now." We get no further information what that different place might be. She wears a loose, high-waisted dress. Could she be pregnant after all? She does not look happy or say anything of another relationship. While the audience gets a glimpse of her crying, Fred insists that she give him another chance and he asks for her number to which she gives in and allows him to text her. They walk in opposite directions but soon stop to text each other. The film ends with this shot, hinting at a new attempt at a serious and lasting relationship. Mindy's profile of her dress bulging in the middle might even suggest that she is pregnant—or might hope so for the future.

Emergency contraception, or the "morning-after pill," was marketed in the United States after 1998, was approved for over-the-counter access without prescription in 2006, and has quickly become an "$80-million industry in the United States and throughout the Western world" (Prescott cover). The fact that a relatively high number of women did not take the required second dose was one of the reasons for its initial rejection for open access by the FDA (United States Government Accountability Office 27). In 2010, when the film was made, a newer version of emergency contraception was already available that consists of only one dose and is marketed as most effective when taken within three days (the most popular brands being "Plan B One Step" and "Next Choice One Dose"). In 2009, the FDA stated that both men and women could obtain "Plan B One Step" without a prescription if they were older than 17 years of age (Kee, Hayes, McCuistion 860). In the film, the pharmacist correctly asks for Mindy's identification but does not give the required information about side effects until Mindy has left. The availability of emergency contraception is credited with a recent decline in the number of abortions (Wind). Khoury stated that the film "helps build awareness for EC, for emergency contraception" (Khoury, "An Interview"), but the two-dosage aspect, which is the driving plot device, makes its information already outdated.

Although produced as an independent micro-budget film and initially marketed mostly on digital platforms, the film was an immediate success and highly popular both with critics and the audience (Khoury "An Interview"). It also won several awards, such as the "NY Emerging Talent Award" and the "Audience Award" at the New York Gen Art film festival (*The Pill*, Website). The writer-director-producer, who characterized himself as a single man in New York City and "professional hypochondriac," insisted that the idea was based on something that happened to him and that the film should be very "real" and relatable (Khoury, "An Interview"). Romantic comedies love New York; as Deborah Jermyn writes, "New York (and Manhattan more specifically) has evolved as the pre-eminent and most memorable location adopted by the Hollywood rom-com"; with its dynamic context and aura of adventure, it offers "the perfect milieu to explore the most potent of modern Western culture's mores; the belief that somewhere, out there, is the someone who is 'the one'" (10, 12). Despite its beginning with a casual sexual encounter and linking the need for post-coital contraception with the fleeting relationship, the film reinforces the deeply romantic belief that obstacles can be overcome, such as dead-end relationships, and true love can be found, and that such love still includes the possibility of children.

Although the romantic comedy has traditionally been viewed as a genre for and about women, recently a type has emerged that has a male central character and may include male audiences. Tarmar Jeffers McDonald has observed that the "homme-com," as she terms it, tends to re-infuse into the sexless romcom the subject and depiction of sex, including sexual humor, which she considers necessary for the survival of the genre (159). She laments, however, the return to a pre-feminist sexual double standard where "men want sex, and women withhold it from them, urging them to grow up and settle down" (159). *The Pill* has both a male and female protagonist who are equally important to the plot. The film differs from the examples McDonald analyses (*The 40-year-old Virgin*, 2005; *Wedding Crashers*, 2005) in that the women in it want sex at least as much as the men: Mindy takes advantage of Fred's half-conscious state when she initiates intimacy, and in another scene it is the girlfriend Nelly who is initiating if not commanding sex. In another interview, Khoury said that he tried to challenge the American "middle-class morality hanging over our heads" (Ong).

The films by Woody Allan with male (anti-)heroes have had substantial influence on the genre of romantic comedy.[11] Fred is also a hypochondriac and worrier with neurotic tics, and Noah Bean in the role of Fred talks in the manner of Woody Allan, in a comic and often defensive and self-deprecating way. This dynamic plays well against Mindy's eccentricity, her huge need for freedom as well as for a relationship, her vulnerability, feelings of pressure from cultural norms, and resulting mood swings. Fred's attempts to impress Mindy against his own convictions are not really funny but convey his ambivalences, fear, immaturity, and insecurity. Fred wants to leave Mindy but sticks around to make sure he can leave without a pregnancy; she does not believe in relationships and yet challenges him, and is possibly not opposed to the prospect of a child without a father. She confesses that she ended a relationship that felt too "needy," and yet she admits to Fred that she needed him at the family gathering because of her younger sister, Rose. Rose just got engaged and brags openly about "having found the one sooner rather than later when things would have been more pressing"—remarks clearly directed at a rather sad looking Mindy who feels her "biological clock" ticking. At the end, he gets another chance and does not remain impassive when the woman he clearly is attracted to and adores walks away.

Koury's independent film *The Pill* introduces the serious topic of emergency contraception into the genre of romantic comedy and fits well with other developments to include issues of feminism in a post-feminist era, masculinity in crisis, and changing attitudes toward gender and romance, while still upholding the ideal of true love.

Infertility, Ambivalences and Joys of Fatherhood

The German film *Joys of Fatherhood* (2014) that Matthias Schweighöfer (born 1981) directed and produced, and in which he also played the main character, is based on a 2012 bestseller of light and humorous entertaining fiction, *Frettsack* (which may translate loosely as "Ferret Balls"). It was the debut novel of Murmel Clausen (born 1973, pseudonym for Claus-Henric

Clausen), who was already known as a scriptwriter for successful film and television comedies. Its main character named Jens Fischer is a man in his late 30s living in Munich, the author's hometown. He has had no luck with women, has no steady job, and shares a messy apartment with another single man. Melancholic and disillusioned, wondering whether he will ever have a family of his own—and needing money—he lets himself get talked into donating sperm, hoping that this way he will "live on," even if anonymously. However, his roommate has two ferrets for pets and one day a ferret accidentally castrates Jens. No longer able to father children, he becomes desperate to meet the woman who supposedly received a treatment with his sperm and is now pregnant. It takes a few criminal acts, but the corresponding, overbearing grifter character gets the name and address of the woman. He goes out of his way to "coincidentally" become friends with the recipient of his sperm, Maren Heinze, and her husband, but suffers a few major setbacks. Jens finally has a goal in life, namely to win the heart of Maren and become the father of "his" child. He ends up, however, with her girlfriend, Jessie, who in the course of his roller coaster rapprochement with Maren, had sex with his roommate while on drugs and alcohol. Predictably, Clausen wrote a sequel, *Frettnapf* ("Ferret Bowl"), in which their relationship continues on a rollercoaster of emotions and hilarious social situations.

The author weaves some serious thoughts about men's desire for children and fatherhood especially in the middle section of the novel, reflecting cultural norms, fatherhood and identity, the complex relationship between fathering and masculinity, and how being a parent could provide the sense of manliness that he lacks and desires. He impresses his love interest by becoming an expert in pregnancy and babies while showing no sexual interest in her.

Men's reaction to infertility and to "emergent" forms of fatherhood made possible by reproductive technologies, leading to the birth of children for men who would otherwise have remained sterile, childless, or both, has only recently been addressed in sociological research.[12] In fiction, it has been attempted in more "serious" genres of novels and plays, for example in the plays *ICSI* and *Taboos* (2008) by Carl Djerassi, or documentary films and dramas such as the Swiss documentary *Ma Na Sapna* (*A Mother's Dream*, 2013) by Valerie Gudenus. Mainstream fiction, such as the thriller *Gone Girl* (2012) by American writer Gillian Flynn, only owes an occasional plot twist to infertility treatment. In Clausen's novel, the characters are not very developed. Jens likes to make jokes, especially sexual jokes, but most often they embarrass him.

In both novel and film, the legal situation in Germany is correctly explained: the sperm donor does not have any rights of a biological father (Clausen 36).[13] Novel and film find different solutions in order not to give the impression that such claims are easily pursued or even a good idea. The film is clearly aimed at a young audience,[14] wanting to be cheeky, sexy, romantic, non-stop funny and have a charming protagonist—all achieved according to the review in the major German mass paper *Bild* (Körzdörfer). The scriptwriters made major changes and completely rewrote the plot for the film adaptation.[15] Above all, the protagonist is an attractive, charming young man rather than a melancholic, pathetic loser, an important feature for a film aiming at a broad viewership.[16] While the novel had several ironical and self-critical remarks about the genre of romantic comedy, the film neatly fits the definition. Matthias Schweighöfer (born 1981), German cinema's new *Wunderkind* (Körzdörfer), so the paper *Bild* declares, is cast as the male protagonist, aptly renamed Felix ("fortunate"), a very popular surname. Felix enjoys his life as a single man and has an active sex life; the film opens with a sex scene in which he is quite upset about the idea of fatherhood rather than longing for it in solitude. The young woman, obviously a casual encounter, lets him know she is no longer on the pill, after which he immediately stops the act. Even the ferret bite happens during a casual encounter with another woman. It is gradually revealed that years ago he lost a pregnant girlfriend in a car accident and is traumatized from this experience. The part of the funny, chaotic, and often drunk roommate with the crazy ideas and pet ferret is assigned to a brother named Henne (Friedrich Mücke), replacing the novel's crazy drug experimenter and lab worker. Maren Heinze (performed by Isabell Polak, age 32 at the time of the filming), the recipient of his sperm, is not a housewife and former waitress, but a successful sports reporter who is not yet married. After a lot of confusion and the revelation that Maren's boyfriend did not want children at all and was cheating, resulting in a breakup of the relationship, the end brings a different twist as well. Felix finds out that his sperm was not used and he is not the biological father of Maren's child after all. Following his wise father's advice ("families aren't made of blood relations, families are born of love"), he overcomes his reservations about a child "not his own" and fights for romance. The film ends with a brief scene five years later (intertitle) in which Maren is pregnant again. Henne explains to a cute little girl—who shares his reddish locks, suggesting he may be the biological father—about sperm banks and how children are made with the help of such sperm in a metaphor of cars and garages.[17] He says that for the new baby, Felix's original cars were used. The audience cannot be sure that this "secret" is the truth, though, but it is possible because earlier the film showed how the woman gets to choose among donors with the help of descriptions and pictures. This may not be accurate; in German sperm banks, the choice is only by facts such as eye and hair color, height, weight, education, and blood type of the donor ("Behandlung mit einer Samenspende") but international organizations such as Cryos International offer a much wider choice and have sparked the debate about designer babies. At the film's end, everyone is happy. The first child is decidedly not his biologically but Felix got the girl, as is expected in a romantic comedy, and appears to be happy in the role of father. In the end, though, biological fatherhood is upheld in spite of the earlier message about acceptance of non-biological fatherhood and love. The film, marketed as a family film, is more traditional here than the novel where biological fatherhood is not important in the end.

Conclusion

Betsy Stirratt, artist and adjunct curator at the Kinsey Institute for Research in Sex, Gender, and Reproduction, writes: "Forms of humor have always been an important way for people to communicate about sex. Humor about sex continues to be part of our everyday lives, and it remains one of the few acceptable ways that sex can be discussed in polite company" (Stirratt vii). This statement applies even more to films in the genre romantic comedy or date films.

Humor is definitely gendered as Delia Ciaro and Raffaella Baccolini have begun to demonstrate.[18] Although I cannot delve deeper within this essay it is remarkable that all the examples found for humorous treatment of birth control were written and directed by men. Male writers and directors from several cultures have addressed ambivalences and vulnerabilities about fatherhood and fecundity using a humorous approach. In the 1970s, women's use of humor proved a revolutionary tactic, especially in the genre of cartoon novels, to address issues important to women's lives including contraception and abortion (Tiefer 25). In fact, the women's movement has so effectively changed social norms that many sexual jokes from earlier in the 20th century are no longer found funny but instead awful and offensive. In the early 21st century, more "feminist" humor has moved into mass fiction and mainstream media. Although the number of female filmmakers is growing, it appears, however, that women are less likely to write or direct women in funny roles when it comes to contraception, especially sabotaged contraception, or medically assisted reproduction, maybe because women are the ones where such humor can most easily offend, upset, or hurt. The male comic protagonists in *The Pill, Joy of Fatherhood*, and also *The Priest's Children* follow a well-established pattern where "the male comic portrays something of the innocent child in his facial features and demeanor" (Chiaro and Baccolini 8). International differences when it comes to reproduction and humor definitely need to be explored further.

Hugh Mill's pill-swapping mix-up resulting in lots of babies and happily married couples, read 50 years later, leaves a quaint impression with the humor markedly tied to class and thus very British. It reads like an experiment in openness to sexual encounters outside of marriage, tamed with the help of contraception and its manipulation, showing that the pill does not destroy traditional family structures and therefore might as well be accepted. It should become legal for unmarried women, or they might find creative and illegal ways to obtain it, causing harm to others. The forced marriage due to failed contraception has a comeback in the context of changing societies, the role of the Catholic Church, and population decline, as shown in the Croatian black comedy. The spiritual "father" who sabotages contraception in a tumultuous post–Communist country reaches his goal of increasing the birth rate in his community and gets much admiration from his superiors, but he is forced to acknowledge the major social and psychological problems that accompany the unintended pregnancies as well as the sufferings and responsibilities they bring. Much of the comedy engages (male) humor at the expense of women and their sexuality but also includes naïve men who are not part of this controlling group. In the end, the priest regrets his playing God and enforcing the traditional dogma against contraception over secular contemporary rights. Indeed, sabotaged contraception is no laughing matter to many. According to a recent U.S. study with females ages 16 to 29 years, "15% reported birth control sabotage" (Knox and Schacht 301) such as a male partner who disposed of her pills, poked holes in condoms, or prevented her from getting contraception. The disturbing experiences lying under the film's comic surface are at least as provocative, drawing attention not only to religious teachings but ongoing strong social pressures for women to have children. The fact that the film is not distributed in the United States and not available on streaming sites reveals the distributors' assumption that an American audience may not share its humor. U.S. women for whom, in stark contrast to most European women, contraception has until the "Affordable Care Act" been a privilege rather than a right, are more sensitive when it comes to violations of this right and have no sense of humor about it.

    The romantic comedy *The Pill*, despite advocating for the use of birth control, still upholds the romantic belief in true love—and family. The last film (*Joys of Fatherhood*) promotes younger men's openness to new forms of "emergent fatherhood" in reaction to male infertility, using reproductive technology, but also affirms men's wishes for biological fatherhood and a traditional family, with the family-friendly-rated film adaptation being more conservative than the novel. While addressing infertility and sperm donation, a relatively taboo subject for light entertainment, it takes liberties regarding the rights of sperm donors. The accidental vasectomy may be a bizarre idea and some viewers may find the casual attitude to sex offensive but the comedy also contributes to fighting the stereotype of Germans having no sense of humor.

152   Part 3. From Unplanned to Planned Pregnancies

Although the stories depicted through these forms of fiction and media vary in exact subject matter, they all revolve around contraception and planned and unplanned pregnancies, which are complicated and uncomfortable subject matters for public representation. Humor has continued to be an effective method to ease the tensions surrounding these issues creating a greater chance for understanding and prevention of complicated and difficult situations.

Notes

1. Another choice would be David Lodge's 1965 novel *The British Museum Is Falling Down* in which the high risk of pregnancy with the so-called rhythm method features prominently. However, there is already scholarship on Lodge's works and use of humor available. *Prudence and the Pill* allows me to expand on an aspect only mentioned in the article by Jessica Borge in this volume.

2. For the "irreverence for marriage" in restoration comedy, see for example Perry 207.

3. See for example the survey of scholarship in Inhorn et al., *Reconceiving the Second Sex*, 1–7.

4. The film is also examined in the essay by Jessica Borge in this volume.

5. Also see Gosell. Information on "Ortho Novin" was provided by Jessica Borge.

6. In January of 2016, the subtitled DVD become available in the UK but not in the United States, the marketing reflecting an assumption that American viewers might not find the subject and treatment funny. The German-dubbed version ("*Gott verhüte!*" meaning "May God prevent!") was distributed in cinemas, on DVD, and streaming on *Amazon.de* in 2014, recommended for an audience older than 12 years.

7. Cf. the director's commentary on the German-language website of the film, *Gott verhüte*. Brešan is alluding to the interview series *Light of the World* (2010) which even before publication made headlines in the global press because the Pope did not speak out against condom use in connection with the risk of HIV infection (188).

8. For details on the changes in Croatia, see Ramet et al.

9. Remarkably, in 2015 the Dutch Labor Party, PVdA, has taken up the idea of pricking holes in condoms in a campaign ad about the shrinking population of the province of Zeeland (Jaarsveldt).

10. Crnkovic has come to a similar result with regard to earlier films by Brešan and attested them "'Enlightenment' values of one's own critical thinking with one's own head" ("The Museum Spills Out," 200).

11. Cf. Jermyn 9–10.

12. For sociological research on "infertile fatherhood" and "emergent fatherhood," see the respective chapters in Inhorn, *Globalized Fatherhood*.

13. For a detailed legal study, see for example Rütz. There has been as least one case in California where a new legal precedent was set for the rights of a sperm donor not married to the mother of the child (Gershman).

14. The German coding is "suitable for persons over 6 years" which is approximately equivalent with the American PG rating, suggesting parental guidance.

15. Although only Clausen is named in the credits as screenwriter, in interviews Schweighöfer spoke of a team as common in film work, in this case a "laughing team" ("Lach-Team") of three men and two women including himself (Körzdörfer).

16. The latter is something several reader reviews on booksellers' platforms such as Amazon.de criticized about the novel.

17. Therapists do indeed recommend informing children at the age between two and five if their legal father is not their biological one (Klar and Trinkl 57), because they have a right to learn the identity of the sperm donor.

18. See Chiaro and Baccolini who have published representative analyses from inter-

disciplinary and international perspectives. Some of the following thoughts were inspired by the essays in this volume.

Works Cited

Bancroft, John. "Sex and Humor: A Personal View." *Sex and Humor: Selections from the Kinsey Institute*. Ed. Catherine Johnson, Betsy Stirratt, and John Bancroft. Bloomington: Indiana University Press, 2002. 5–13. Print.
Beadle, Amanda. "United Nations Declares Access to Contraception A 'Universal Human Right.'" *ThinkProgress*. Center for American Progress Action Fund, 14 Nov. 2012. Web. 5 Oct. 2016.
"Behandlung mit einer Samenspende." *Familienplanung*. Bundeszentrale für gesundheitliche Aufklärung. 8 Dec. 2015. Web. 5 Oct. 2016.
Brešan, Vinko. Interview. *Cineuropa*. Cineuropa. Web. 7 Oct. 2016.
_____, dir. *Gott verhüte!* (*Svecenikova djeca*). Script Mate Matisic, based on his own play. Perf. Kresimir Mikic, Niksa Butijer, Marija Skaricic, etc. Dubbed in German. 2013. Neue Visionen, 2014. DVD.
_____, dir. *The Priest's Children/Svecenikova djeca*. Script Mate Matisic, based on his own play. Perf. Kresimir Mikic, Niksa Butijer, Marija Skaricic. English subtitles. 2013. Arthaus, 2016. DVD.
Capo, Beth Widmaier. *Textual Contraception: Birth Control and Modern American Fiction*. Columbus: Ohio State University Press, 2007. Print.
Chiaro, Delia, and Raffaella Baccolini. "Humor: A Many Gendered Thing." *Gender and Humor: Interdisciplinary and International Perspectives*. Routledge Research in Cultural and Media Studies 64. New York: Routledge, 2014. 1–11.
Clausen, Murmel. *Frettnapf: Roman*. Munich: Heyne, 2013. Print.
_____. *Frettsack. Roman*. Munich: Heyne, 2012. Print.
Cook, Matt. "Sexual Revolution(s) in Britain." *Sexual Revolutions*. Ed. Gert Hekma and Alain Giami. Genders and Sexualities in History. New York: Palgrave Macmillan, 2014. 121–40. Print.
Crnkovic, Gordana P. "The Battle for Croatia: Three Films by Vinko Brešan." *Democratic Transition in Croatia: Value Transformation, Education, and Media*. Ed. Sabrina P. Ramet and Davorka Matic. College Station: Texas A&M University Press, 2007. 247–75. Print.
Crnkovic, Gordana P. "The Museum Spills Out on the Square, the Past's Challenge to the Present: The Films of Vinko Brešan." *Post-Yugoslav Literature and Film: Fires, Foundations, Flourishes*. New York: Continuum, 2012. 175–201. Print.
United States Government Accountability Office, [Crosse, Marcia.] "Food and Drug Administration: Decision Process to Deny Initial Application for Over-the-Counter-Marketing of the Emergency Contraceptive Drug Plan B Was Unusual: Report to Congressional Requesters." *GAO*. US Government Accountability Office, 2005 (GAO 06–109). Web. 4 Oct. 2016. PDF.
"Demographic Picture." *Croatia.eu*. The Miroslav Krleža Institute of Lexicography, n. d. Web. 5 Oct. 2016.
Draitser, Emil. *Making War, Not Love: Gender and Sexuality in Russian Humor*. New York: St. Martin's, 1999. Print.
Gershman, Jacob. "Paternity Rights of Sperm Donors Expanded in Actor's Custody Dispute." *Law Blog. The Wall Street Journal*. Dow Jones, 14 May 2014. Web. 5 Oct. 2016.
"Gallery: The Pill." *American Experience: The Pill*. Companion website to the film. PBS. Public Broadcasting Service, n. d. Web. 5 Oct. 2016.
Gosell, Patricia Peck. "Packaging the Pill." *Manifesting Medicine*, ed. Robert Bud. *Artefacts*. Artefacts Consortium, 1999. 105–21. Web. 5. Oct. 2016. PDF.
Gott verhüte. Gottverhuete.de. Web page. Neue Visionen Filmverleih, Berlin 2014. Web. 5 Oct. 2016.
Inhorn, Marcia C., Wendy Chavkin, and Jose-Alberto Navarro, eds. *Globalized Fatherhood*. Fertility, Reproduction, and Sexuality 27. New York: Berghahn, 2014. Print.

Inhorn, Marcia C., Tine Fjornhoj-Thomsen, Helene Goldberg, and Maruska la Cour Mosegaard, eds. *Reconceiving the Second Sex: Men, Masculinity, and Reproduction.* Fertility, Reproduction, and Sexuality 12. New York: Berghahn, 2009. Print.

Jaarsveldt, Janene Van. "Poke Holes in Condoms, Increase Zeeland Population: Labour Joke." *NlTimes.nl.* NlTimes, 11 Mar. 2015. Web. 5 Oct. 2016.

Jermyn, Deborah. "I ♥ NY: The Rom-Com's Love Affair with New York City." *Falling in Love Again: Romantic Comedy in Contemporary Cinema.* Ed. Stacey Abbott and Deborah Jermyn. London: I.B. Tauris, 2009. 9–24. Print.

Johnson, Catherine, Betsy Stirratt, and John Bancroft, eds. *Sex and Humor: Selections from the Kinsey Institute.* Bloomington: Indiana University Press, 2002. Print.

Jütte, Robert. *Contraception: A History.* Trans. Vicky Russell. Cambridge: Polity, 2008. Print.

Klar, Sabine, and Lika Trinkl, eds. *Diagnose: Besonderheit: Systemische Psychotherapie an den Rändern der Norm.* Göttingen: Vandenhoeck & Ruprecht, 2015. Print.

Kee, Joyce LeFever, Evelyn R. Hayes, and Linda E. McCuistion. *Pharmacology: A Patient-Centered Nursing Process Approach.* St. Louis: Elsevier, 2014. Print.

Khoury, J. C. "A Conversation with JC Khoury—Writer/Director of *The Pill*." Video recording, posted on *YouTube* by MYMHM[.tv],[movies you may have missed.com], 2012. Web. 5 Oct. 2016.

Khoury, J. C. dir. *The Pill.* Script J. C. Khoury. Perf. Noah Bean, Rachel Boston, Anna Chlumsky, etc. Shoot First Entertainment, 2011. *Netflix.* Web. 5 Oct. 2016.

Knox, David, and Caroline Schacht. *Choices in Relationships: An Introduction to Marriage and the Family.* 12th ed. Boston: Cengage Learning, 2016.

Körzdörfer, Norbert. "*Vaterfreuden.* Schweighöfer von Frettchen entmannt!" Review. *Bild.* Bild, 6 Feb. 2014. Web. 5 Oct. 2016.

McDonald, Tamar Jeffers. "Homme-Com: Engendering Change in Contemporary Romantic Comedy." *Falling in Love Again: Romantic Comedy in Contemporary Cinema.* Ed. Stacey Abbott and Deborah Jermyn. London: I.B. Tauris, 2009. 146–59. Print.

Mills, Hugh. *Prudence and the Pill.* Philadelphia: Lippincott, 1966. Print.

Mills, Hugh, script. *Prudence and the Pill.* Dir. Fielder Cook. Perf. Deborah Kerr, David Niven, Robert Coote. 1968. Turner Classic Movies. Video recording.

"Natural Change in Population in the Republic of Croatia." *Dzs.hr.* Croatian Bureau of Statistics, 2006–2015. Web. 5 Oct. 2016.

Ong, Michelle. "J.C. Khoury's Pill Street Blues." *Interview.* Interview Magazine, n. d. [2010]. Web. 5. Oct. 2016.

Perry, Ruth. *Novel Relations: The Transformation of Kinship in English Literature and Culture, 1748–1818.* Cambridge: Cambridge University Press, 2004. Print.

Pope Benedict XVI, and Peter Seewald. *Light of the World: The Pope, the Church, and the Signs of the Time. A Conversation with Peter Seewald.* San Francisco: Ignatius, 2010. Print.

Prescott, Heather Munro. *The Morning After: A History of Emergency Contraception in the United States.* Critical Issues in Health and Medicine. New Brunswick: Rutgers University Press, 2011. Print.

Price, Curtis Alexander. *Henry Purcell and the London Stage.* New York: Cambridge University Press, 1983. Print.

"Prudence and the Pill." Review. *Kirkus Reviews.* Kirkus Media, n. d. Web. 5 Oct. 2016.

Ramet, Sabrina P., Konrad Clewing, and Renéo Lukic, ed. *Croatia since Independence: War, Politics, Society, Foreign Relations.* Munich: Oldenbourg, 2008. Print.

"The Rights to Contraceptive Information and Services for Women and Adolescents." Briefing Paper. *UNFPA: United Nations Population Fund.* UNFPA and the Center for Reproductive Rights, 2011. Web. 5 Oct. 2016.

"Reproductive and Sexual Coercion." Committee Opinion No. 554. *Obstetrics & Gynecology* 121 (2013): 411–15. *ACOG.org.* American College of Obstetricians and Gynecologists. Web. 5 Oct. 2016.

Rütz, Eva Maria K. *Heterologe Insemination. Die rechtliche Stellung des Samenspenders: Lösungsansätze zur rechtlichen Handhabung.* Berlin: Springer, 2008. Print.

Schweighöfer, Matthias, dir. *Vaterfreuden / Joys of Fatherhood.* Script Murmel Clausen (after

his novel, *Frettsack*). Perf. Matthias Schweighöfer, Friedrich Mücke. English subtitles. Warner Home Video, 2014. DVD.
Simon, Alissa. "Film Review: *The Priest's Children*." *Variety*. Variety Media, 22 July 2013. Web. 5 Oct. 2016.
Stirratt, Betsy. Foreword. *Sex and Humor: Selections from the Kinsey Institute*. Ed. Catherine Johnson, Betsy Stirratt, and John Bancroft. Bloomington: Indiana University Press, 2002. Vii. Print.
Tiefer, Leonore. "The Capacity for Outrage: Feminism, Humor, and Sex." *Sex and Humor: Selections from the Kinsey Institute*. Ed. Catherine Johnson, Betsy Stirratt, and John Bancroft. Bloomington: Indiana University Press, 2002. 22–39. Print.
The Pill: A J.C. Koury Film. Website. *Shoot First Entertainment*. J.C. Khoury, n. d. Web. 5 Oct. 2016.
Ward, Stuart. "'No nation could be broker': The Satire Boom and the Demise of Britain's World Role." *British Culture and the End of Empire*. Ed. Stuart Ward. Studies in Imperialism. Manchester: Manchester University Press, 2001. 91–110. Print.
Wind, Rebecca. "Emergency Contraception (EC) Played Key Role in Abortion Rate Declines." *Guttmacher Institute*. Guttmacher Institute, 17 Dec. 2002. Web. 5 Oct. 2016.

PART 4. ABORTION ACROSS CULTURES:
REPRODUCTIVE CHOICE, DUTY OR CRIME

When Abortion Was Illegal
*Remembrance and Advocacy
in Recent Films from Romania
and Mexico—and "I Had an Abortion"
Storytelling on the Web*[1]

WALTRAUD MAIERHOFER

In 2006, the rock musical *Spring Awakening* (music by Duncan Sheik and lyrics by Steven Sater), an adaptation of Frank Wedekind's German play of 1891, became an unforeseen, wildly popular Broadway hit. It won eight Tony awards, which resulted in many more productions, including internationally, and made the original play in a new translation by Jonathan Franzen (2007) a popular high school reading in the United States. The musical kept the setting in the past when abortion was illegal and drew a "parallel between the repression of the 1890s and the sexual repression that is still rampant today" (Sater, Preface ix). The plot, with the death of its female teen protagonist due to a lack of sexual education and a resulting clandestine abortion, hit a nerve with many criticizing abstinence-only education. Because of changes in the details about sexuality, it can also be read as a "criticism of male control over women's reproductive rights" (Harelik 73). The popular adaptation enabled many U.S. teenagers to openly reflect about abortion in a new way. While "the subject [was] more polarizing than ever" in the United States, as film critic Stephen Farber noted in 2012, Hollywood films were remarkably silent or evasive on the issue. Parley Ann Boswell has already begun to argue that "the films that focus on real people dealing with abortion have been produced or financed outside of the United States" (181).[2] This essay examines three post–2000 films from Romania and Mexico that thematize abortion and the respective reproductive rights situations.[3] The films vary in artistic quality, and the goal is not a detailed film analysis but rather to show what arguments filmmakers presented that thus possibly influenced public opinion.

It is noteworthy that both directors are male. Do women, where they want to make an argument about abortion, tend to choose media with more immediate effect? Anne Zohra Berrached's film *24 Wochen* (*24 Weeks*, 2016) telling the story of a woman struggling with the option of late-term abortion, may be a groundbreaking exception. Three of four recent European documentary films advocating for abortion access—*Abortion Democracy: Poland/South Africa* (Diehl 2008); *Droit à l'avortement* (*Abortion, a Human Right*, Vicky Claeys, 2014); *Abortion: Ireland's Guilty Secret* (reporter Alys Harte, 2015); and *Vessel: Abortion in International Waters* (Dieana Whitten, 2014)—were directed by women or featured a female reporter. In the meantime, many women around the world seeking abortion (especially where it is illegal) have turned to another form of self-administering with the medication Misoprostrol, also known in the United States as the "Mexican abortion pill." It has led to a new form of global advocacy and access through the Web, with women sharing their stories in unheard-of numbers. This kind of new storytelling will be contrasted with the films by way of conclusion.

4 Months, 3 Weeks and 2 Days *and Abortion in Romania's Past and Present*

4 luni, 3 săptămâni și 2 zile (*4 Months, 3 Weeks and 2 Days*, 2007), directed by Cristian Mungiu, is set in 1987 Communist Romania. Although the plot focuses on an abortion, the audience sees signs of distress, of unmet needs, and unhappiness throughout the entire film. These aspects make the film a powerful tool to remind its international audience of what it felt like to live in Romania at this time, what led to the revolution, and the high hopes for a better life afterward. Director Mungiu implies that the "burdens of the dictatorship have imposed a grey pall on the country, putting most of the citizenry in a perpetually sour mood," noticed *Time* film critic Richard Corliss (1).

The Communist party with Nicolae Ceausescu, who was head of state from 1967 to 1989, enforced strict abortion and birth control laws that limited many women's options to practically zero when it came to safe sex and terminating an unintended pregnancy.[4] The biggest change was in 1966, when abortion was made illegal, and contraceptives (including their import) were also illegal. While the Communist regime promoted women's equality in the workforce, it strictly controlled women's fertility and access to contraception and abortion. From today's perspective Ceausescu's regime abolished fundamental rights of women, especially reproductive rights. However, the numbers of both legal and illegal abortions rose. For example, in 1983 the number of abortions (421,386) exceeded the number of live births (321,489), and only 9 percent had the required justification ("Demographic Policy"). In 1985, two years before the film takes place, the policy was made even more strict: The only legal way to receive an abortion was if the woman had more than five children already living under her care, or if she was over 45 years of age. High taxes were levied on those over 25 that did not have children and monthly gynecological exams were required of any woman of childbearing age, including pubescent girls, to ensure all pregnancies were caught and monitored to term ("Demographic Policy"). In addition, spontaneous abortions and miscarriages were often investigated to make sure that they were not hidden induced abortions. If someone was caught performing illegal abortions, it was punishable by prison and even death ("Demographic Policy").

At the outset of the film *4 Months, 3 Weeks and 2 Days,* we meet Gabita (Laura Vasliu) and Otilia (Anamaria Marinca), two pretty students in their early 20s. Gabita is pregnant and is getting ready to have it terminated. We get no past information of Gabita's love life, how she made the decision, or even about the father of the child. Otilia, Gabita's good friend and roommate in her very small and sparse lodgings, is her accomplice in pulling off the illegal stunt. A lot of the responsibility falls on Otilia, while her friend makes a naïve and childlike, helpless impression. Otilia borrows additional money from her own boyfriend, arranges for a hotel room for the procedure to take place, and meets with the abortionist Mr. Bebe (Vlad Ivanor) before leading him to the hotel. His name, likely an alias, ironically translates to "baby." We find out almost nothing about him and how they found him, just like the women themselves. A friend of a friend of Gabita had also consulted him for the procedure, they had agreed on the phone before, and Gabita mentions that he was known for offering the procedure even after three months. Also, it is Otilia who is left to dispose of the evidence—without getting caught. Otilia's helpfulness and loyalty are tested even more when Gabita reveals that she is much more than two months pregnant—exactly four months, three weeks, and two days—as she originally told her friend and the abortionist, making the procedure even more dangerous in terms of her health and its illegality.

Everything about the procedure is abhorrent, emphasizing the risk and danger everyone involved faces. Mr. Bebe acts extremely cold and repulsive when he explains the procedure and pressures the two women with an ultimatum into the advance payment for his "help," namely sex with both. The procedure consists of a vaginal probe which delivers an abortifacient, and Gabita is supposed to lie absolutely still until it shows effect after about an hour, then go to the bathroom to avoid a mess in the hotel room. The "outcome" is not to be buried because dogs might dig it up, nor put down the toilet as it would clog and get them all in trouble. In case of fever, he recommends aspirin. Calling an ambulance in case of heavy bleeding or another unplanned effect would get them all "half way to the prison," and he forbids it. The two women show growing fear and disgust, though they no longer dare to respond. When he mentions they could call him for help, we know they would want to avoid that. He then leaves them alone to wait for the abortifacient to take effect. All of the deception and irresponsibility on Gabita's part places high demands on her friend Otilia and tests their friendship to the limit.

Director Christian Mungiu uses a visual style that keeps the mystery and drama going without sensationalism. It is "familiar to serious European cinema: just about every scene, no matter how long, is shot without cutting" (Corliss 3). This technique allows the audience to view the characters' struggles, both individually and as a pair, as a continuous sequence, leaving out anything that is unimportant to their predicaments. At the same time, this technique increases the intensity and the drama in the film by allowing the audience to be fully involved in what is going on, making the film very naturalistic.

Another technique is the use of storytelling off screen. Through long stretches, we only see one character while simultaneously something very important is happening to the other that we know about but do not witness directly. An example of this technique is seen when Bebe receives "payment" in the form of intercourse. As Emma Wilson argues, "What's critical is that the action takes place off-screen. We are obliged to experience it vicariously, through the fear and projection of the protagonist who is outside the bedroom" (21). This technique is also applied instead of showing Gabita going through the physical abortion process. Otilia leaves to have dinner with her boyfriend's family at his insistence, and we watch Otilia's obvious nervousness and growing tension. It is a situation that only she knows, but has to keep secret, especially as Gabita is not answering the phone and Otilia was supposed to not leave her alone. "The rigor of the director here, refusing any cut-away to Gabita, is devastating," writes Emma Wilson in her analysis of the film (22). It builds the intensity of the film as we are led to assume various scenarios of what could be happening to Otilia's friend.

The last and possibly most shocking technique to further the intensity of the story is when Otilia finally returns to the hotel. After finding that her friend is in fact alive, though totally exhausted and apathetic, Otilia remembers that she must get rid of the evidence from the procedure, the body of the crime they just committed. Her long blank gaze into the bathroom conveys her conflicting emotions but does not prepare the audience for the following shot. This time the film does not spare the audience the direct shocking view of what lies in front of Otilia, the aborted fetus. Though half-covered by towels and blood, the head is clearly visible and its size apparent when Otilia's hands quickly wrap it up and put it in a bag, with Gabita's weak voice in the background asking to bury it. Otilia, "the resourceful heroine of the film," takes the bus through the city, wanders around for a good spot, and disposes of it finally by dropping it into a trash chute on the roof of a high rise as Mr. Bebe had suggested: "The thud of the flesh package as it drops to the ground comes as a dull aftershock and reminder of the gravity of the act" (Wilson 22).

The ending does not answer all the questions of the viewer. One critic stated, "Mungiu sets his abortion drama in the register of the everyday and shows its irresolution with a matter-of-factness that borders on absurd" (Wilson 23). Otilia returns to the hotel finding her friend in the restaurant waiting for her meal, ironically with a wedding party seen in a room behind. Otilia does not want to tell Gabita what she did with the fetus, and the two promise each other to never speak of the events that had taken place that day. When the waiter brings Gabita a serving of the wedding meal, the various meats on the plate may remind her and the viewer of the human flesh and blood just discarded. The film ends in silence. Richard Corliss points out that Mungiu's film is "right and realistic—and far from the ending Hollywood would devise, if it ever dared to make a movie like *4 Months*" (3).

Indirectly, the film seems to make a stronger pro-life argument than any major U.S. film about young women experiencing unintended pregnancies such as the comedies (!) *Knocked Up* (directed by Judd Apatow, 2007) or *Juno* (directed by Jason Reitman, 2007)—both of which avoid the discussion of abortion and even the word. Instead of promoting a happy life with a baby, Mungiu's film uses graphic images and major moral dilemmas to possibly deter the audience from accepting abortion. As Wilson notes, "*4 Months, 3 Weeks and 2 Days* not only fails to spare us its characters' distress, but also includes a harrowing and unavoidable image of a tiny aborted fetus.... The explicitness connects the film with extremist pro-life campaigning materials which aim to appall" (Wilson 18).[5] A pro-life stance would expect the women to get caught or punished. Both women are shown suffering in silence after the sexual violence they had to endure as a form of payment. Even if they do not get caught for the illegal act, they already feel punished. The film did very well at international festivals and with critics, winning many awards including the Palme d'Or at the Cannes Film Festival and Best European Film and Best Director at the European Film Awards. Examining its reception in Romania and in the United States, Oana Godeanu-Kenworthy and Oana Popescu-Sandu argue that the film took on new meanings for viewers in both countries because it could be imbedded in a larger national debate over reproductive rights: It "was transformed from an act of amoral probing of Romanian individual and collective memory about communism, into a film about the controversial nature of particular individual choices within the liberal capitalist paradigm" (225). It became the director's most popular film (Pop 218).

Within this paradigm, the film remarkably manages to convey a standpoint that is not simply for or against abortion. Usually, the decision to end a pregnancy takes many factors into account. For instance, the woman may think of her health, her financial stability, and the quality of life that the child may have if she decides to continue with the pregnancy. However, in the film, we are not a part of the original thought process of Gabita when she decides. It is reflected, however, in the argument that Otilia, still in shock from what happened earlier, gets into with her boyfriend after the birthday celebration; they rely on withdrawal and she is thinking about what she would do if she, like Gabita, became pregnant. It seems she wants to break up with him although he insists he would marry her. She does not feel ready to settle down if she could not continue her studies and thus hope for a better life. This tense moment conveys that women are left alone with decisions of great consequence and suffer either way. We are to assume that Gabita made the choice on her own terms, very well presenting a strong argument for a woman's right to terminate a pregnancy. Despite this one decision, Gabita acts helpless and thoughtless and is portrayed as very impractical and irresponsible throughout the film. She mentions her parents but it is obvious that she does not want them to know and possibly influence her. This leads the audience to believe that Gabita might have made the decision solely based on her own fears, needs, and hopes, not to mention any consideration that might dominate U.S.–American discussion about whether or not a fetus is a person and has rights. The only indication that she does consider the fetus as human is the fact that she twice asks about its burial. Both arguments are strong in the film, which leaves it to the viewer to determine meaning and draw conclusions.

The film with its scenario of life under a pronatalist dictatorship shows how important it is for the well-being of women to have access to reliable birth control options and safe and legal abortions where they fail. Most Communist countries allowed abortion; in fact, in countries such as the Soviet Union and China abortion was a major part of birth control, as the article in this volume by Shelley Chan also points out. In Romania, however, the population was declining from the 1960s on, and in order to counter this trend the party enforced a pronatalist population policy, "Decree 770" (1966–1967), which made contraception and abortion illegal with very few exceptions. Contraceptives were no longer manufactured in Romania and all import of them stopped. Sex education was non-existent. The expected sharp increase in the birth rate, however, lasted only briefly, and after a year it began to steadily fall again.⁶ These statistics suggest that it took only a year for abortions to move underground, thus leading to many risk factors for women and to criminal activity, as the film portrays.

Abortion in Romania was legalized through a decree of the provisional revolutionary government only days after the 1989 uprising, "and the sudden liberalization gave Romania one of the highest abortion rates in Europe" (Stan and Turcescu 181). Today, abortion is legal in Romania without restriction as to reason up to 14 weeks of gestation ("The World's Abortion Laws Map 2013 Update"). However, in 2003 a modification was added mandating "women must undergo a psychological check-up before having an abortion," and doctors conveyed that this was "meant to convince women to carry the pregnancy to term" (Stan and Turcescu 182). In the post–Communist decade, Romania did not know anti-abortion protests as common in the United States or Ireland. Remarkably, the film was made as such protests first surfaced in 2005 after a synod of the Orthodox Church issued a statement on social issues including abortion (Stan and Turcescu 184, 185). Romanian feminist scholar Mihaela Miroiu reminds us:

> Despite the memory of the lack of reproductive freedom in communist Romania, strong pro-life movements, linked to religious conservative groups, have emerged. Their agenda is the same as in other countries: the banning of the right to abortion. Women's rights and human rights organizations joined hands in the Coalition for Reproductive Rights and, since 2011, have been fighting together for the preservation of women's right to choose [99].

Beyond the discussion of women's and reproductive rights, the strict anti-contraception and anti-abortion policies of Romania have gained notoriety in studies by economists. They claim that the legalization of abortion in the United States led to reduced crime rates 12 to 22 years later when a cohort who would have been born into low socio-economic circumstances would have reached peak crime-age (Donohue and Levitt). Romania was the subject of a counter-study that showed that "children born after the ban on abortions had worse educational and labor market achievements as adults" (Pop-Eleches); a chapter in the popular book *Freakonomics* spread the idea that the abortion ban may have been the reason why the Romanian revolution, largely carried out by the generations born after 1966, was particularly violent (Levitt and Dubner).

Abortion in Mexico, The Crime of Padre Amaro *and* Fresh Start

Mexico is among a large number of countries where since the 1970s contraceptive use has risen sharply and family planning is emphasized by government programs. These changes led to a decrease in fertility which has fallen from nearly seven in 1950 to currently around 2.5 per woman of childbearing age.[7] According to an article by Marcy Bloom in 2007, contraceptive use by married women of reproductive age in Mexico was at 44 percent. The most recent data (no date provided) on "acceso universal a la salud sexual y reproductiva" (universal access to sexual and reproductive health) provided by Mexfam (Fundación Mexicana para la Planificación; Mexican Association for Family Planning), Mexico's leading reproductive and health provider, shows that sterilization ranks as the most common method of birth control in the country, with a percentage of 43.3. The next most common form of birth control is the IUD with a percentage of 17.7, followed by oral contraceptives at 15.3 percent, and the remaining 23.7 percent represented the use of injectable or traditional methods of contraception if any at all. The statistics also show that 20 percent of women from a rural background have an unmet need for contraception in contrast to 9 percent of women living in urban areas. The leading contraceptive method in rural areas remains the drinking of traditional herbal tea believed to have abortifacient properties, or withdrawal. Women in these areas lack modern contraceptive information and services. According to Mexfam, the unmet need for contraception is nearly 27 percent among adolescents and over 21 percent among indigenous women, and adolescent pregnancy rates remain high.

A 2008 study showed that over the prior 30 years, fertility had declined in nearly every country of Latin America, and contraceptive use had risen dramatically, but abortion still remained a common practice among women, though it was still illegal in most countries of the region (Singh and Sedgh). According to Leila Darabi, between the years 1990 and 2006, the number of abortions carried out in Mexico increased by one-third, with numbers shifting from 533,000 to 875,000 (n.p). A 2009 news release reporting the findings of a study conducted by El Colegio de Mexico, the Population Council Mexico Office, and the Guttmacher Institute emphasized that "many abortions in Mexico take place under unsafe conditions, resulting in serious health consequences for women" (Darabi). In particular, "seventeen percent of the Mexican women who obtained abortions in 2006 were treated in public hospitals for complications" (Darabi). The high abortion rate reflects the fact that awareness of reliable contraceptive methods and access to family planning services remain low in rural areas.

The laws covering abortion in Mexico vary among the states and the Federal District. Abortion had been officially deemed a crime in the 1931 penal code, punishable with one to eight years imprisonment for the woman and helper, depending on circumstances. In 2007, abortion became legal in the Federal District (Mexico City) for a wide array of reasons, including the woman's sole desire to not continue the pregnancy. The Grupo de Información en Reproducción Elegida (Information Group on Reproductive Choice) was founded in 1991 and became one of the main driving forces behind legislative change. Their pamphlet explains the eight laws of abortion in Mexico, and more specifically which regions of Mexico uphold these laws.[8] Only in the state of Yucatán is abortion allowed for socioeconomic reasons. Opposed to a staggering 61 percent of the worldwide population that lives in countries in which abortion is allowed due to the sole will of the mother, as previously stated, only in the Federal District of Mexico has this cause allowed a legal abortion within the first 12 weeks of gestation since 2007. The procedure is free of charge at any public health clinic within the district (Gaestel), and the legal abortions carried out here have "almost no complications, providing a sharp contrast to the clandestine procedures that occur in the rest of the country" (Juárez).

One of the reasons for the legal change in the Federal District was a 2003 study which found that nationally complications from "clandestine abortions are the fourth leading cause of maternal death ("Abortion").[9] The media contributed to this public debate and forming of opinions. The Mexican film *El Crimen del Padre Amaro* (*The Crime of Father Amaro*), which ends with a clandestine abortion and the death of a young woman, was released in August of the year 2002 and quickly became a record-selling box office hit, "the highest-grossing Mexican film in its native country" (Munoz), reflecting the enormous interest. The Mexican Catholic Church generated a "massive campaign" against it (De la Mora 176). It caused controversy and protests not only in Mexico but in Latino communities in the United States as well. Not only Mexican clergy but also Catholic bishops in the United States spoke out against watching this film, calling it "morally offensive," due to its sacrilegious nature and negative portrayal of priests (Yarri).

It is remarkable that this film by director Paco del Toro was based on a 19th-century classic (like the musical success *Spring Awakening*), the naturalistic Portuguese novel with the same title, *O Crime do Padre Amaro* (*The Sin of Father Amaro*, 1876), written by José Maria Eça de Queiróz (1845–1900). The approach to adaptation is different from the musical *Spring Awakening* in that it clearly transfers the location to Mexico and several aspects of the plot to today's culture but the gender roles, sexual behavior, lack of contraceptive knowledge, and coping with the pregnancy remain unchanged.[10] The actor Gael García Bernal (born 1978), who has since become an international celebrity, stars in the title role as Amores Perros, addressed as Father Amaro, a good-looking, idealistic young man, newly ordained in priesthood. He arrives for his first assignment in the small rural town of Los Reyes where he is to assist an aging, very popular priest. He quickly becomes disillusioned by the older priest's involvement in drug dealing and his open relationship with a woman. Amaro falls to temptation, becoming secretly involved with a pious young woman named Amelia (Ana Claudia Talancón). When she becomes pregnant, he pressures her to have an abortion in a questionable establishment. She wants to carry the pregnancy to term and suggests starting a new life with her elsewhere, but the "Father" insists on his profession being more important and that his education should not be in vain. She even volunteers to marry a village man to hide their relationship and give the child a legitimate father but the man in question, who was in love with her before, rejects her. The abortion leads to complications and her sudden dramatic death on the way to a hospital. His crime, the film makes very clear, is not his breaking the vow of celibacy, but his urging her to have an abortion, knowing the risk, in order to save his own reputation and career.[11] In the end, he even comes away in the congregation as the one who tried to save her, not her downfall. Amelia wanted to keep the baby, her wishes were not heard, not to speak of her rights.

The film seems to make an argument in favor of access to birth control and safe abortions which would at least have saved the woman's life. It also raises ethical and theological questions on religion and traditions within the Catholic Church beyond the issue of celibacy and the relationship between spirituality and sexuality. Mexico's population is 82.7 percent Roman Catholic, and the Catholic Church "remains an ever-present political force to be reckoned with" (Lori Brown 62). Although church and state are officially separated, only Mexico City, where the PRD (Party of the Democratic Revolution) has been dominant since the late 1990s, has gained a liberal abortion law (and in 2009 the legalization of gay marriage), while in many states the church and PAN (National Action Party) politicians "have become more assertive in introducing religion into the public sphere" (Orvis and Drogus 665).

The legality of abortion, however, does not necessarily make it more accessible. According to Juárez, due to the intense stigma surrounding abortion, many healthcare professionals flat-out refuse to provide abortion even in the rare cases when the procedure is legally protected. Instead of easing access throughout Mexico, the 2007 legislature in Mexico City created a dramatic conservative backlash throughout the rest of the country, and since 2008 "sixteen states have reformed their constitutions to protect life from the point of conception" (Gaestel). Where abortion is illegal, most women are hesitant to report their attempts, although "restricting abortion does not prevent it from happening: despite it being highly legally restricted everywhere except for the Federal District, an estimated one million clandestine abortions were performed in Mexico in 2009" (Juárez). Because of the legal repercussions involved, women are often reluctant to seek out the post-abortion medical attention they need.

The Crime of Padre Amaro was not the only Mexican film to contribute to the debate. Opponents to abortion got their own film later in 2002 which openly centered on Christian beliefs and received support by the Church. *Punto y Aparte* (*Fresh Start*, 2002) tells the story of two teenage women in a Mexican city who get pregnant without any intention, one of them because her boyfriend pressures her to prove her love, and the other by an act of violence. It shows how filmmakers take different stances in debates about reproductive choice. This film has explicit Catholic overtones, following the Catechism which states: "Formal cooperation in an abortion constitutes a grave offense. The Church attaches the canonical penalty of excommunication to this crime against human life" (part 3, section 2, chap. 2, article 5).[12] This film did not receive much critical reception, especially outside of Mexico, and there is no subtitled DVD available. The plot contrasts two young women, Alina from a well-to-do business family and in school, and Miroslava living in a crammed place with her parents, helping her mother with several younger siblings and manual labor in the household. When her parents find out, Miroslava is sent to live with her boyfriend but both he and his mother verbally and physically abuse her until she runs away. She finds a room for herself and a low-paying job. Both young women contemplate abortion. Only the wealthy one consults a doctor, and her boyfriend breaks up with her after she refuses to submit to his wish. Devastated, she later tries an herbal tea from the market. When that has no effect, her girlfriends take her to the hospital, where she gets preferred access instead of waiting in the long line. She probably has the means to convince her doctor that she qualifies for one of the legal reasons to have the abortion. The procedure is surgical, the dilation and evacuation method under general anesthesia, usually performed when the last period was more than 16 weeks ago as opposed to the (vacuum) aspiration method which is used up to 16 weeks.[13] There is also an injection given which kills the fetus before the surgery, although this is not explained. The film is very graphic about it, juxtaposing scenes from the surgery with the birth, the dead fetus with the newborn, the anesthesized woman and the happy mother. The fetus, which the audience sees being slowly put piece by piece, limb by limb, onto a flat surface, was clearly more than 12 weeks old, more like the 19-weeks-old as in the Romanian film. The pregnancy did not appear so advanced at all, nor is it logical that the woman or her doctor would have waited so long with the procedure, but this is clearly not of concern to the filmmaker. The cinematography is aimed at drama and an effect of shock. We don't need to go into details of fetal development here, but during the rapid growth period in weeks 13 to 16 the limbs lengthen and develop clearly, the head grows to a third of the size of the fetus, and fetal movement begins in week 17.[14] Thus, the graphic detail about the abortion is due to a gap or inaccuracy in logical plot development. The film clearly makes a point about the fetus being a human being that is cut up and discarded in an inhumane if not criminal way.

The film reinforces this anti-abortion message in its depiction of the outcomes for both young women. Alina, who had the abortion, clearly is in pain and barely able to walk when she leaves the hospital accompanied by her girlfriends, while Miroslava walks out alone with her baby and takes a bus. Alina breaks down when her mother has a visitor who is happily expecting a baby. She hemorrhages the very next night, is found unconscious and is brought to the hospital where her mother finds out about what happened. She has nightmares about the fetus she now believes she murdered. The rest of the film focuses on how both women cope with the decisions they made. Both have already lost their boyfriends. It is significant that the "selfish" Alina goes through much grief and doubt while the poor but happy single mother, Miroslava, is forgiven and taken back in by her family, finds work and support and above all happiness in the love of her baby. Sharing her story and her love for the baby with her employers, she makes them forgive their own pregnant daughter whom they had thrown out of the house. In the final scene, Miroslava shares her joy in the baby with Alina, leaving the audience with the feeling that Alina will want to be pregnant again. The audience is supposed to admire Miroslava, who grows stronger through the pregnancy. Alina, on the other hand, while having plenty of resources and support to care for a baby, seems selfish and can only be forgiven because of her regret and suffering.

The direction of *Punto y Aparte* is clearly to discourage abortion for ethical and religious reasons, while in the film *El Crimen del Padre Amaro*, as in the original Portuguese novel and also in the play and musical *Spring Awakening*, access to contraception would have saved a young woman's life. The social commentary of *Padre Amaro* is more on the involvement of the church with political corruption, the hypocrisy of celibacy, and the subservient role of women in the Catholic church.

What is clear is that abortion is very much a part of the lives of women in Mexico, and whether sought openly or clandestinely, no film, no matter how negatively the abortion is portrayed, has put a halt to it. To give just one example, in 2007 a woman named Adriana Manzanares was convicted of manslaughter after an alleged abortion, although she insisted that she miscarried naturally, and sentenced to 27 years in jail (Gaestel). Manzanares was exceptionally vulnerable within the legal system—as a native speaker of Tlapaneco, an indigenous language, she was not fluent in Spanish, the language used in court procedures. Although human rights' activists became aware of her case and fought successfully to shorten her sentence, many other women in similar situations of poverty and lack of resources have not been so fortunate (Gaestel).

"I had an abortion" on the Web

Because of its high rate of unintended pregnancies, Mexico was one of the four countries in which emergency contraception was piloted in 1996. Women's organizations in Mexico have campaigned to make it more known among young women. In 2014, Mexico City passed a law that made emergency contraception (the "morning-after pill") free to 12- to 29-year-olds (Vazquez-Mellado). Increasing access to contraception is the priority of health organizations. The hope is that it will truly make stories like those the films discussed above tell a thing of the past. The reality, however, is that between 1990 and 2014 "abortion rates declined significantly in the developed world" while they stagnated in the rest of the world ("Abortion Rates...").

There is another development, however, that has significantly reduced the number of complications and death after self-induced abortions in Mexico and other countries especially in South America where abortion is illegal: Misoprostol, a prostaglandin and common medication treating ulcers and arthritis, is sold over the counter in Mexican pharmacies (Juárez). In the United States, it is known under the brand name Cytotec and requires a prescription. One of the side effects is contraction of the cervical muscles and thus abortion in the early stages of pregnancy up to nine weeks of gestation. This information has spread since the late 1980s in Brazil and has led to an enormous underground phenomenon of self-administered medical abortion that has even extended to Texas and other parts of the United States where funding of clinics that provide abortion services has been cut.[15] Medical studies have investigated its impact on maternal mortality due to abortion (for example, Harper et al.; Wilson, Garcia, and Lara) and argued for putting "Misoprostol in women's hands" as "a harm reduction strategy for unsafe abortion" (Hyman et al.). While its success rate of 80 to 85 percent for inducing abortion is not as reliable as the mifepristone and misoprostol combination in the standard medical abortion, it is widely available[16] and relatively inexpensive, and many women see it as a safe alternative to seeking out a willing medical professional or trying their luck with a coat hanger or other blunt-force abdominal trauma (Hellerstein). The International Women's Health Coalition spreads information about aborting with Misoprostol. Grassroots organizations such as the Dutch Women on Web advocate for and provide access to safe abortions globally. They have set up telephone hotlines and websites informing women how to safely abort with Misoprostol ("Como..."), watched critically by health organizations and researchers (for example Francome).

Twenty-first-century women utilize the Web and social media to spread information and access to safe abortions worldwide, lessening mortality from abortion and the stigma around it. Women also take advantage of technology and new media for telling their personal stories. Film is just one form of media influencing and reflecting popular culture and perceptions of reproductive rights. In 1971, when abortion was still illegal in West Germany, the popular weekly magazine *Stern* launched a campaign in which 374 women from all walks of life including public figures and celebrities admitted to having had an abortion. "Ich habe abgetrieben" ("I have had an abortion") was modeled on a similar campaign in the French *Nouvel Observateur* in April of that year. It had a big impact on the public discourse and initiatives to change the law and is regarded as one of the milestones in the German women's movement (T. Brown 301). Similar initiatives were begun in 1972 by the American *Ms.* magazine and in Poland in the 2000s.

In the early 21st century, women share their abortion stories on the web and on social media. In the fall of 2015, two Californian students, Lindy West and Amelia Bonow, began the twitter movement #ShoutYourAbortion in order to fight the stigma in the United States. It gained attention in the national news when abortion and funding of *Planned Parenthood* clinics was once again a topic of debate in the presidential election campaigns. For example, the *Washington Post* hailed it for "transforming the reproductive rights conversation" (Gibson). The Dutch organization Women on Web may have the largest such interactive site with global reach, "I Had an Abortion," where women from many countries share their stories in many languages, some extremely short, others elaborate, negative as well as positive experiences. Some stories have as much dramatic potential as the ones told in the films mentioned in this essay, others not much more than the statement of the fact. The organization states its goal as "When you participate, you will help to end the systematic shaming of women around the world" ("I Had an Abortion" project). The web offers a voice to ordinary women, democratizing the narration about abortion and providing access to many positive and encouraging stories to women all around the world.

Notes

1. Parts of this essay originated from projects written by Alexandra Cordes (BA Psychology, 2016), Maritza Penida (BA Theater Arts and Italian, 2016), and Cohen Lewis-Hill (Dance and Spanish) in my Honors seminars at the University of Iowa. They deserve praise for their work and thanks for allowing me to incorporate and revise sections of their papers.
2. Over the last decade, American television has included more abortion-related plots as shown by Sisson.
3. Further examples are Claude Chabrol's *Un Affaire de Femmes* (*The Story of Women*, 1988), set in Nazi-occupied France, and *Vera Drake* (directed by Mike Leigh, 2004), set in 1950s England, but both focus on the abortionist and for reasons of volume are omitted here. See for summaries Boswell 181–2.
4. For the extent, mechanisms, and effects of "Controlling Reproduction in Ceausescu's Romania" see the monograph by Kligman.
5. Andrusko, reviewer for the *National Right to Life News* (!), considered the film therefore for the category "The Most Persuasive Anti-Abortion Argument."

6. See the graph "Total Fertility" for Romania, especially 1950 to 2000, generated on the interactive data selection on *World Population Prospects*.

7. See the graph "Total Fertility" for Mexico, generated on the interactive data selection on *World Population Prospects*.

8. In cases of a pregnancy being the result of rape, an abortion is legal in every single territory of Mexico. In cases when a woman has an incomplete miscarriage, abortion is valid in 30 of the 32 Mexican states. Twenty-nine states allow abortions if the pregnancy puts the mother's life at risk, 14 view abortion as legal if the fetus has genetic malformations, 11 if the mother's life is at risk, and 12 for other causes such as the pregnancy being a result of artificial insemination without consent, the woman living in poverty, already has at least three kids, and the woman is in her first 12 weeks of gestation. See also Juárez.

9. See the 2008 Report "In the Supreme Court of Mexico" 3.

10. See Susan Sotelo who examines in detail the film as an adaptation of the novel; Garcia Orso studies the religious aspects.

11. A similar opinion is expressed in the interview by Munoz.

12. Considering birth defects caused by the Zika virus, Pope Francis conceded in early 2016 that "avoiding pregnancy is not an absolute evil" but that "directly procured abortion" was (quoted in Hoffman).

13. There are several websites that provide good information about the surgical procedure options, such as by Planned Parenthood.

14. There are many good websites on fetal development; see for example actual size illustrations in "Review of Medical Embryology" 28.

15. This has led to headlines in 2015 when an Indiana woman was charged for feticide after using the medication; the verdict was overturned in 2016 (see Liss-Schultz).

16. See Owens and Burke.

Works Cited

"Abortion Rates Declined Significantly in the Developed World between 1990 and 2014." News release. *Guttmacher Institute*. Guttmacher Institute, 11 May 2016. Web. 5 Sept. 2016.

Andrusko, Dave. "'The Most Persuasive Anti-Abortion Argument' Ever? (*4 Months, 3 Weeks and 2 Days*)." *National Right to Life News* 35.3 (Mar. 2008): 2. Web. 20 Oct. 2016.

Berrached, Anne Zohra, dir. *24 Wochen*. Perf. Julia Jentsch, Bjarne Mädel. Script Carl Gerber and Berrached. Berlin: zero one film, 2016. Film.

Bloom, Marcy. "Contraception in Mexico." *Rewire.news*. Rewire, 24 Mar. 2007. Web. 20 Oct. 2016.

Boswell, Parley Ann. *Pregnancy in Literature and Film*. Jefferson, NC: McFarland, 2014. Print.

Brown, Lori A. *Contested Spaces: Abortion Clinics, Women's Shelters and Hospitals: Politicizing the Female Body*. 2013. 2nd ed. New York: Routledge, 2016. Print.

Brown, Timothy Scott. *West Germany and the Global Sixties: The Anti-Authoritarian Revolt, 1962–1978*. New York: Cambridge University Press, 2013. Print.

Carrera, Luis Carlos, dir. *The Crime of Father Amaro/ El Crimen Del Padre Amaro*. Perf. Ana Claudia Talancon, Ernesto Gomez Cruz, Sancho Gracia, Gael Garcia Bernal. Sony Pictures Home Entertainment, 2003. DVD.

Catechism of the Catholic Church. Vatican. Citta del Vaticano: Libreria Editrice Vaticana, 1993. Web. 1. Sept. 2016.

Claeys, Vicky, dir. *Droit à l'avortment / Abtreibung—ein Menschenrecht*. Arte, 2015. TV film. *Dailymotion*, 18 Mar. 2015. Web. 21 Mar. 2015.

"Como puedo hacer un aborto con fármacos (Misoprostol, Cytotec)?" *Women on Waves*. Women on Waves, n.d. Web. 30 Sept. 2015.

Corliss, Richard. "How Not to Have an Abortion." *Time*. Time, 1 Feb. 2008. Web. 14 Dec. 2013.

Darabi, Leila. "Despite Being Largely Illegal, Abortion in Mexico Is Far More Prevalent Than in the United States." *Guttmacher Institute*. Guttmacher Institute, 2 Feb. 2009. Web. 16 May 2013.

De la Mora, Sergio. *Cinemachismo: Masculinities and Sexuality in Mexican Film*. Austin: University of Texas Press, 2006. Print.
De Queiróz, José Maria Eça. *The Sin of Father Amaro*. Trans. Nan Flanagan. Aspects of Portugal. Manchester: Carcanet, 1994. Print.
Del Toro, Paco, dir. *Punto y Aparte*. Perf. Evangelina Sosa, Mauricio Islas. Video Mercury Films, 2002. DVD.
"Demographic Policy." *Romania: A Country Study*. Ed. Ronald D. Bachman. *Country Studies US*. GPO for the Library of Congress, Washington, 1989. Web. 20 Oct. 2016.
Diehl, Sarah, dir. *Abortion Democracy: Poland/South Africa*. 2008. Berlin: Sarah Diehl, 2008. DVD.
Donohue, John J. III, and Steven D. Levitt. "The Impact of Legalized Abortion on Crime." *The Quarterly Journal of Economics* 116. 2 (2001): 379–420.
"Facts About Abortion: Worldwide Abortion Statistics." *Guttmacher Institute*. Guttmacher Institute, 26 May 2011. Web. 1 May 2013.
Farber, Stephen. "A Movie Breaks the Abortion Taboo." *The Daily Beast*. The Daily Beast, 10 Apr. 2010. Web. 20 Oct. 2016.
Francome, Colin. *Unsafe Abortion and Women's Health: Change and Liberalization*. Farnham: Ashgate, 2015. Print.
Gaestel, Allyn, and Allison Shelley. "Mexican Women Pay High Price for Country's Rigid Abortion Laws." *The Guardian*. Guardian News and Media, 1 Oct. 2014. Web. 30 Sept. 2015.
Garcia Orso, Luis. "Observer of Everyday Life: Carlos Carrera and *El Crimen Del Padre Amaro* (The Crime of Father Amaro)." *Through a Catholic Lens: Religious Perspectives of Nineteen Film Directors from around the World*. Ed. Peter Malone. Communication, Culture, and Religion Series. Lanham, MD: Rowman & Littlefield, 2007. 97–102. Print.
Gibson, Caitlin. "How #ShoutYourAbortion Is Transforming the Reproductive Rights Conversation." *The Washington Post*. Washington Post, 15 Nov. 2015. Web. 12 Oct. 2016.
Godeanu-Kenworthy, Oana, and Oana Popescu-Sandu. "From Minimalist Representation to Excessive Interpretation: Contextualizing *4 Months, 3 Weeks and 2 Days*." *Journal of European Studies* 44.3 (2014): 225–48. LexisNexis Academic. Web. 20 Oct. 2016.
Harelik, Elizabeth. "'Masculine Stirrings,' 'The Bitch of Living,' and 'Bodily Filth': Representations of Adolescence and Adolescent Sexuality in *Spring Awakening* and Its Adaptations." M.A. thesis, Ohio State University, 2012. *OhioLINK*. Ohio Library and Information Network. Web. 20 Oct. 2016.
Harper, Cynthia, Kelly Blanchard, D. Grossman, J. Henderson, P. Darney. "Reducing Maternal Mortality Due to Abortion: Potential Impact of Misoprostol in Low-resource Settings." *International Journal of Gynecology and Obstetrics* 98 (July 2007): 66–69. Web. 20 Oct. 2016.
Hart, Alys, reporter. *Abortion: Ireland's Guilty Secret*. Producer Shabnam Grewal. BBC documentary, 2015. *YouTube* post, 4 Feb. 2015. Web. 12 Oct. 2016.
Hellerstein, Erica. "The Rise of the DIY Abortion in Texas." *The Atlantic*. The Atlantic Monthly Group, 27 June 2014. Web. 29 Sept. 2015.
Hoffman, Matthew Cullinan. "Pope Francis' Mexico Trip Ends on a Controversial Note." *The Catholic World Report*. Joseph Fessio, 19 Feb. 2016. Web. 8 Sept. 2016.
Hyman, Alyson, Kelly Blanchard, Francine Coeytaux, Daniel Grossman, Alexandra Teixeira. "Misoprostol in Women's Hands: A Harm Reduction Strategy for Unsafe Abortion." *Contraception* 87.2 (2012):128–30. Web. 20 Oct. 2016.
"I Had an Abortion." Project. *Women on Web*. Women on Web (Amsterdam), n. d. Web. 20 Oct. 2016.
"Ich habe abgetrieben." *Stern*, 6 June 1971. Title. Print.
"In the Supreme Court of Mexico. Acción de Inconstitucionalidad. 146/2007." Comments by National Abortion Federation. *Prochoice.org*. National Abortion Federation (Washington, D.C.), 5 Feb. 2008. Web. 20 Oct. 2016.
"In-clinic Abortion Procedures." *Planned Parenthood*. Planned Parenthood Federation of America, 2016. Web. 20 Oct. 2016.

Juárez, Fatima, et al. "Unintended Pregnancy and Induced Abortion in Mexico: Causes and Consequences." *Guttmacher Institute*. Guttmacher Institute, n.d. Web. 30 Sept. 2015.
Kligman, Gail. *The Politics of Duplicity: Controlling Reproduction in Ceausescu's Romania.* Berkeley: University of California Press, 1998. Print.
Levitt, Steven D., and Stephen J. Dubner. *Freakonomics: A Rogue Economist Explores the Hidden Side of Everything.* New York: Harper Perennial, 2005. Print.
Leyes Del Aborto En México. Coyoacán: GIRE, 2008. *Gire.org.* Grupo de Información en Reproducción Elegida (Mexico City), Nov. 2008. Web. 1 May 2013.
Liss-Schultz, Nina. "An Indiana Court Just Said Women Can't Be Jailed for Ending Their Own Pregnancies." *Mother Jones.* Mother Jones and the Foundation for National Progress, 22 July 2016. Web. 20 Oct. 2016.
Mexfam. "Acceso universal a la salud sexual y reproductiva." Fact sheet, n.d. *Mexfam.* Fundación Mexicana para la Planificación (Tlalpan, México), 2015. Web. 20 Oct. 2016.
Miroiu, Mihaela. "On Women, Feminism, and Democracy." *Post-Communist Romania at Twenty-Five: Linking Past, Present, and Future.* Ed. Lavinia Stan and Diane Vancea. Lanham, MD: Lexington, 2015. 87–106. Print.
Mungiu, Cristian, dir. *4 Months, 3 Weeks, and 2 Days / (4 luni, 3 săptămâni și 2 zile).* 2007. IFC Films, 2008. DVD.
Munoz, Lorenz. "Director Deflects Fire and Brimstone: Carlos Carrera's Controversial Film." *The Los Angeles Times,* 15 Nov. 2002: E17. Print.
Orvis, Stephen, and Carol Ann Drogus. *Introducing Comparative Politics: Concepts and Cases in Context.* 3rd ed. Thousand Oaks: CQPress, 2015. Print.
Owens, L., and A. Burke. "Online Availability of Mifepristone and Misoprostol." *Contraception* 90.3 (2014): 309. Web. 20 Oct. 2016.
Pop, Doru. *Romanian New Wave Cinema: An Introduction.* Jefferson, NC: McFarland, 2014. Print.
Pop-Eleches, Cristian. "The Impact of an Abortion Ban on Socioeconomic Outcomes of Children: Evidence from Romania." *Journal of Political Economy* 114.4 (2006): 744–73. Web. 20 Oct. 2016.
"Review of Medical Embryology Book by Ben Pansky." *LifeMap Discovery: Embryonic Development Database.* LifeMap Sciences, 2013. Web. 29 Sept. 2016.
Sater, Steven. Preface. *Spring Awakening.* By Sater and Duncan Sheik. New York: Theatre Communications Group, 2007. Print.
Singh, Susheela, and Gilda Sedgh. "The Relationship of Abortion to Trends in Contraception and Fertility in Brazil, Colombia and Mexico." *Guttmacher Institute.* Guttmacher Institute, Mar. 1997. Web. 1 May 2013.
Sisson, Gretchen, and Katrina Kimport. "Facts and Fictions: Characters Seeking Abortion on American Television, 2005–2014." *Contraception* 93.5 (2016): 446–51. Web. 20 Oct. 2016.
Sotelo, Susan Baker. "Father Amaro's Crime: From the Portuguese Novel to the Mexican Film." *Studies in Honor of Lanin A. Gyurko.* Ed. Ken Hall, Ruth Muñoz-Hjelm, Miguel Méndez. Juan de la Cuesta Hispanic Monographs 32. Newark: Juan de la Cuesta, 2009. 247–61. Print.
Stan, Lavinia, and Lucian Turcescu. *Religion and Politics in Post-Communist Romania.* Oxford: Oxford University Press, 2007. Print.
Vazques-Mellado, Sofia. "Mexico City Passes Law to Give Free Morning-After Pills to 12-Year-Olds." *Lifesitenews,* LifeSite, 20 June, 2014. Web. 20 Oct. 2016.
Wedekind, Frank. *Spring Awakening. A Play.* Trans. Jonathan Franzen. New York: Farrar, Straus and Giroux, 2007. Print.
Whitten, Diana, dir. *Vessel: Abortion in International Waters.* With Rebecca Gomperts. Filmbuff, 2014. DVD.
Wilson, Emma. "*4 Months, 3 Weeks, and 2 Days*: An 'Abortion Movie'?" *Film Quarterly* 61.4 (2008): 18–23. Print.
Wilson, Katherine S., Sandra G. Garcia, Dian Lara, "Misoprostol Use and Its Impact on Measuring Abortion Incidence and Morbidity." Publications. *Guttmacher Institute.* Guttmacher Institute, n. d. Web. 4 Oct. 2016.

"The World's Abortion Laws Map 2013 Update." *The World's Abortion Law*. Center for Reproductive Rights (New York), 2015. PDF. Web. 20 Oct. 2016.
World Population Prospects, the 2015 Revision. United Nations. United Nations Department of Economic and Social Affairs—Population Division, 2015. Web. 12 Oct. 2016.
Yarri, Donna. "The Crime of Father Amaro." Review. *Journal of Religion & Film* 8 (2004). Digital Commons University of Omaha at Nebraska. Web. 15 Sept. 2016.

The Forbidden Pregnancy and the Abandoned Children
On Mo Yan's Fiction About the One-Child Policy and Abortion in China

SHELLEY W. CHAN

Population Policies

Politics and science are two seemingly unrelated fields, yet they are in fact difficult to separate, as science is more often than not politicized in governmental policymaking. As David H. Guston asserts: "Science advising in government is unavoidably political, but we must make a concerted effort to ensure that it is democratic" (Guston). Unfortunately, the process of science advising is not always democratic. Some governments permit "a political agenda to dictate the scientific process" (Finkel 1) and family planning in China is one such case. When people in the United States discuss Planned Parenthood and debate "pro-life" or "pro-choice" beliefs on abortion, they do so largely based on ideological or religious stances, and they can choose to hold whatever position out of their own free will. In China, however, family planning has been a collective and political behavior that is based entirely on the needs of the nation. It is by no means a democratic plan coming from the will of people, who, especially women, have not had a choice for several decades. Since its implementation in the late 1970s, the controversial One-Child Policy has been enforced as a national strategy of paramount importance in China. Whereas it is often assumed to have effectively controlled the rapid increase of China's population over the past three and a half decades, this policy has also caused many social problems, such as gender-specific abortion, infanticide of female babies, sex imbalance, and the emergence of a special group of people, the *shidu* parents who have lost their only child for various reasons after they are past childbearing age. As a result, this policy has been widely discussed and severely criticized abroad.

According to feminist critics, family is never merely a private and personal domain, or more precisely, "the personal is political" (Satz). Since "the state cannot choose not to intervene in families: the only question is how it should intervene and on what basis" (Satz). Science is never above politics in China. Instead, as Susan Greenhalgh suggests, "the party erased the boundary between the social sciences and party politics, making social science part of Marxian ideology/party politics" (48). During the decades of wars in China in the first half of the 20th century, including the war fighting against Japanese invasion as well as the civil war that intensified the last two or three years before the Communists took power in Mainland China, there was indeed a need to replenish the population. In addition, Mao Zedong (1893–1976) firmly believed that population growth would empower the country. As a result, after the establishment of the People's Republic of China in 1949, the population of China grew rapidly largely due to Mao's policy of encouraging childbearing, to an extent that the population situation in China was what Greenhalgh and Edwin Winckler called the "'socialist birth problem': socialist institutions that encouraged more births than they could support" (Greenhalgh and Winckler 46).[1] Susan Greenhalgh provides us with the following picture in her study *Just One Child*:

> In the first decade of the PRC, China's population field, though small, possessed a variety of logics (theories, hypothesis, historical cases) and techniques (for data processing, calculation representation) that could have helped the new government understand the dynamics of population growth, problematize the population issue, and work out the complexities of state planning and policymaking. But China's experts on population would not be allowed to provide those services. Instead, they would find their careers and in some cases also their lives destroyed [47].

Ma Yinchu (1882–1982), a well-known Chinese economist, was one such expert. After examining the trend of population increase under Mao's policy, Ma suggested government control of fertility in his famous essay entitled "New Population Theory" published in 1957. However, "although Ma's essay used the Marxian formulation of 'contradictions' between consumption and accumulation, stressed the 'errors' and 'bankruptcy' of Malthusian theory, and advanced a then-politically correct policy" (Greenhalgh 57), it still suffered from open attacks, as his theory did not match Mao's political ambition of having a bigger population so as to increase productivity to make China surpass the United Kingdom and catch up with the United States. As a result, Ma was removed from the position of the president of Peking University, the most prestigious university in China and the cradle of the May Fourth Movement. Demography thus became a forbidden zone from that moment onward. Not until the 1970s when the government officials woke up to the pressure of population growth did they take Ma Yinchu's population control theory into serious consideration—once again science was under the dictatorship of politics. Finally, in 1979, the One-Child Policy was implemented.

After more than three decades of implementation, besides causing the above-mentioned social problems, the One-Child Policy has also resulted in an aging population that will seriously hinder China's economic development. According to the World Health Organization,

> by 2050, 35% of the population will be 60 years of age or older. That means China will be ... a largely grey-haired society with fewer people available within the workforce to support the cost[ly] health burden of an aging population [which] put[s] additional stresses on [the country]. Pension payouts, rising healthcare costs, cognitive impairment leading to long-term care solutions are all part and parcel of intended or unintended population control policies. At the same time revenue from taxes takes a hit as fewer citizens are available in the workforce [Rosen].

Consequently, in November of 2013, the central government of China lifted the ban for the single-child couples, i.e., if both the husband and the wife were the only child of their original families, they were allowed to have a second child. Following this tentative loosening of restrictions, the One-Child Policy finally came to an end on October 29, 2015: the Chinese Communist Party's 18th Party Congress announced in its Fifth Plenum Communiqué that China would allow all couples to have two children. In other words, they replaced the One-Child Policy with a Two-Child Policy. Like its implementation, the ending of the One-Child Policy is entirely the result of political considerations of the national apparatus. To be precise, what the decision-makers care about is how well a woman's uterus can be used as a tool to serve the state rather than her own well-being. Whether or not to bear children and how many children to bear is a completely personal decision in the private space, but it has been violated by the public space in the name of the nation.

Despite its importance and great impact, the One-Child Policy has not been a frequently explored topic in Chinese literary creations, especially by mainstream writers. In other words, pens do not always write about pills in China, probably due to the highly politically sensitive nature of the subject. Yet there are still writers who try to step into this forbidden zone, and one of them is Mo Yan, the winner of the 2012 Nobel Prize in Literature, who wrote about this topic very early on when he started his writing career in the 1980s.[2] Moreover, it seems that this subject had been haunting him for almost three decades, so much that after writing a few shorter stories on it, he finally produced a full-length novel, *Frog*, in 2009, which is exclusively about the One-Child Policy. While the length of his stories varies, descriptions on themes such as abandoned children, unplanned births, and forced abortions, etc., are detailed and vivid, and some of them are developed fully in the novel, arguably turning it into a political allegory as it may well be interpreted as an implied condemnation of the Tiananmen Square incident on June 4, 1989. Disclosing the novelist's serious criticism, these writings serve as a good source of reference for a reader who revisits the policy after its termination.

One Child and "Abandoned Child"

An early attempt of Mo Yan's writing about the One-Child Policy was his short story "Abandoned Child" published in 1986, less than ten years after the implementation of this policy. The story is about a PLA (People's Liberation Army) officer, the first-person narrator, who found and saved an abandoned female infant from a sunflower field on his way home for a visit. Needless to say, the baby girl became a big burden for the narrator: he could not keep the baby as his parents and wife showed strong displeasure with her. He already had a daughter; everyone in his family was urging him to have a second child in the hope that it would be a son. As an officer, however, the narrator had to follow the One-Child Policy, and therefore he placed himself in a very awkward and tense situation in his family. Neither could he send the baby back to where she was found as she would very likely starve to death. As a result, the narrator decided to find a home for the abandoned infant, but he had no luck at all as no family was willing to adopt a girl. Seeking help from his aunt, an obstetrician working for the clinic in his hometown, the narrator ended up witnessing another baby girl's abandonment in the clinic.

Apparently, the main theme of the story is to criticize the traditional concept of preference for sons over daughters. At the same time, in this early attempt of writing about the One-Child Policy, Mo Yan already demonstrates the impacts that the policy has had on people's lives: girls are unnecessary and unwelcome, even more so than in the old times before Mao Zedong advocated for equality between the sexes. It is true that infanticide of baby girls has been a common practice in Chinese history, especially in rural areas where a male labor force is in great demand. In addition, the Confucian notion of filial piety plays an important role. A couple that has no sons is considered most unfilial, since only male descendants count as carriers of the family line. Whereas women's social positions were raised after 1949, the One-Child Policy has exposed the deep-rooted tradition and obviously increased the cases of "gendercide," i.e., "to abort female foetuses and ensure baby girls don't survive."[3] As a result, there has been a significant decline in female births, and the world is "missing 100 million baby girls" (Hausegger). Sex-selective abortion, baby girl abandonment, and female infanticide have caused a high sex ratio: "Since the onset of the one-child policy, there has been a steady increase in the reported sex ratio, from 1.06 in 1979, to 1.11 in 1988, to 1.17 in 2001. There are marked and well-documented local differences, with ratios of up to 1.3 in rural Anhui, Guangdong, and Qinghai provinces" (Hesketh, Lus and Xing). One of the results of the sexual imbalance is that many male citizens of marriageable age find it difficult to get proper wives. The following episode in Mo Yan's "Abandoned Child" is very disturbing. In the story, when the first-person narrator was trying very hard to find a home for the baby girl, he ran into a childhood classmate who was now in his early thirties. When questioned, this classmate told the narrator that he was still single because "there just aren't enough women to go around" (182). Five days later, this single man approached the narrator "with obvious embarrassment, he said, 'Why not ... why not give me the baby? I'll raise her till she's eighteen.... When she's eighteen ... I'll only be fifty ... and who says I can't...'" (182). Undoubtedly, this request is ridiculous, absurd, and unacceptable to both the narrator and the reader. While the reader is relieved to see the narrator reject the request, he or she is left to question the legitimacy of the policy and its particularly negative impacts on the individuals of the country.

Ironically, although the imbalance of sexes creates a high demand for marriageable women, girls are still given up by parents who want a son. In the story, when the family members of the narrator discovered that the abandoned child was a girl, they showed no surprise at all:

> "It's a girl!" Mother said.
> "If it wasn't, who would be willing to throw it away?" Father said darkly as he banged the bowl of his pipe on the floor [164].

And the narrator sighs sadly, "Girls, girls, unwelcome girls everywhere" (166).

Indeed, the novelist attributes the abandonment of female infants to deep-rooted tradition. His narrator sighs: "On the surface, it appeared that some parents were forced into acts of inhumanity by rigid family planning restrictions. But upon closer examination, I realized that the traditional preference for boys over girls was the real culprit" (172). Then the novelist ends the story with the following remarks: "Doctors and the Township Government can work in concert to force sterilization upon men and women of child-bearing age, but where might we find a wonder drug capable of uprooting and eliminating the petrified notions that cleave to the brains of people in my hometown?" (189). Nevertheless, the serious social problem caused by the high sex ratio that has been accelerated and intensified by the One-Child Policy is inevitably revealed by the story. Ironically, while the criticism of traditional culture treating women as reproduction machines for producing male heirs has become a cliché, now the male narrator has a similar predicament:

Mother, no, everyone in the family, was hoping against hope that my wife and I would produce a son so I could fulfill my responsibilities as a son and a husband. It had become such a powerful demand, accompanying my wife and me without letup over the years, that you could cut the tension with a knife. It was a noxious desire that had begun to poison the mood of everyone in the family; the looks in their eyes tore at my soul like steelyard hooks [164–65].

Here, to fulfill his responsibilities as a son and a husband means to ignore the government rule and to mate with his wife so as to produce a son. But he cannot, as an army officer: "Time and again I was on the verge of laying down my arms and surrendering, but I always stopped myself" (165). He stopped himself simply because the potential son would not be approved by the state due to the One-Child Policy.

"Tunnel" of Triumph

While "Abandoned Child" deals with an unwelcome female life that has already been born, the short story "Didao" ("Tunnel," 1990), another of Mo Yan's attempts to write about the family planning policy in China, describes the resistance to the policy by villagers. Fang Shan was a peasant who already had three daughters, and his wife was pregnant again. In order to avoid a forced abortion, Fang Shan spent six months digging a tunnel under his own house where he could hide his wife when the officials of the Family Planning Committee came. The story described how the officials captured the pregnant women in the village and sent them to the clinic for abortions. They went so far as to tear down the house of a villager with a situation similar to that of Fang Shan: having three girls and a wife that was pregnant with a fourth child. Fang Shan's wife was competing with the officials—she was in labor inside the tunnel when the officials were looking for her and trying to tear down her house as well. Eventually she gave birth to a boy successfully. The story ends with Fang Shan's proud declaration: "A son! A son!... My dear wife, we have won!" (Yan, "Didao" 480; my translation). It is notable that the story is written in a playful and happy tone, which carries a Bakhtinian carnivalesque playfulness that challenges and subverts the authority. When the public space invades the private space, i.e., when the governmental staff deconstructs their home in the name of national interests, Fang Shan's tunnel, an outcome of his wisdom, serves as a sub-private space to reject the invasion. Interestingly, the characters are teased, but none of them is demonized. Nevertheless, the sympathetic attitude of the author is demonstrated by the birth of the baby boy, which is regarded as a victory by the boy's father. Furthermore, despite the light atmosphere of the story, readers who are familiar with revolutionary literature and art will be reminded of a popular film titled

Tunnel Warfare, a film that takes place during the Great Proletarian Cultural Revolution (1966–1976), about a guerrilla in a Chinese village fighting against the Japanese invaders during the War of Resistance against Japan from 1937 to 1945. In the beginning of Mo Yan's story, the tranquility of an early morning was disturbed by the barks of dogs in the village along with villagers' shouting and screaming. Then the alerted Fang Shan jumped down from his bed to check and told his wife: "Here they are!" (471). This is a typical *guizi jincun* ("Jap devil coming into the village," which has become a popular expression describing scenes in those anti–Japanese war films) scene in films such as *Tunnel Warfare*. In fact, the fictional characters, Fang Shan and his wife, mention this famous movie to tease each other when they were hiding in the tunnel. In the disguise of a light and joking writing style, people from the Family Planning Committee, important personas that implement the population policy, are juxtaposed with the most hated and made-fun-of negative characters of the war film—the Japanese invaders.

After Mo Yan won the Nobel Prize in Literature in 2012, debates on his deservedness of the prize flooded the literary field in China and abroad. One of the many accusations is Mo Yan's employment of the revolutionary language and writing style without conscious criticism. The above discussion of "Tunnel" shows that what he does in the story is an alternative kind of residue of the Maoist discourse (MaoSpeak, *Mao wenti*, or *Mao-ti*) left to Mo Yan, which appears to be satirical of the most important national policy of Mao's successors, quite a contrast to Anna Sun's accusation that "Mo Yan's writing is in fact a product of the aesthetic ideologies of Socialist China … an example of a prevailing disease that has been plaguing writers who came of age in what can be called the era of 'Mao-ti,' a particular language and sensibility of writing promoted by Mao in the beginning of the revolution." I argue that Mo Yan is actually "making use of Mao-ti in a poignantly ironical manner," to use Sun's own words when she comments on the writers who have her approval.

Experiments of "Explosions"

As early as 1985, Mo Yan wrote the novella "Explosions," a story about forced abortion. Similar to "Abandoned Child," the first-person narrator also served in the army and had a daughter; his parents and wife also all urged him to have a second child in the hope that it would be a son. As an army officer, the narrator had no choice but to follow the One-Child Policy imposed by the government. Although he used contraceptive measures when he visited home, his wife still managed to get pregnant. After returning to the army, the narrator received a telegram informing him of his wife's unexpected pregnancy and urging him to go home to take care of it. The entire family strongly opposed the abortion, but the narrator insisted on taking his wife to the clinic in which his aunt worked as an obstetrician.

Mo Yan describes the abortion scene in a very special way. Readers may expect reading things such as the woman screaming in pain, family members worrying, doctors and nurses being busy, etc. Indeed, we can find all these in the story, but what makes it unique is the detailed descriptions of the fetus in a woman's abdomen. At this point I borrow a term, "prememory," from Johnnie Gratton. In his studies of Patrick Modiano, the French novelist who won the 2014 Nobel Prize in Literature, Gratton discusses "the idea of a memory that goes back beyond one's own birth," and believes that "it embodies the aspirations of postmemory, but now in the form of a belief that, through what [Marianne] Hirsch calls a 'deep personal connection,' one has somehow inherited or acquired a *pre*memory." Interestingly, "prememory" seems to fit this first person narrator of Mo Yan's novella. When the narrator and his wife were waiting outside the delivery room in which a woman unknown to them was in labor, the narrator imagined that he was the unborn baby, or "remembered" his experience of being an unborn baby: "I ache to become that fetus. I see myself and shudder with terrible, uncontrollable fear..." (Yan, "Explosion" 38). The male narrator suddenly had a tight connection with the woman in labor, to be precise, with the unborn baby inside her body. Whenever the woman tried to exert her utmost, the narrator became the fetus pushing a heavily laden cart up the mountain. When the doctor and nurse urged the laboring woman to push hard, the narrator took it as an order to himself as the fetus to push the cart on a mountain path:

> I am pushing a heavily laden cart up the mountain. The mountain path twists and turns, precipitous. I brace myself, planting my legs firmly, the muscles feel as if they're going to split. I grasp the cart handles in both hands, shut my eyes and grit my teeth. My cheeks straining and puffing, I suck all my pent-up breath into my belly; things go white then black before my eyes, the ends of my hair crackle, the wooden cart handles grow, the sun spins around my head and cries of cicadas fill the air.... The cart wheels roll along by inches. Push! Push hard! Harder! Just a little way now and we'll be at the top.... Put some muscle into it! Yes, that's right, that's right ... oh, no.... I can't make it.... [38].

As if the fetus needed to take a break, the memory of being born was interrupted at the point that the woman fell apart, and the narrative switched back to the present with the narrator being the army officer again, who was waiting outside the room hearing what was happening inside: "The woman in labor falls apart again. Aunt and Nurse An stand to one side panting..." (38). Nevertheless, the officer remained half way staying in his memory, as he felt that the mountain road had left him extremely tired and his muscles were sore: "The precipitous mountain road has left me exhausted. Muscles flaccid, I stand midway up the mountain, imagining the fragrant grass at the top with fear and longing" (38). After a short while, the woman in labor started to work hard again, and the narrator returned to his memory of being the fetus:

> I push the cart up the mountain, each and every muscle slack as a worn-out spring. I'm not straining my muscles, I'm straining my frame, my teeth, my porridge-thick consciousness. The distance from the slope to the mountain top is short and thin as a knife-edge. I feel the brink of the flat summit through the cart-wheels. I smell the raw scent of the wild grass and flowers. The honeybees' golden down-covered bodies attack the gently drifting butterflies like whistling bullets... [40].

When the baby was finally born, the narrator became the officer again: "Good, Aunt shouts. The infant's head, ugly and elongated from the pressure of the birth canal, is bathed in the warm bright atmosphere of the world. Aunt pulls on its arms and the baby, like a round slippery eel, swims out. I feel thoroughly revolted and gratified" (41).

Interestingly, the male narrator makes his "identity related to the body," a female body in labor (Brooks 2). This body, instead of being "at once the subject and object of pleasure," in Peter Brooks' words (1), is at once the subject and object of pain—the physical pain suffered by the laboring body and the psychological pain imagined or remembered by the fetus-narrator-author. It is certainly painful for Mo Yan who shares the experience with the narrator in the story of having his child aborted. Mo Yan confessed to *Der Spiegel* in an interview after he won the Nobel Prize in Literature: "I am guilty.... I even asked my wife to have an abortion for the sake of my own future.... As a father, I have always felt that everybody should have as many children as he likes. As an officer, however, I had to obey the rule which applies to every official: one child, no more. China's population issue is not solved easily. I am sure of one thing only: Nobody must be stopped from having a child by means of violence" (Zand).

Through the switching of the narrator's identity, the tension between the unborn baby as a helpless individual and the One-Child Policy representing the controlling state apparatus is very well displayed. Even though the fetus is not the narrator's own child that is going to be taken away soon, it can represent all the fetuses facing the same fate of being aborted: how much the outside world wants to end his life, and how strong his desire of becoming a real human being to breathe the air of the outside world. That the fetus is not the narrator's own child and is eventually successfully born discloses the author's pain that afflicts him and his willingness to see victory on the child's side. At the same time, the experiment of two diegetic levels of the same first-person narrator whose identity is switching back and forth from the perspective of a man ready to put his unborn baby to death to that of the fetus eager to survive, is an innovative, powerful and effective way to bring a new reading experience to the reader, leaving him or her to ponder fundamental issues such as life and death and placing politics and the interests of the state above human nature and human rights. The "prememory" of the narrator can also be "an imaginative investment and creation," to borrow the words that Marianne Hirsch used to describe "postmemory" (22). In the words of Johnnie Gratton, "the resources of both postmemory and prememory are deployed precisely in order to place oneself in the position of those whose language is lost and whose memory, therefore, is absent." The use of prememory in the birth-giving scene in this story reveals a sense of guilt in the novelist that generates a strong impulse of writing more on this topic, which resulted in his writing of the full-length novel *Frog* in 2009.

Formation of Frog

An accumulation of his thoughts and retrospectives on the One-Child Policy over the prior two decades, *Frog*, the novel that one scholar described as "an anarchic, brutal book about the inhumanity of servants of the Communist state, the inadequacy of Chinese men and the moral vacuum at the heart of post–Mao China" (Lovell), is seen by Mo Yan as a "self-criticism" (Zand). As mentioned above, Mo Yan feels guilty as he asked his wife to abort a baby for the sake of his future. Perhaps by narrating a traumatic past related to his own is a way of healing for him: "literature can be thought of as multi-functional when it comes to traumatic history: as *healing*, in that it restores meaning where it has been destroyed" (Schweiger, emphasis original). Indeed, "even though we have left the 20th century, the 20th century has not yet left us; on the contrary, its historical burden remains with us" (Schweiger). Likewise, even though the Chinese people on the whole and the novelist in particular have left the One-Child Policy behind, the One-Child Policy has not yet left them. That the novel was written before the relaxation of the policy made it a catharsis for the author's painful past, which was a continuous presence for many Chinese citizens. When the one-sided propaganda and official narrative fail to represent the flaws of the policy, or try to black box them, people may "almost naturally turn to literature as an alternative medium through which to convey the meaning of the past" (Schweiger), as "literature, particularly fiction, can be drawn on as a complementary *and* contesting discourse" (Wang 2). Consequently, literature lends the novelist as an individual its healing function, "integrating suppressed voices and painful, forgotten experiences into collective memory," and the result is his creation of *Frog* (Schweiger).

Mo Yan usually likes to set his stories in his own hometown, Northeast Gaomi Township, and *Frog* is no exception. The novel consists of five books in "a one-sided epistolary" structure (Sheehan). Except for the last book, each of the other four books begins with a letter from the first-person narrator, Wan Xiaopao (pen-named Tadpole), to a fictional Japanese writer, Sugitani Akihito, who is modeled on the prototype of Kenzaburo Oe, the winner of the Nobel Prize in Literature in 1994. Book Five is a nine-act play focusing on an absurd and miserable case of a surrogate mother.

The novel is primarily about the life of its female protagonist, Gugu (the pronunciation of the word "aunt" in Chinese), Tadpole's aunt, with a timespan of more than half a century. Gugu was born and raised during the Japanese occupation of China in the Second World War, and had the experience of being captured and imprisoned by the Japanese. After the People's Republic of China was established in 1949, Gugu received education and training to become an outstanding obstetrician in her hometown. This character, i.e., an aunt who works as an obstetrician at a country clinic, also appears in both "Abandoned Child" and "Explosions" as a supporting character. In *Frog*, this main character was described as half angel, half devil. On the one hand, as a brilliant modern obstetrician, she fought against the traditional midwives whose old methods of midwifery were often dangerous to the mothers and babies, and brought thousands of healthy babies into the world in the early stage of the People's Republic when Mao encouraged reproduction. On the other hand, however, as a loyal member of the Communist Party, she faithfully carried out the One-Child Policy after its implementation and committed countless abortions (including late-term). As a result, although she was worshipped as a child-giving goddess earlier, she also conducted many abortions and inductions of labor later in her career, and was therefore condemned as a baby-killing demon. In her remaining years, Gugu no longer showed interest in the family planning policy, especially after two pregnant women died at her hands, one being the wife of her own nephew, the narrator Tadpole. Instead, she indulged her passion for clay dolls—she married an artisan who followed her instructions to make clay dolls to represent the babies she had aborted. The last book, a nine-act play, is largely where the title of the novel comes from: it is about a surrogacy center in the disguise of a bullfrog raising farm, with the major characters from the previous four books appearing in the play.

The title, *Frog*, its original pronunciation *wa* and written as 蛙 in Chinese, has different dimensions of meanings. First of all, it is a homophone to *wa* (娲) in the name of *nüwa* (女娲), the legendary goddess who created human beings and patched up the sky. Second, the frog character *wa* 蛙 is very close to another character *wa* 娃, which means "child" in Chinese: the only difference in pronunciation lies in the tones: the frog character is in the first tone and the child character is in the second tone. Third, frogs are known for being fertile and therefore are totemic animals in certain areas of China, such as Mo Yan's hometown, Northeast Gaomi Township of Shandong Province. Besides, the penname of the narrator, Tadpole, is also symbolic as the shape of a tadpole is suggestive to that of a sperm. Using a fertile totemic animal with the shape of a sperm as a metaphor for a legendary female human creator to whom all children, generation after generation, owe their lives, the novelist suggests that giving birth and having descendants is a law of nature and human rights that needs to be protected and that therefore no political agenda should violate. Furthermore, the nine-act play that concludes the novel is a highly concentrative and intensified social commentary: Chen Mei was a young woman who was seriously disfigured by a big fire at the sweatshop in which she had worked in order to pay off the debt that her parents had owed the government at her birth; her mother was another pregnant woman who died at Gugu's hands. Now Chen Mei worked secretly for a bullfrog farm-surrogacy center as a surrogate mother. Being the surrogate mother of the baby of Tadpole and his second wife, Little Lion, an enthusiastic follower of Gugu, Chen Mei was not only deprived of the right of motherhood, but also exploited and deceived by the surrogacy center as the money for surrogacy was denied. Heavily loaded with social criticism, the play displays the harmful effects of the One-Child Policy that lasted into the commercialized, grotesque post–Mao China, a society filled with endless materialistic desires, in which the bottom line of morality is challenged by greedy blood suckers as well as people of "spiritual homelessness" with "a general sense of non-belonging" (Schweiger).

Besides fictional characters, such as Gugu, some plots and details from Mo Yan's earlier stories also reoccur and are fully developed in the novel. For instance, in "Tunnel," the Family Planning Committee tore down the houses of the families with illegal (in the sense of the One-Child Policy) births and pregnancies as a punishment, including that of Fang Shan's wife. In *Frog*, the threat extends beyond the house of a targeted family to include the neighbors' properties—they made the neighbors put pressure on that family. Gugu shouted loudly to the neighbors:

> All you neighbours of Wang Jinshan, listen carefully. In accordance with special regulations issued by the commune family-planning committee, since Wang Jinshan is shielding his daughter, who is maintaining an illegal pregnancy in defiance of the government, and insulting authorised workers, we will now pull down the houses of his neighbours on all sides. You can go to Wang Jinshan to recoup your losses. If you do not want your houses to be destroyed, now is the time to persuade him to have his daughter come out [150–51].

Increasing the tension between the authorities and the ruled, this more effective way plays tricks on Chinese people's mentality—in a collective culture in which the notion of "face" is critical to interpersonal relationships, people always place their positions in the crowd. Doubtlessly, neighbors are important social relations, and the popular saying that "a close neighbor means more than a distant relative" is known to all. If one gets his innocent neighbors into trouble, it would not only harm the harmonious relationship but also make one lose face, which is one of the things that the Chinese are most reluctant to do. Obviously, the novelist creates smarter officers represented by Gugu in *Frog* who not only used violence but also knew how to manipulate people's way of thinking.

Another example is the abortion surgery of Tadpole's wife. Tadpole's identity and experience are similar to that of the narrator in "Explosions," but his wife was not as lucky as the narrator's wife in the novella. Tadpole, an army officer with a daughter, had to take his pregnant wife to the clinic for an abortion. Mo Yan makes a much bigger scene in the novel when he describes the resistance that Tadpole encountered. Not only his family opposed the abortion, his wife's parents were so determined to keep the baby that they decided to hide their daughter. In the novel, as mentioned above, Gugu was the leader of the Family Planning Committee who delivered the order to tear down the properties of their neighbors. Under such enormous pressure, Tadpole's wife had no choice but to surrender herself to Gugu. Eventually, while the wife of the narrator in "Explosions" survived the abortion surgery, Tadpole's wife died at Gugu's hands during the surgery. The changes in this episode serve to disclose the author's more obvious criticism on forced abortion, and his stronger concern for the wellbeing of pregnant women in China.

As Julia Lovell observes, although Mo Yan "has been attacked both inside and outside China for his collaboration with the Communist literary establishment" since he was awarded the Nobel Prize in Literature in 2012, "readers will find little in 'Frog' ... that validates the society created by the Communist Party." In fact, the sensitive reader may even find this book a harsh criticism that steps in a strictly forbidden zone. Some subtle details invite the reader to make daring interpretations.

As one book reviewer asserts, "*Frog* is a startlingly dramatic book because of its clashes between prospective parents and family planners (read: government abortionists) who truly believe they are doing what is best, not just following orders" (Maslin). Indeed, Gugu was a flesh and blood human being who had no bad intentions. While she strictly followed orders from the Party, she truly believed that she was doing the most correct and the best thing for the country. Yet she was tortured by her own internal conflicts as both a loving woman and a committed party member later in the book. She did not get married until pretty late, deciding to marry a clay doll craftsman. After marriage, she asked her husband to make 2,800 clay dolls for her, each representing one aborted baby who had died because of her; this gesture can be interpreted as an act of her repentance for her former sins. When Tadpole and Little Lion, who had helped Gugu tremendously in the implementation of the One-Child Policy, visited Gugu in her country house, they saw the following scene:

> Gugu pulled the chain on a hundred-watt bulb near the wall, bringing the room into sharp focus. Every window in the three rooms was bricked up. Latticed wooden racks fronted the eastern, southern, and northern walls, each little square occupied by a clay doll.
>
> Gugu placed the doll in her hands into the last square on the wall, then stepped back, lit three sticks of incense on an altar in the centre of the room, fell to her knees, brought her palms together, and muttered prayerfully [309].

Naturally, these squares on the walls remind the reader of the funerary caskets at a crematory.

What is more, Tadpole's fifth letter to Sugitani Akihito has the following remark followed by two questions: "Every child is unique, irreplaceable. Can blood on one's hands never be washed clean? Can a soul entangled in guilt never be free?" One is tempted to ask: whose hands and soul is he referring to? Does the blood merely represent the unborn babies? Most importantly, why is this letter dated June 3, 2009, the eve of the 20th anniversary of the Tiananmen Square incident of June 4, 1989? The letter as a part of the fabrication thus is fictional, and the novelist could have dated it on any of the other 364 days. Why does he choose to date it on that particular day? In Mainland China, the democratic movement in 1989 is still a big taboo, and "June 4" has become a banned phrase. That is why an implicative new date has been invented by netizens in China when they need to mention June 4: May 35. In fact, the army was ordered to open fire at the protesting students after midnight of June 3, and since it was after midnight, it was recorded as June 4. Therefore, dating the letter on June 3 could be at once an indirect and a direct way to signify the tragedy in 1989. As a result, the reader has reasons to read Tadpole's remark and questions in the letter as a mournful speech on the eve of the 20th anniversary of the Tiananmen Square massacre. This is particularly true when we consider that earlier in the story, in his letter to the same Japanese writer that opens Book Three, Tadpole had the following comments when he discussed his wife's death and the responsibility of Gugu with Sugitani Akihito: "Even though she's expressed remorse more frequently in recent years, saying she had blood on her hands, that's history, and history is all about effects, not what caused them" (171). The event that occurred in the summer of 1989 has become history, and it seems that what or who caused it is important to nobody in present-day China that suffers from a "state-sponsored amnesia," as Yan Lianke, another prominent contemporary Chinese writer, puts it.

By the same token, the clay dolls that Aunt asks her husband to make to commemorate all the babies she has aborted could be understood as miniature monuments to the young people and students who lost their lives in Beijing 20 years prior to Tadpole's specially dated letter.

188   Part 4. Abortion Across Cultures

In conclusion, the publication of *Frog*, "a rich and troubling epic—and a very human story" (Maslin) that summarizes and develops Mo Yan's criticism of the One-Child Policy for three decades and eventually evolves into a political allegory, is another example of Mo Yan's speaking up for his fellow Chinese citizens and his eagerness to explore controversial and sensitive topics, such as the One-Child Policy and, at least in the implicit dimension, the biggest political taboo in China today, the June 4 Tiananmen massacre.

Notes

1. In their 2005 book *Governing China's Population*, Greenhalgh and Winckler wrote, "At the meso level of institutions and discourses, the CCP soon encountered a 'socialist birth problem' (our term). As the CCP socialized first urban and then rural areas, it discovered that, by providing modest subsidies to urban areas and by helping secure basic needs in rural areas, socialist institutions tended to encourage more births than socialist institutions could support" (60).

2. Another full-length novel on this topic is *The Dark Road* written by the exile author Ma Jian, which was published in English in 2012.

3. See Haussegger. "Gendercide" is a coined word used in her article with the lead line, "An Inconvenient Truth: Women Are Just Not That Important."

Works Cited

Brooks, Peter. *Body Work: Objects of Desire in Modern Narrative*. Cambridge: Harvard University Press, 1993. Print.

Finkel, Madelon Lubin. *Truth, Lies, and Public Health: How We Are Affected When Science and Politics Collide*. Westport, CT: Praeger, 2007. Print.

Gratton, Johnnie. "Postmemory, Prememory, Paramenory: The Writing of Patrick Modiano." *French Studies* 59.1 (2004): 1–7. ResearchGate. 26 Dec. 2015. Web.

Greenhalgh, Susan. *Just One Child: Science and Policy in Deng's China*. Berkeley: University of California Press, 2008. Print.

Greenhalgh, Susan, and Edwin A. Winckler. *Governing China's Population: From Leninist to Neoliberal Biopolitics*. Stanford: Stanford University Press, 2005. Print.

Guston, David H. "Forget Politicizing Science. Let's Democratize Science!" *Issues in Science and Technology* 21.1 (2004): 25–28. Web.

Haussegger, Virginia. "Acts of shame as girls die." *The Canberra Times*. The Canberra Times, 20 Mar. 2010. Web. 23 Dec. 2015.

Hesketh, Therese, Li Lu, and Zhu Wei Xing. "The Effect of China's One-Child Policy after 25 Years." *The New England Journal of Medicine* 353 (2005):1171–1176. Web. 24 Dec. 2015.

Hirsch, Marianne. *Family Frames: Photography, Narrative and Postmemory*. Cambridge: Harvard University Press, 1997. Print.

Lovell, Julia. "Mo Yan's *Frog*." *New York Times*. New York Times, 6 Feb. 2015. Web. 28 Dec. 2015.

Maslin, Janet. "In Mo Yan's *Frog*, a Chinese Abortionist Embodies State Power." *New York Times*. New York Times, 25 Feb. 2015. Web. 1 Jan. 2016.

Mo Yan. "Abandoned Child." *Shifu, You'll Do Anything for a Laugh*. Trans. Howard Goldblatt. New York: Arcade, 2001. Print.

_____. "Didao" ["Tunnel"]. Mo Yan *wenji*. Vol. 5. *Dao shen piao* [*The Way, the God, and the Whoring*]. Beijing: Zuojia chubanshe, 1995. Print.

_____. "Explosions." Trans. Janice Wickeri. *Explosions and Other Stories*. Ed. Janice Wickeri. Hong Kong: Chinese University of Hong Kong, 1991. Print.

_____. *Frog*. Trans. Howard Goldblatt. New York: Viking, 2014. Print.

Rosen, Len. "Population Tinkering: Why China Abandoned Its One-Child Policy." *The Futurist: A Magazine of Forecasts, Trends, and Ideas About the Future*. World Future Society, 3 Nov. 2015. Web. 22 Dec. 2015.

Satz, Debra. "Feminist Perspectives on Reproduction and the Family." Rev. ed. *Stanford Encyclopedia of Philosophy.* Ed. Edward N. Zalta. Center for the Study of Language and Information (CSLI), Stanford University, Winter 2013. Web. 19 Nov. 2015.
Schweiger, Irmy. "From Representing Trauma to Traumatized Representation: Experiential and Reflective Modes of Narrating the Past." *Frontiers of Literary Studies in China* 9.3 (2015): 345–68. Web. 27 Dec. 2015.
Sheehan, Jason. "Do You Have to Read *Frog*? No, but You Might Want To." Review. *NPR.* NPR, 26 Jan. 2015. Web. 27 Dec. 2015.
Sun, Anna. "The Diseased Language of Mo Yan." Review. *Kenyon Review.* The Kenyon Review, Fall 2012. Web. 26 Nov. 2015.
Wang, David Der-Wei. *The Monster That Is History: History, Violence, and Fictional Writing in Twentieth-Century China.* Berkeley: University of California Press, 2004. Print.
Yan Lianke. "On China's State-Sponsored Amnesia." Opinion. *New York Times.* New York Times, 1 Apr. 2013. Web. 27 June 2014.
Zand, Bernhard. "Nobel Laureate Mo Yan: 'I Am Guilty.'" *Spiegel Online.* Spiegel online, 26 Feb. 2013. Web. 27 Dec. 2015.

Part 5. Legacies

Woman Rebel
Margaret Sanger and American Popular Culture

Beth Widmaier Capo

Evil eugenicist or valiant reformer? Sinner or savior? The name of American birth control activist Margaret Sanger (1879–1966) is often invoked in ongoing debates over reproduction and contraceptive access in America. For many feminists, she was a heroic example of activism, a "woman rebel" and "woman of valor," a "crusader" and a revolutionary.[1] But for many religious and political conservatives she was, and still represents, a racist advocating abortion and a "culture of death." Her name is invoked without context or any nuanced understanding of the history of reproductive rights in America, and she is often quoted out of context.[2] For instance, a 2012 political cartoon by Mike Lester entitled "A Woman's Right to Choose" depicts an angel quoting the Biblical commandment "Thou shalt not kill" into a woman's ear while the devil whispers the quote, misattributed to Sanger, "more children from the fit, less from the unfit—that is the chief issue in birth control" in her other ear.[3] Winning the 2009 Margaret Sanger Award from Planned Parenthood for her support of women's health was used against Hillary Clinton by opponents in her 2016 presidential campaign. Sanger and her legacy loom large in contemporary discussions of reproductive rights.

This essay analyzes the fascinating polarization of Margaret Sanger as cultural icon in American public discourse and popular culture. Sanger is a malleable symbol, useful to various positions in ideological debates that center on judgments of women's reproductive autonomy. Whether the topic is abortion, contraception, sex, eugenics—even Wonder Woman!—Margaret Sanger's name is asserted, her influence implied. Recent biographers have revealed Sanger's complicated and mercurial life (discussed below). Her legacy as a cultural touchstone is equally complex, and understanding its manifestations illuminates contemporary debates on reproductive rights while providing an interesting case study of one symbol across a variety of cultural mediums, including biography, nonfiction, drama, film, TV, fiction, and graphic novels.

Margaret Sanger and the attendant issues her name connotes (reproductive and sexual freedom, women's roles as mothers and political activists) are associated with feminism in popular culture. Of course, there is no singular "feminism" but rather a variety of interests creating contemporary "feminisms." Even within self-proclaimed feminist circles, Sanger is a contested figure. When feminist Gloria Steinem received the Presidential Medal of Freedom in 2013, she said her award was "retroactive in honoring the work of Margaret Sanger."[4] In contrast, Catholic theologian and self-named feminist Angela Franks argues that Sanger is "antithetical to a liberating feminism" (237). As a movement and an ideology, feminism has had a conflicted relationship with the media, which enjoys unparalleled power in shaping public opinion. Consider the damage Rush Limbaugh's creation of the term "Feminazi" still does as its tentacles reach into the minds of today's "I'm not a feminist, but..." generation, or the powerful spectacle of Beyoncé's "feminist" performance at the 2014 MTV Video Music Awards. As young generations are immersed in popular media, academics and others have expressed the fear that they will forget (or never learn) history, and feel an entitlement not grounded in the struggles of (still living) women. This work contributes to critical studies since the 1970s on images of women in the media. As other cultural scholars have noted, audiences do not always respond in the intended way and may interpret texts in surprising and subversive ways.[5]

What the Scholars Say: Biography and Cultural History

The "real" Margaret Sanger was a complex historical figure, both a "sinner" and a "saint." Educational and scholarly projects usually reflect an academic interest in historical context and present Sanger as an important but conflicted social reformer. The Margaret Sanger Papers Project, a historical editing project based at New York University and dedicated to making Sanger's writing available, has since 1985 located, collected, edited, published, and commented on her writing.[6] In addition, a number of well-written print biographies explore the more controversial aspects of Sanger's life, such as her pugnacious personality, her lovers, and her relationship to the eugenic movement. As their titles reveal, they ultimately provide positive judgments: Ellen Chesler's 1992 study names Sanger a *Woman of Valor*, and Jean Baker's 2011 study is subtitled *A Life of Passion*. A similar treatment can be found in documentary films such as the NEH–funded *Margaret Sanger* (1998), which emphasizes the reform crusader (representative lines include "she fought for the right to birth control," "fought the Catholic church," and "reveled in controversy").[7] These documentaries, like the biographies, put Sanger's eugenics and free love in the context of those widespread historical social movements. Several recent cultural studies have appeared on the history of the birth control pill, such as work by Elaine Tyler May and Jonathan Eig.[8] These works, written for a broader reading audience, discuss Sanger's instrumental role in the development of hormonal contraception. May, for instance, depicts Sanger as an "elderly activist in the women's rights movement," a "birth control pioneer" and a "lifelong feminist" who advocated the pill as a necessary component for "women's emancipation" (4, 14, 14, 34). A "feisty socialist and militant feminist," Sanger was also a "romantic" whose beliefs and "words reflected the views of many sex reformers throughout the 1920s and 1930s" (17, 76).

Jonathan Eig's recent study of four individuals involved in the production of the pill, *The Birth of the Pill*, "sexes" up Sanger's life, emphasizing sexual freedom as her motivation. This focus is evident from the book's first page, describing the moment in 1950: "She was an old woman who loved sex and had spent forty years seeking a way to make it better.... She wanted a scientific method of birth control, something magical that would permit a woman to have sex as often as she liked without becoming pregnant" (1). Sanger's vision of the pill was "nothing less than a revolution. No guns or bombs would be involved—only sex, the more the better. Sex without marriage. Sex without children. Sex redesigned, re-engineered, made safe, made limitless, for the pleasure of women" (6). Like other writers mentioned here, Eig contextualizes Sanger in the movements for sexual reform, free love, and eugenics in the early 20th century, but he places sex at the center of Sanger's crusade and comments extensively on her personal sexual activity. He calls her "obsessed," and titles chapter eight "The Socialite and the Sex Maniac," with Katherine McCormick as the socialite. Perhaps to add interest to his study, he situates Sanger as a "sex advocate.... Yet in the grandest sense of all, Sanger's goal had been to make sex better—more pleasurable and loving—and by 1960, she had done just that" (276, 306).

Margaret Sanger also plays a surprisingly large role in Jill Lepore's 2014 historical study *The Secret History of Wonder Woman*, a fact noted by many reviews.[9] The book, a narrative of William Moulton Marston's invention of comic book character Wonder Woman, unearths Sanger's relationship to Marston's lover Olive Byrne and posits that Wonder Woman is, in part, based on Sanger. Any historian of the birth control movement will recognize the name Byrne—Sanger's sister Ethel Byrne was a key part of the early radical movement, undergoing a publicity-inducing hunger strike after her 1916 arrest alongside Sanger for opening a birth control clinic. Lepore integrates the history of Sanger's birth control movement to create context and explain relationships. Marston's wife, Sadie "Betty" Holloway Marston, for instance, was a "New Woman" expecting equality in marriage, a figure made possible in part by Sanger's activism. Margaret Sanger delivered her niece Olive in 1904, and played an important role in Olive's life, including paying her college fees and visiting her throughout her life. Lepore posits that Sanger's belief in free love was manifest by Olive, who lived in a triangular relationship with Marston and his legal wife.

William Moulton Marston himself was greatly influenced by Sanger, in 1937 naming her "as the second-most-important person on the planet (second only to Henry Ford), as measured by 'contributions to humanity'" (187). Lepore also reports that "years later, when Marston hired a young woman named Joyce Hummel to help him write Wonder Woman, Olive Byrne gave Hummel a copy of [Sanger's] *Woman and the New Race*. Read this, she told her, and you'll know everything you need to know about Wonder Woman" (103; see also 247, 218). Like Eig, Lepore makes much of the "kinky" and sexual aspects of Sanger's life.[10] "Sex sells," as the saying goes, and this spin surely sells more books to a general readership shaped by a voyeuristic culture steeped in female sexuality and personal censure of public figures. It also, inevitably, can lead to ad hominem attacks and a distraction from the legacy of Sanger's advocacy for birth control; she can be more easily dismissed as a sex-obsessed radical, devaluing the political, social, and economic contributions of her work. The same dynamic recurs in current discussions of women's reproductive rights, as evidenced by Rush Limbaugh's 2012 comments on Sandra Fluke's testimony on insurance coverage for contraception (Glass).

While most biographies and cultural histories for general audiences provide a contextual treatment of Sanger that is ultimately positive, even with increased attention to her personal life, several exceptions exist. Some scholars have published biographical and cultural studies that focus on oppressive aspects of Sanger's personality and her crusade. One example, which reveals an ideological split between liberal feminists and self-identified conservative feminists, is *Margaret Sanger's Eugenic Legacy* by the above-mentioned Angela Franks. The works outlined in the previous paragraphs are all careful to discuss Sanger's strategic alliance with the popular eugenics movement, balancing quoting her published writing with analysis of her actions and larger cultural beliefs. Ultimately, these writers find Sanger a positive figure. Franks does not follow this pattern. She critiques Sanger's elitism, sex-centeredness, and an "ideology of control" that is, she argues, "antithetical to a liberating feminism" (237). To Franks, birth control is fundamentally eugenic and demeaning to women: "Instead of accepting this radical misogyny, feminism should value the female body as something with a unique dignity" (239). By emphasizing eugenics, Franks interprets Sanger as a negative symbol who sought to control women, akin to the "killer angel" of conservative religious thinkers.[11]

Similarly, while most academic works see the birth control pill as a positive development, a blog-turned-book by Holly Grigg-Spall, *Sweetening the Pill: or How We Got Hooked on Hormonal Birth Control*, condemns it as an addictive drug that enslaves women to patriarchy and capitalism. Sanger is not the real target of Grigg-Spall's work (she is mentioned only four times), but like Franks, she refutes the argument that Sanger and her work, which culminated in the development of the birth control pill, are feminist. Rather, these works see Sanger as a symbol of oppressive ideologies, eugenics and patriarchy.[12]

Screen and Stage: Film, TV and Drama

The history of birth control and its struggle for legality transcend scholarly books and documentaries. Film and television bring the issue to wider public audiences but oversimplify Sanger and her legacy. For instance, the 1994 made-for-TV film *Choices of the Heart: The Margaret Sanger Story* stars an often pained-looking Dana Delany. The film offers a straightforward yet sentimental portrayal and may be judged as melodramatic propaganda by a more skeptical 21st-century viewer. This hagiography portrays Sanger as a loving mother who, through her work as a nurse, becomes an advocate for birth control and fights the tyrannical religious monomaniac Anthony Comstock. Two quotes capture this dynamic: "I am God's warrior," Comstock gasps on his deathbed (1:09:44). Against this masculine religious certitude, Sanger defends her work to her husband in the guise of women's traditional role as caretaker of life, saying in an anguished voice, "I am doing this for my children" (35:22). The narrative voiceover of son Grant describes "Mother's journey," positioning her as a mother in a flattering light, and many scenes depict Sanger loving on her kids while providing unflattering presentations of husband William Sanger and Anthony Comstock. Much is made of the story of Sanger's original impetus, the death of Sadie Sachs from illegal abortion after being denied contraceptive information by a doctor.[13] The film heightens the emotional drama with swelling music counterpointed to the husband weeping, while Sachs' young daughter leans against Sanger as the other hungry, gaunt children enter the room to gaze on their mother's corpse. As she leaves the home, Sanger sags against the wall, her tears mixing with the rain. As the title forecasts, Sanger is making "choices of the heart." By focusing on the early years of 1914 to 1916, the movie avoids Sanger's involvement in the free love and eugenic movements and whitewashes her complicated personality, painting her as a sappy, scrappy fighter for justice. Cartoonist Peter Bagge remarks, in his essay on sources for his own work on Sanger, "In typical Lifetime-channel fashion," *Choices of the Heart* "not only presents her as a martyr and a saint, but unfairly portrays her father and first husband as patriarchal oppressors.... Like, why even go there?" (Bagge "Who's Who"). Indeed, this treatment can be contrasted to documentaries like the NEH-funded *Margaret Sanger* (1998), which depicts Sanger's free love as well as her desire for public attention.

More recently, the period drama *Boardwalk Empire*, an HBO original series which debuted in 2010, used the birth control movement as part of the historical setting of Prohibition Era Atlantic City. In Season 1, an episode entitled "Family Limitation" references Sanger's 1914 publication of that name. The character Margaret, who later becomes the wife of main character Nucky Thompson, is offered a copy of Sanger's "Family Limitation" by a woman at the Temperance League: "This contains useful knowledge," the woman tells her, "I highly recommend that you read it." Although Sanger never appears as a character, she influences the character of Margaret throughout the series. Season 1 shows Margaret douching with Lysol as a birth control method, clearly concerned about preventing pregnancy. In Season 3, Margaret Thompson opens a women's health clinic that offers birth control, much as Sanger did in 1923, and Sanger is explicitly mentioned in a later episode when Margaret receives an issue of Sanger's periodical *The Birth Control Review* in the mail.[14] Margaret Thompson in many ways references Sanger: she is a determined woman horrified by the lengths women will go to to prevent pregnancy, and she works for women's reproductive health despite a lack of support from her husband and the medical community. "While Margaret's feminist activism is a sub-plot," according to Leigh Kolb, it is also "an important, sobering reminder of our history and provides context for much of what propels current conversations on reproduction and women's health." Importantly, Margaret Thompson is an admirable character in a show populated with shady bootleggers, violence, and crime. While men, including her husband, sleep with prostitutes while expecting their wives to procreate, female characters such as Margaret Thompson reveal the real situations faced by women "underneath the surface" of American history and the show's main plots (Kolb).[15]

Similarly, in live staged drama, Monica Byrne's 2012 play *What Every Girl Should Know* invokes Sanger as a saintly figure to four girls in a Catholic Reformatory in 1914 New York City.[16] Images advertising the play picture Sanger in a stained glass window. The title is a reference to a series of articles Sanger published in the socialist newspaper *New York Call* in 1912–1913. In Byrne's play, the girls, age 14–15, have all been sexually molested by different men, including the reformatory priest who hears their confessions. They have read in the newspaper about Sanger's arrest "for distributing obscene material" and adopt her as their patron saint: "I have made an offering, and therefore canonized her, and now she's the patroness of the room," declares one character (25, 35). They toast her by drinking absinthe out of a diaphragm (61). Praying to her for deliverance, they create a "cult of Margaret Sanger," as one review title read (Begley). The ads for this play, as mentioned above, play on iconography of saints by depicting Sanger and the main characters in stained glass. In the end, three of the four girls escape the reformatory, saying, "What does it really mean to follow Margaret Sanger? Do we make up stories or do we live them?" (Byrne 82). Sanger never appears in the play, but she stands as a positive force for female empowerment and the desire for autonomy. And although the play is set in the past, the issue of young women's sexuality and access to contraception are very contemporary.[17] Reviewers such as Hurwitt note the play as "timely" and "pertinent," a connection to contemporary reproductive rights that Byrne intended: "One of the things I realized as I was writing this play is that the life these girls envisioned for themselves, the life they fantasized about themselves, is the life that I am leading now, one century later. And it's because of the efforts of people like Margaret Sanger who believed that women should lead a life of their choosing," she states (Woods).

From Fact to Fiction: Sanger in Novel Form

The publication of Peter Bagge's graphic novel in 2013 was the impetus for my research on Sanger and contemporary popular culture. At the time I was surprised to discover no depictions of Margaret Sanger in contemporary fiction, although there were two recent novels set in the 19th century focused on the history of birth control and abortion, Marge Piercy's *Sex Wars: A Novel of Gilded Age New York* (2005) and Kate Manning's *My Notorious Life* (2013). Since Bagge's work, however, one novel presenting a fictionalized history of Sanger herself, Ellen Feldman's *Terrible Virtue*, and a second graphic novel, Sabrina Jones' *Our Lady of Birth Control: A Cartoonist's Encounter with Margaret Sanger*, have been published.

Ellen Feldman's 2016 *Terrible Virtue* is a historical novel told from the point of view of Sanger herself with some sections offered from other perspectives. The novel is accurate in its historical particulars and typical of the generally positive depictions described above, with plenty of space given to Sanger's conflicted mothering, her lovers, her ambition, and birth control as her passionate cause. "All my life people have been asking me the same question," the Prologue begins. "What made you sacrifice everything, husband, children, a normal life—whatever that's supposed to be—for the cause?" But, she asserts to the reader, "it was not a sacrifice" (1). Throughout the novel the narrator delights in her sexuality and details her exploits without shame, such as early in her marriage when the "house simmered with sex" (24). Feldman incorporates information on birth control as Sanger learns of it, from her early introduction to French Letters (condoms) through her research in Europe. It skillfully addresses the two most common charges against Sanger, abortion and eugenics: in the novel Sanger explains that "contraception was the tool that would make abortion unnecessary" (150) and that, at the time, "eugenics was a reputable science" and "I was hoping the science of eugenics would paste a fig leaf of decency over the naked effrontery of contraception" (243). The novel's value is in providing contemporary readers access to the period and a first-person account of Sanger's strategies in a time when reproductive rights in America are under increasing attack. As reviewer Ann Mayhew notes, "While *Terrible Virtue* suffers from pacing issues, often feeling rushed, Feldman still presents stunning moments that remind us what is at stake when men seek to restrict the bodily autonomy of women."

Two recent graphic biographies also bring Sanger to contemporary audiences. The techniques and tropes of graphic novels, the visual rhetoric they utilize, and their emergence as a popular alternative medium enable a surprisingly complex portrait of Sanger to a new audience.[18] Graphic novels are sustained "visual, narrative mediums" (Wolk 16) that call upon readers to simultaneously interpret text and image.[19] In *Understanding Comics*, Scott McCloud describes cartooning as "a form of amplification through simplification": "When pictures are more abstracted from 'reality,' they require greater levels of perception, more like words" (McCloud 30, 49).[20] Thus, reading a graphic text requires interpretive strategies that engage an awareness of visual cues, the use of color and line, the narrative pacing within and between panels, and other elements in an active reading process. We read a graphic text differently than a written text, our eyes running back over images and words recursively, picking up information as we unconsciously analyze the relationship of word to image, panel to panel, icon to meaning. This also differs from "reading" a film or television show, in that interaction with the book medium allows for interruption and return; although a viewer must relate image and words (along with other cues, such as soundtrack) to interpret film, the viewer cannot easily manipulate the linear sequence created by the director.

In his explanatory essay "Why Sanger?" Peter Bagge states that he wrote *Woman Rebel* to counter the untrue depictions of Sanger in other media, especially the false negative claims made by Internet wingnuts. Bagge is a libertarian political cartoonist and has published cartoons for *Reason* magazine since 2001. His highly accessible graphic biography introduces Sanger, in what he calls a "warts-and-all portrayal," to a younger audience attuned to the visual cues of graphic novels (Bagge "Why Sanger?"). *Woman Rebel* uses Bagge's signature style[21] of caricature, relying on exaggeration rather than realism. This simple, symbolically abstract style engages readers in the rich process of meaning construction more than realistic representations such as photographs. "When you look at a comic book," according to Wolk in *Reading Comics: How Graphic Novels Work and What they Mean*, "you're not seeing either the world or a direct representation of the world; what you're seeing is an interpretation or transformation of the world, with aspects that are exaggerated, adapted, or invented" (20). Bagge's style of "'ugly' cartooning" is "a conscious choice to incorporate a lot of distortion and avoid conventional prettiness" (52). In effect, this style "makes you consider both what you're looking at and what's wrong with it" (58). In *Woman Rebel* everyone is ugly, flailing, and grotesque. The visual shorthand of rubbery limbs, fish lips, knobby knees, overstated facial expressions, and cartooning conventions such as radiating lines and bulging eyes express exaggerated emotion and hyperbolic drama. This style seems fitting for a historical figure like Sanger, remembered for her outsized emotions and determination. For instance, in one panel, depicting Sanger as a young nurse unable by law to give information about birth control to a woman who almost died from a self-induced abortion, Bagge shows Sanger with angrily slanted eyes and gritted teeth, arms akimbo, kicking a can on the pavement as thick black lines of frustration radiate from her head (15). Throughout the biography Bagge exaggerates Sanger's emotional states with contorted facial expressions and physical postures, making her a comedic protagonist.

On occasion Bagge takes the abstraction further, with 40 of the 503 panels using full or partial black silhouettes. For example, in the middle panel of a 3 × 3-grid page depicting the Sadie Sachs story, Sachs and her children are a lumpy black silhouette in the bed, Sanger a dark standing shadow to the left (14). While the silhouettes are recognizably the grotesque bodies of characters, the monochrome palette rests the eye and lets the bright colors of the other panels pop. It also reinforces the tone of this event: the women and children are faceless, literally "in the dark" in their legally enforced ignorance of contraception. The exaggerated style accomplishes the author's objective, to inform and entertain. While the likeness isn't flattering, neither is it degrading, as all figures are drawn in this manner. As one reviewer notes, "Bagge's cartoonish style doesn't debase or demean the subject matter, it helps enliven it" (Mautner). Indeed, "the overblown aesthetic also fits perfectly with the story of a woman who pissed off everyone she knew on a regular basis," as another reviewer remarks (Brown). This treatment is a far cry from the sappy hagiography of *Choices of the Heart*, or the dense prose of written biography, but has a narrative affinity with Lepore's lively take on Wonder Woman.

Another unique aspect of graphic narrative is the pacing constructed via the ratio of words and images, the placement of panels on the page, and the use of white space between panels. Together, these elements provide the spatial and temporal boundaries of the narrative. Bagge's graphic biography covers almost all of Sanger's life, opening with an image of Sanger as a young girl in Corning, New York in the 1880s and ending with an image of an aged and bedridden Sanger in the year of her death, 1966. To fit this all within 72 pages, Bagge constructs crowded pages with a high ratio of text to image. A fast-paced narrative is created by a sequence of discrete panels, showing space, time, and change over both. Jumps in the narrative are signaled by small "scene markers" at the top of some panels, such as "one year after the wedding" and "New York City, 1912" (10, 12). Sanger's aging face, signaled by wrinkles and jowls, and shifts in fashion also cue the rapid advancement of time. As one reviewer noted, this "hectic pace effectively mirrors Sanger's own frantic work ethic" (Mautner). This design has been hailed by reviewers as showing "tremendous concision and vigour" while being "brilliantly economical" (Cooke).

As a graphic biography, Bagge's narrative is accurate of the historical facts, although much like other recent biographers he highlights her personal foibles alongside her political accomplishments. A "Who's Who and What's What" provides additional information, archival photographs, and explanation of primary sources at the end of the book. As Bagge states in his brief "Why Sanger?" essay, "My hardest task was deciding what parts of her life not to include—and so much of it was literally *action-packed* that all I could think of was 'comic book!' whenever I read of her exploits." He titled it "Woman Rebel" in reference to her first short-lived radical periodical and a general description of Sanger's attitude. The narrative engages some points of controversy regarding Sanger's life while eliding others: He explains, "I don't perceive Sanger as some kind of a saint or intend to pass her off as such" ("Why Sanger?"). Text, image, and episode selection show a conscious choice to depict Sanger as imperfect. Bagge follows the lead of biographers in describing Sanger as a flawed parent and wife who loved her children but often ignored them in favor of her work. In one panel, for instance, daughter Peggy says, "Other mommies don't work," and Sanger, with her back turned as she heads out the door, replies, "Yes, well this one does, and you'll just have to get used to it" (12). Bagge also acknowledges ambition, jealousy, and a taste for the limelight as elements of Sanger's personality.

What interpretation of Margaret Sanger does Bagge bring to a wider, younger audience? This graphic biography emphasizes Sanger's involvement in free love and downplays her involvement in the eugenic movement. Like the recent work by Eig and Lepore discussed above, Bagge highlights Sanger's sexual activity, a result perhaps of our contemporary openness if not voyeurism. For instance, Eig writes, "She fell in love with Henry Havelock Ellis, one of the world's preeminent sexual psychologists…. She was a sexy slip of a woman, a redheaded fireball of lust and curiosity, and in Europe she was freer than ever to explore her passions" (41). Hillary Brown seems to be commenting on the emphasis on Sanger's sexual activity when she describes Bagge's work in her review for *Paste Magazine* as "unvarnished in presentation and juicy in content." Bagge allots 18 panels to her relationship with Havelock Ellis and his sexual fetishes, and 16 panels to Sanger literally in bed with H.G. Wells. In one panel Sanger is so enamored of Havelock Ellis she offers to urinate in front of him to satisfy his fetish. In contrast, far fewer panels cover events of historical and personal significance. For instance, there are two panels for her publication *Family Limitation*, nine for her grief at the death of her daughter Peggy, and four for her 1921 world tour. Bagge also downplays proportionally Sanger's involvement with eugenics, allotting three pages overall, two of those pages in a sympathetic portrayal of Sanger's explanation of eugenics in an interview and one page of a 1926 presentation to the women's auxiliary of the Ku Klux Klan. Some of these scenes may be intended as humorous (or, as Cooke writes in her review, "played for laughs") while also offering insight into the state of ignorance Sanger was trying to address. For instance, as Sanger demonstrates how to insert a diaphragm on her plastic gynoplaque, one of the KKK women asks, "What's a vagina?" (Bagge 56). Overall, his portrayal of Sanger may be criticized for lacking dignity in both the graphic style and narrative emphasis, but it is an accurate representation of her virtues and flaws and does not diminish Sanger's accomplishments.

Sabrina Jones' 2016 graphic biography *Our Lady of Birth Control: A Cartoonist's Encounter with Margaret Sanger* is more visually subdued, produced in black and white with bold lines and crowded pages.[22] Like Bagge, the style of the work has been positively reviewed. Kelly writes that the "bold, stark drawing style accentuates Sanger's own boldness and brazen, joyous lack of delicacy." The images, however, are more generic than Bagge's exaggerated style, and Sanger's face is neither particularly accurate nor memorable. This graphic style supports the more positive, less exaggerated treatment of Sanger that the feminist narrative offers, but also makes the work less visually interesting. The title again indicates Sanger as saint, and full page images depicting Sanger in various heroic poses, such as the Statue of Liberty (Jones 100), clearly demonstrate Jones' admiration.

One advantage of *Our Lady of Birth Control* is how it ties Sanger's work to contemporary reproductive rights debates over sex education, abortion, and sexual freedom. Jones inserts herself and her own work for reproductive rights into the text (chapters 7, 16, 19, 22), situating Sanger's historical activism and demonstrating its continued resonance. Like Bagge's *Woman Rebel*, Jones offers a high-speed treatment, breezing quickly through Sanger's early years.

Sanger's neglect of her children (such as panels on pages 70, 83, 97, 117, and 149) and involvement in free love are not ignored, with several panels depicting conversations held in bed with various lovers (pages 75, 82, 93, and 132). However, these panels are fewer proportionally than in Bagge's biography, and offer a less sensational depiction. Jones takes on directly the "False Charges" against Sanger, as chapter 18 is titled, noting the work Sanger did with African American support and putting eugenics into context. Overall, the biography covers less detail of Sanger's life than *Woman Rebel* but situates it more widely in the history of reproductive rights.

While Jones' style is distinct from Bagge, she shares his motivation to create the graphic biography. In an interview, Jones states, "I was intrigued that such a great do-gooder was also quite a bad girl in private" (Kelly). Her work is meant to educate the public in the face of false accusations that taint Sanger's legacy. The work is a feminist tribute, as the introductory note clearly states it is intended to be. This tone carries throughout. "Margaret Sanger stood for the right of all women to control their own bodies, lives and sexuality," Jones writes. "Isn't that what my slanderers are afraid of?" a naked Sanger asks in the accompanying image (142). By depicting it matter-of-factly and without sensation, Jones validates Sanger's sex-positive legacy for contemporary readers still embedded in a slut-shaming culture. She states in an interview, "I hope my stories and images affirm our right to experience sex, love and relationships in whatever form is right for us" (Kelly).

If, as Douglas Wolk argues, "cartooning is, inescapably, a metaphor for the subjectivity of perception," then graphic biographies can shape perceptions of Margaret Sanger for a younger audience (21). The visual rhetoric of these texts reinterpret Sanger as a flawed yet forceful historic personality. Although, as a feminist scholar of literature and history, I shook my head at some of Bagge's and Jones' choices, I must admit that perhaps what has been missing from earlier depictions of Sanger is just this, what one reviewer called "a heckuva lot of fun" (Mautner) and another "a great read, full of politics, sex, controversy, yelling, feminism, and, of course, history" (Brown). In a similar way, Margaret Thompson on *Boardwalk Empire* brings an exciting dramatic version of birth control in American history into contemporary consciousness. Representations of Margaret Sanger in the media have been largely dichotomous, sketching the extremes of divided politics, but recent work by Bagge, Jones, Feldman, Lepore, and others offers fresh influence on the popular imagination in the ongoing debate over Sanger's legacy.

Like any individual, Margaret Sanger was a complicated person who filled many roles as a mother, wife, nurse, lover, friend, activist, and writer. She is invoked most often in today's popular discourse to stake a position on issues of reproductive rights, but this naming reveals more about the flexible act of interpretation than it pinpoints the truth about this mercurial woman and her historical legacy. In July 2012 *Time* magazine named Sanger on its list of "20 Most Influential Americans of All Time." As issues of reproductive rights from abortion access to insurance funding for birth control continue to swirl in America, and as our popular culture dives deeper into exploration and exploitation of sex and sexuality, Margaret Sanger will remain a lightning rod, her name loaded with variant meanings, symbols, and ideologies.

Notes

1. This favorable depiction is evident in several book titles, including Chesler's *Woman of Valor: Margaret Sanger and the Birth Control Movement in America* (1992) and Eig's *The Birth of the Pill: How Four Crusaders Reinvented Sex and Launched a Revolution* (2014). By feminists, she is invoked as an early freedom fighter for reproductive choice, such as in Nicole Glass's article "Sandra Fluke Continues Battle That Margaret Sanger Began."

2. Sanger is often quoted out of context by conservative politicians, such as Representative Christopher H. Smith (R-NJ), as a racist eugenicist ("Food for Thought"); on culture of death see Abbott. A 2009 documentary, *Maafa 21: Black Genocide in 21st Century America*, links Sanger and birth control to slavery, abortion, and "Nazi-style eugenics" (Goldberg). In August 2016, NFL player Ben Watson claimed that "the whole idea with Planned Parenthood and Sanger in the past was to exterminate blacks" (Smith).

3. According to Planned Parenthood, this statement was made "by the editors of *American Medicine* in a review of an article by Margaret Sanger. The editorial from which this appeared, as well as Sanger's article, 'Why Not Birth Control Clinics in America?' were reprinted side-by-side in the May 1919 *Birth Control Review* (Sanger, 1919b)."

4. Shortly afterward the CNS News service, an offshoot of the Media Research Center which claims to be a "balanced" news source fighting the "liberal bias" of most media outlets, ran an article about the award that emphasizes Sanger as an advocate of eugenics and quotes her out of context on eugenics as a way to stop the "unfit" from breeding. The article is couched as objective journalism but through emphasis and omission slants coverage of both Steinem and Sanger negatively. The web article contains a link to Steinem's brief acceptance speech. More explicitly right-wing sites refer to Sanger as "baby murderer" and "Mother of the American Abortion Holocaust," such as the conspiracy-theory anti–Semitic site First Light Forum.

5. For instance, see Hollows.

6. The Project has produced microfilm, published collections, a newsletter, and an excellent online site with the same title.

7. Another example is the documentary *Margaret Sanger: A Public Nuisance* (1992). The PBS documentary *The Pill* (2003) also gives Sanger positive if cursory attention for her role in the invention of the birth control pill.

8. See also Hajo, Rowbotham, and Simmons. Hajo discusses Sanger in the context of the clinic movement: "Under the leadership of Margaret Sanger, the birth control movement was a juggernaut that rapaciously collected any and all rationales defending a woman's right to choose," but Sanger is only a bit-player in the complete text (2). Rowbotham's 2010 *Dreamers of a New Day: Women Who Invented the Twentieth Century* about "rebels and reformers," "dreamers and adventurers" who "criticized" and "subverted" briefly discusses Sanger as a "sex reformer" and "birth controller"; "defiant," "resolved," and "defiantly" "revolutionary" (3, 92). Simmons, in *Making Marriage Modern* (2009), claims that Sanger embodied the sex radicalism of Greenwich Village.

9. In a review of Lepore's book, the *New York Review of Books* printed David Levine's drawing of Sanger bouncing on a diaphragm trampoline while dressed as Wonder Woman.

10. The "kinkiness" has been duly noted by reviewers; Katha Pollitt's review in the *Atlantic*, for instance, is titled "Wonder Woman's Kinky Feminist Roots."

11. Similarly, George Grant's short biography of Margaret Sanger, *Killer Angel*, focuses on her sexuality and her eugenic agenda, comparing her to Hitler.

12. This book was savagely reviewed by Lindsay Beyerstein in *Slate*.
13. Sanger tells the story of "Mrs. Sachs" in both *My Fight for Birth Control* and *The Autobiography of Margaret Sanger*.
14. In episode eight of Season 3, the woman Margaret Thompson saw in the hospital who inspired her to open the clinic admits that she purposefully drank E. Coli infected milk to induce a miscarriage, and she asks for "one of those Dutch caps, that go up here"; throughout the series "men's reactions to birth control and family planning have been venomous" (Kolb).
15. Another period drama, Showtime's *Masters of Sex*, which depicts the lives of sex researchers William Masters and Virginia Johnson, ignores their debt to Sanger, according to the Margaret Sanger Papers Project ("Masters & Johnson & Sanger"). The show debuted in 2013.
16. *What Every Girl Should Know* was commissioned by Little Green Pig Theatrical Concern and premiered at the Cordoba Center for the Arts, Durham, North Carolina, in April 2012.
17. Another recent dramatic work features Margaret Sanger: In August 2014, actress Pamela Daly staged the one-woman show *Sanger*, a play compiled of Sanger's own words. See the website *Sanger: One Woman, One Story*.
18. Graphic novels rose to mainstream acceptance out of the subculture of alternative comics in the last few decades, growing in popularity, critical reception, and audience. According to Wolk, we are currently enjoying a Golden Age of comics, the audience expanding beyond the masculine subculture of comic book geeks (70). They are now a recognized genre of academic study, as evidenced by interdisciplinary journals such as the *International Journal of Comic Art*, *Journal of Graphic Novels and Comics* and *Studies in Comics*.
19. Wolk argues that "comics aren't a genre; they're a *medium*" (11). To read them, one must look at both word and image simultaneously (129). Graphic novels "resist reading" by "reminding readers that they are looking at pictures and are engaged in an intellectual process involving inference, abstraction, conceptualization, recollection, understanding, and pleasure; they are renegotiating a medium with a social history; they are holding a (book) object; and perhaps even that they, themselves, are a material reality" (Joseph 455).
20. Stuart Medley explains the relationship between perception and the degree of realism or abstraction this way: the "continuum—with photographs at one end and abstracted or distilled images at the other—as a means to judge the communicative and instructional potential of pictures as they become more distant from the realistic. Indeed, in experiments intended to determine what kinds of images allow for easy identification of objects, the most realistic image has been persistently demonstrated *not* to be the most communicative" (55). According to Wolk, cartooning's "chief tools are distortion and symbolic abstraction" (120).
21. Wolk explains that "a consistent, aestheticized distortion, combined with the line that establishes that distortion, adds up to a cartoonist's visual style" (123). Bagge's use of caricature makes sense, as his cartoons have a decidedly political slant. As Medley defines it, caricature are "picture whose important details have been exaggerated…. Best known as the province of the political cartoonist" (Medley 65).
22. My treatment here is much more cursory than the extended analysis of Bagge's *Woman Rebel* for two reasons: it was published shortly before the deadline for this piece, whereas Bagge's work was the original spark for my research, and Jones' treatment is less interesting to me personally, both because it lacks the caricature element and layers of analysis that Bagge's visual style offers and because it is more positive in its narrative.

WORKS CITED

Abbot, Matt C. "'The Pill' That Gave Birth to the Culture of Death." *RenewAmerica*, RenewAmerica, 20 Dec. 2014. Web. 16 Aug. 2016.

Bagge, Peter. *Woman Rebel: The Margaret Sanger Story*. Montreal: Drawn & Quarterly, 2013. Print.

Baker, Jean H. *Margaret Sanger: A Life of Passion*. New York: Hill and Wang, 2011. Print.
Begley, Sarah. "The Cult of Margaret Sanger." *The Daily Beast*. The Daily Beast, Nov. 2013. Web. 16 Aug. 2016.
Beyerstein, Lindsay. "The Truth About the Pill." *Slate*. The Slate Group, 3 Sept. 2013. Web. 16 Aug. 2016.
Brown, Hillary. "Woman Rebel: The Margaret Sanger Story by Peter Bagge." *Paste Magazine*. Paste Media Group, 18 Oct. 2013. Web. 16 Aug. 2016.
Byrne, Monica. *What Every Girl Should Know: A Full Length Play*. 2012. MS 1741. Dramatists Play Service, New York.
Chesler, Ellen. *Woman of Valor: Margaret Sanger and the Birth Control Movement in America*. New York: Simon & Schuster, 1992. Print.
Choices of the Heart: The Margaret Sanger Story. Dir. Paul Shapiro. Writ. Matt Dorff. Perf. Dana Delany. 1995. Power Pictures, 2005. DVD.
Cooke, Rachel. "*Woman Rebel: The Margaret Sanger Story* by Peter Bagge—Review." *The Guardian*. Guardian News and Media, 4 Jan. 2014. Web. 16 Aug. 2016.
Eig, Jonathan. *The Birth of the Pill: How Four Crusaders Reinvented Sex and Launched a Revolution*. New York: Norton, 2014. Print.
Feldman, Ellen. *Terrible Virtue*. New York: HarperCollins, 2016. Print.
"Food for Thought." *Margaret Sanger Papers Project Newsletter* 61 (Fall 2012): 7. New York University, 2012. Web. 3 Nov. 2016.
Franks, Angela. *Margaret Sanger's Eugenic Legacy: The Control of Female Fertility*. Jefferson, NC: McFarland, 2005. Print.
Glass, Nicole. "Sandra Fluke Continues Battle That Margaret Sanger Began." *The Huffington Post*. TheHuffingtonPost, 9 Apr. 2012. Web. 16 Aug. 2016.
Goldberg, Michelle. "Awakenings: On Margaret Sanger." *The Nation*. The Nation Company, 7 Feb. 2012. Web. 16 Aug. 2016.
Grant, George. *Killer Angel: A Short Biography of Planned Parenthood's Founder, Margaret Sanger*. Nashville: Cumberland House, 2001. Print.
Grigg-Spall, Holly. *Sweetening the Pill: or How We Got Hooked on Hormonal Birth Control*. Winchester: Zero Books, 2013. Print.
Hajo, Cathy Moran. *Birth Control on Main Street: Organizing Clinics in the United States, 1916–1939*. Urbana: University of Illinois Press, 2010. Print.
Hollows, Joanne. *Feminism, Femininity and Popular Culture*. Manchester: Manchester University Press, 2000. Print.
Hurwitt, Robert. "'What Every Girl Should Know' Review: Teen Rebellion." *SFGate*. Hearst Communications, 15 Sept. 2013. Web. 16 Aug. 2016.
Jones, Sabrina. *Our Lady of Birth Control: A Cartoonist's Encounter with Margaret Sanger*. Berkeley: Soft Skull, 2016. Print.
Joseph, Michael. "Seeing the Visible Book: How Graphic Novels Resist Reading." *Children's Literature Association Quarterly* 37.4 (Winter 2012): 454–67. Print.
Kelly, Kim. "The Amazing Life of Margaret Sanger, 'Our Lady of Birth Control.'" *Salon*. Salon Media Group, 30 July 2016. Web. 16 Aug. 2016.
Kolb, Leigh. "'Boardwalk Empire': Margaret Thompson, Margaret Sanger, and the Cultural Commentary of Historical Fiction." *Bitch Flicks*. Bitch Flicks, 14 Nov. 2012. Web. 16 Aug. 2016.
Lepore, Jill. *The Secret History of Wonder Woman*. New York: Knopf, 2014. Print.
Lester, Mike. "A Woman's Right to Choose." Cartoon. *Cartoonist Group*. The Cartoonist Group, 12 Feb. 2012. Web. 16 Aug. 2016.
Levine, David. "Margaret Sanger." *The New York Review of Books*. NYRev, 20 Nov. 2014. Web. 16 Aug. 2016.
Manning, Kate. *My Notorious Life: A Novel*. New York: Scribner, 2013. Print.
Mautner, Chris. "Woman Rebel: The Margaret Sanger Story by Peter Bagge." *The Comics Journal*. The Comics Journal, 27 Nov. 2013. Web. 16 Aug. 2016.
Margaret Sanger: A Public Nuisance. Dir. Terese Svoboda and Steve Bull. Women Make Movies, 1992. Film.
Margaret Sanger. Dir. Bruce Alfred. Cobblestone Films, 1998. TV documentary film.

Margaret Sanger Papers Project. The Margaret Sanger Papers, New York University, n.d. Web. 16 Aug. 2016.

"Masters & Johnson & Sanger." *Margaret Sanger Papers Project Newsletter,* Fall 2013: 6–7. New York University. Web. 3 Nov. 2016.

May, Elaine Tyler. *America and the Pill: A History of Promise, Peril, and Liberation.* New York: Basic Books, 2010. Print.

Mayhew, Ann. "New Novel 'Terrible Virtue' Tells the Story of Margaret Sanger's Life." *Bitchmedia.* Bitch Media, 25 Apr. 2016. Web. 16 Aug. 2016.

McCloud, Scott. *Understanding Comics: The Invisible Art.* New York: HarperCollins, 1993. Print.

Medley, Stuart. "Discerning Pictures: How We Look at and Understand Images in Comics." *Studies in Comics* 1.1 (2010): 53–70. Print.

Piercy, Marge. *Sex Wars: A Novel of Gilded Age New York.* New York: William Morrow, 2005. Print.

The Pill. Dir. Chana Gazit. PBS American Experience, 2003. Film.

Planned Parenthood of America. "Opposition Claims About Margaret Sanger." Fact Sheet. *Planned Parenthood.* Planned Parenthood Federation of America, Oct. 2004. Web. 16 Aug. 2016.

Pollitt, Katha. "Wonder Woman's Kinky Feminist Roots." *The Atlantic.* The Atlantic Monthly Group, Nov. 2014. 51–56. Print.

Rowbotham, Sheila. *Dreamers of a New Day: Women Who Invented the Twentieth Century.* London: Verso, 2010. Print.

Sanger: One Woman, One Story. Sangerplay.com. Home page. Pamela Daly, n.d. Web. 5 Nov. 2016.

Sanger, Margaret. *The Autobiography of Margaret Sanger.* Mineola, NY: Dover, 1971. Print.

_____. *My Fight for Birth Control.* New York: Farrar & Reinhart, 1931. Print.

Simmons, Christina. *Making Marriage Modern: Women's Sexuality from the Progressive Era to World War II.* Oxford: Oxford University Press, 2009. Print.

Smith, Samuel. "NFL Star Ben Watson: Planned Parenthood Was Created to 'Exterminate Blacks' and 'It's Working.'" *The Christian Post.* The Christian Post, 4 Aug. 2016. Web. 16 Aug. 2016.

Wolk, Douglas. *Reading Comics: How Graphic Novels Work and What They Mean.* Cambridge: Da Capo, 2007. Print.

Woods, Byron. "'What Every Girl Should Know' to Play NYC Fringe Festival." *Indy Week.* Indy Week, 8 July 2013. Web. 16 Aug. 2016.

From the Pill to the Pen to the Pill, Again
Carl Djerassi's Discursive Constructions of Birth Control

WALTER GRÜNZWEIG

The first book-length study of Carl Djerassi's fiction, drama, and autobiography by Ingrid Gehrke carries the German title *Der intellektuelle Polygamist* (2008). "The intellectual polygamist" is a metaphorical formulation the Austrian-American chemist-turned-author liked to use on himself in order to refer to his divided intellectual interest in, on the one hand, the "hard" natural sciences, and, on the other hand, his literary and dramatic works, for which he invented the genres "science-in-literature" and "science-in-fiction."

Already in his evaluation of the public discourses on and the private interests in contraception—*The Politics of Contraception*, published in 1979, and one of the earliest works Djerassi wrote for non-chemists—he used a version of the "intellectual polygamist" metaphor. In this case, however, it referred to his double interest in chemistry itself and his concern with the social and human consequences of birth control, contraception, and the natural sciences at large. Additionally, he believed that his commercial success applying his findings also raised far-reaching social questions. Appropriately toned down from polygamy to bigamy, he referred to himself in this book as "a person, who for over 20 years has lived a bigamous professional life in serving simultaneously as a professor carrying out basic research and as an industrialist who has had to concern himself with finding worldwide applications for laboratory discoveries" (Djerassi, *The Politics of Contraception* 2).

Carl Djerassi at times complained that he was too frequently addressed as the creator of the pill and received too little attention for his achievements in fiction and drama. He therefore particularly cherished the one honorary doctorate (out of dozens) awarded by the *Fakultät* of Cultural Studies at TU Dortmund University for his literary achievements. But for him, this was not an either/or: whether bigamy or polygamy, the central notion of these metaphors, apart from the moral ominousness common to both, was its simultaneity. Djerassi was a scientist who was conscious of the cultural basis and conditioning of the sciences and of the peculiar characteristics of, as he liked to put it, the tribe of natural scientists.

Following the extensive research into Djerassi's literary works for two decades at TU Dortmund University, this essay explores his non-fictional discursive constructions of the pill. It is not surprising that a writer of fiction and dramatic works should be particularly aware of the intellectual, attitudinal, and linguistic dimension or, as he himself called it, the "software" side of the natural science "hardware" (cf. Djerassi, *The Politics of Contraception* 3). I therefore extend our previous explorations of Djerassi's literary *oeuvre*, most notably in a collection of essays resulting from a symposium on his literary work (cf. Grünzweig, *The SciArtist*), to such works as *The Politics of Contraception* (mentioned above), the *Reflections on the 50th Birthday of the Pill*, entitled *This Man's Pill* (2001), and his autobiographies. Djerassi's complex discourses relating to the pill are at times familiar, at times surprising and unusual, but always relevant for the cultural constructions of contraception and the pill as they have unfolded since the 1960s.

The Pill and Its Impact in Autobiographies

The German title of Carl Djerassi's first major autobiography, *The Pill, Pigmy Chimps, and Degas' Horse* (1992), translates as *The Mother of the Pill* (*Die Mutter der Pille*). Over the years, Djerassi developed an extensive field of metaphors explaining the scientific and industrial development of the pill in familial terms (cf. Djerassi, *In Retrospect* 26–36). There is a paternal grandfather, Ludwig Haberlandt, interwar physiologist at the University of Innsbruck, and several potential grandmothers, including Margaret Sanger and Katherine McCormick. As the organic chemist who first synthesized norethindrone, Djerassi argues in *This Man's Pill*: "I played a maternal role in the birth of the Pill, in Mexico City on 15 October 1951" (5), and "Gregory Pincus—despite the uncertainties of paternity generally—deserves to be called a father of the Pill. The initial rabbit experiments by M.C. Chang in Pincus' laboratory clearly were the sperm that fertilized the chemical egg" (59).

This maternal metaphor not only describes the contribution of the organic chemist, but also a specific attitude toward the scientific project as a whole. In various autobiographical texts, Djerassi says that he is often asked whether he is "really the father of the Pill." He calls this a "phallocentric" question (Djerassi, *In Retrospect* 26), observing that "for a new drug to be born there is needed also a mother and frequently also a midwife or an obstetrician" (*The Pill, Pigmy Chimps, and Degas' Horse*, 49).

Starting in the late 1960s, the "pill" became a target of the women's movement and of prominent feminists. In his 1979 book, Djerassi points to the irony "that a radical fringe of well-meaning, affluent, middle-class members of some women's rights movements now condemn the Pill, seemingly without any awareness of how culture-bound their arguments are" (44). He quotes from an anonymous article claiming that behind the pill

> stands the whole power-penis-potency complex (PPP).... Great new wonder drug! It launches a frontal attack on the pituitary gland (fondly known as the master gland of the body—which means that our entire hormonal system is assaulted) and "saves us from pregnancy" in exchange for a two-page long list of side effects ... which our male pharmacist or male doctor threw in the waste basket, and which we will never see [Djerassi, *The Politics of Contraception* 45–46].

In reaction to such criticism, Djerassi consistently explained research in contraception and birth control as focused on women and on women's interests. He emphasized women contributors to the development of the pill, trying to dispel the notion of a "sexual conspiracy focused on an intimate aspect of [women's] sexuality" (Djerassi, *This Man's Pill* 71). Quoting Margaret Sanger's definition of feminism in her 1938 autobiography—namely, that "women should first free themselves from biological slavery, which could best be accomplished through birth control" (Djerassi, *This Man's Pill* 70)—he connected his research not only to the feminist tradition but also to the great emancipatory and liberatory master narratives of the Euro-American Left. There is a utopian dimension in this project emerging from "a universal and individual wish to improve the quality of life" (Djerassi, *This Man's Pill* 94). This is in line with a gendered redefinition of his long years of work as a scientist: "But on a purely personal level, the Pill also had a monumental effect on me. It has changed me from a 'hard' scientist—an organic chemist, driven by scientific curiosity and the scientist's accompanying baggage of ambition, competition, and the desire for peer recognition of which I have written extensively in my novels—to a 'softer' one" (Djerassi, *This Man's Pill* 5). "Softer" means more self-reflexive, more mindful of social consequences, in short, more feminine as analyzed in Gehrke's article on Djerassi's "regendering of the natural sciences." If he were to start his life again, he would have liked to do so as a woman (see Gehrke, "'If something like a next life'"). As this was not likely to happen, he created, in his novels and plays, some of the most impressive and memorable women researchers in contemporary literature.

The "soft" notion of science fits in well with the serendipitous emergence of the pill. Djerassi emphasizes that initially his group was "not focusing on contraception when we developed an oral progestational compound. Our research was undertaken because at that time progesterone was used clinically for treatment of menstrual disorders" (Djerassi, *This Man's Pill* 51), infertility, and even cervical cancer. The fact that the pill was in a way an incidental side-product undercuts the masculine notions of science as planned, rational, and functional. It introduces a sense of playfulness that permeates all of Djerassi's non-fictional writings on science and characterizes many of his most impressive fictional and dramatic scientist protagonists. It also questions notions of scientific competition, a constitutive quality of Djerassi's scientific tribes that women have a hard time penetrating—but eventually do.

The "soft" science metaphor not only highlights the mother but also the family as a system. If one really wanted to get Carl Djerassi mad, one had to use the initial, no longer applied, German designation of the pill, literally anti-baby pill. "Why," he asked furiously, did the German language singularly adopt "the bitter, almost brutal, '*Antibabypille*'? Did the Church preempt this linguistic terrain before the journalists could settle on the pithy '*die Pille*'?" (Djerassi, *This Man's Pill* 67). If, today, most German uses "dropped the pejorative 'anti–Baby' prefix," this also has to do with Djerassi's elaborate presence in German and Austrian media where he always made the point that his invention was a "'pro-baby Pill,' because its ultimate purpose is to assure that every child is a wanted child" (Djerassi, *This Man's Pill* 67). The pill is pro-family.

There is something that connects this specific concern for family to the large number of 20th-century exiles who had to take refuge in foreign countries. Carl Djerassi was an exile from Austria and, together with Arnold Schwarzenegger, who is not an exile, was probably the most important Austrian American in history. (In spite of the age difference, Djerassi has surely already outlived Schwarzenegger in the estimated permanency of his reputation.)

For my argument in this contribution, I want to link Djerassi to another Viennese refugee, Eva Schmidt-Kolmer, ten years Djerassi's senior and a Communist physician who fled from occupied Austria to Great Britain, where she played an important role in the Free Austrian Movement. After the war, she moved to Communist East Germany, where she became the mother of the *Kinderkrippen* in the German Democratic Republic, the ubiquitous socialist day-care centers that took care of babies from early infancy.

When I interviewed Eva Schmidt-Kolmer in the fall of 1989, a few days before the Berlin Wall came down, I was most impressed by the way she linked her exile experience to the *Krippen* project. She, who had been torn from her family and whose mother was killed in the Maly Trostinets concentration camp, decided that the state had an obligation to ensure the well-being of children and to support familial responsibilities for the next generation.

Carl Djerassi's ideological orientation was, of course, very different, but there is an affinity. It is conspicuous that the pill was a project that emerged from Mexican hormone research and that was conducted by Jewish refugees. Djerassi's colleague at the Mexican firm of Syntex was George Rosenkranz, a Hungarian Jewish refugee, and he was only one of many refugee European scientists who brought relevant knowledge to the New World. While I am not trying to establish a direct connection between Djerassi's pioneering research in Mexico and his status as an exile, there are indirect connections that certainly lead to his overriding concern with family especially in the context of his later discussions of the pill.

I have elsewhere explained that Djerassi's exile experience freed him from traditional patterns of thinking, thus liberating his capacity for innovation and enabling his extraordinary scientific discoveries (Grünzweig, "Carl Djerassi" 250). Djerassi himself has repeatedly explained, with bitter irony, that if "I hadn't been born a Jew, I wouldn't have left Vienna and would doubtless have ended up as an Austrian physician—possibly even one voting for Kurt Waldheim" (Djerassi, *In Retrospect* 151). Here, however, I want to point out a different legacy of the exile, a mixture of personal, familial experience in a humanistic framework, which links his main scientific achievement to the notion of improving—rather than destroying, as many Catholics, and others had it in connection to the pill—the family.

The researcher who has had a bigamous relationship with the pharmaceutical industry for such a long time can hardly be expected to be a Marxist revolutionary, and yet I have found Djerassi's constructions of the pill surprisingly anti-capitalist, or better: anti-corporatist. To begin with, next to using the word "Anti-Babypille," the most effective way to enrage Djerassi was to hint at the possibility "that every contraceptive pill swallowed by the hundred million women who annually use the Pill globally leaves some financial residue in my pocket" (Djerassi, *In Retrospect* 105). Apart from the fact that that was not the way the contract and business with Syntex was set up, Djerassi had always seen his own wealth as an opportunity and a responsibility to promote causes, most impressively manifested in the Djerassi Resident Artist program, which has become one of the major and most eminent artistic residency programs internationally.

But what I appreciate just as much is his criticism of the profit motives of international corporations. Already in the 1980s, Djerassi stated: "Of the eight largest pharmaceutical companies in the world, only one still conducts some contraceptive R&D, and that of the 'me-too' variety; and only one of the top eight sells contraceptive drugs or devices" (Djerassi, *This Man's Pill* 76). The reason for this development is a change in markets in which the affluent industrial world is very much implicated:

The pharmaceutical market, which has changed dramatically during the past decade, has spoken. It now focuses on blockbuster drugs dealing with diseases of aging or deterioration in the increasingly geriatric populations of affluent Japan, North America, and Europe. The needs of poor pediatric societies of Latin America, Asia and Africa cannot be met by market forces alone, which have a very poor track record where poverty is concerned [Djerassi, *In Retrospect* 76–77].

In his criticism of the corporate profit motive that masses of consumers actively contribute to—this being one of the many truly "bitter pills" his books deal with—Djerassi was very much to the point. In weighing options for contraception, he had always considered the specific situation of women in the developing world (and, in fact, accused representatives of the Western women's movement of failing to take this into consideration). Given the profit-driven research focus of major corporations on the diseases of the elderly, the complicity of the privileged "geriatric" part of the world provided him with an impressive example of the collective responsibility of developed nations for the misery of the developing world.

Connected to this critique of democratic capitalism was an awareness of the cultural differences in the area of contraception. Djerassi's move to Mexico upon invitation of Syntex was, of course, primarily a career move. He may have remembered that in 1938 Mexico was the only nation that filed official protest against Hitler's annexation of Austria with the League of Nations in Geneva. However, what seems to be important in hindsight is the fact that "Syntex was the first and possibly the only significant example of important research in such a highly competitive field being conducted in a developing country" (Djerassi, *This Man's Pill* 57–58). Djerassi proudly stated that "in a short while tiny Syntex broke the international hormone cartel.... By the late 1950s, over half the world's supply of steroid hormones originated from Mexico" (34). Although Djerassi became rather enervated when somebody set "chemical" food products against "natural" foods, the connection of his invention with aboriginal Mexican plants, the inedible yam, seems to have had a symbolic quality in addition to the chemical one. There had always been a tendency to "naturalize" contraceptive research, starting with the Austrian Ludwig Haberlandt, who had called periods of infertility "hormonal temporary stabilization" (Djerassi, *In Retrospect* 16).

Safe contraception fundamentally changed human relationships. The pill reduced the risk that sex would lead to pregnancy virtually to zero, thus turning it into pure enjoyment. Sex was liberated from its servitude to the procreative function and became an act in its own right, an end in itself. By grounding its *raison d'être* purely and exclusively in the pleasure principle, sexuality becomes aestheticized. "Man," Djerassi explained in loving detail, "is the sexiest animal on earth." "Among the millions of species, only we have sex for fun. Only we—and perhaps a couple of others such as the Pigmy

Chimp (Bonobo)—are able and willing to have sex 365 days of the year" (Djerassi, *This Man's Pill* 119).

So, the notion of sexuality as an end in itself is already grounded in nature's rejection of the seasonal regulation of sexuality. It continues, another aesthetic dimension, with the "extraordinary size (in relation to body size) of a man's erect penis" (Djerassi, *This Man's Pill* 119). "Why," Djerassi asked, "should we need such an absurdly thick, swollen object to deliver sperm into a woman's vagina—ostensibly the only biologically significant, *reproductive* function of a penis? Clearly, we do not. A very thin, pipette-like structure would do equally well" (119–20).

Thus the pill in fact fulfills the obvious human destiny to turn sexuality into aesthetics in its own right. Never mind that another theoretician of birth control in literature, Norman Mailer, has it exactly the other way around. Mailer *opposes* contraception because it strips away the existential quality of sexuality—the possibility of conception and pregnancy. In a 1968 *Playboy* interview, he stated:

> The problem of birth control is the same as all of the other problems in our technological society. They're all part of the same damn problem; something is insulating us away from our existence.... Since primitive man lived in relation to his life that was more biological—which is to say, he felt everything around him with his own body—he was therefore more intelligent *physically* than he is today .... In our modern life, on the other hand, the body is so deadened at its sexual center by contraceptives and pills that we no longer can afford to be as selective as we used to be [Lucid 287].

The comparison makes Carl Djerassi, born in the same year as Norman Mailer, seem much more politically progressive, although the seemingly polar opposites are probably two sides of the same coin. Whereas Djerassi aestheticizes the sexual act, Mailer focuses on the thrill of the possible consequences. The difference lies in the fact that Mailer looks at the act purely from a male point of view, whereas Djerassi takes a relational as well as female perspective—which comes as no surprise given his frequent self-definition as a male feminist.

Total separation of sex and procreation, however, also requires the "extreme counterpart" of birth control—namely, "to create new life *without sexual intercourse*" (Djerassi, *In Retrospect* 121). This is where the pill somewhat paradoxically meets with the new high-tech possibilities from in-vitro fertilization to Intra-cytoplasmic sperm injection (ICSI), a technology not only compensating for low sperm counts but even for the lack of any mature sperm whatsoever. If the separation of sex and procreation in the case of the pill resulted in pure and unalleviated sexuality, here it results in pure parenthood, allowing couples—through private sperm and egg banks—to postpone parenthood until the fulfillment of their professional careers.

All in all, the discursive constructions of contraception, and specifically the pill, in Djerassi's non-fictional, "soft," non-chemist writings form an unorthodox story of progress. It leads from the liberation of women from biological slavery (which, in addition to freedom, also allows for their enjoyment of sex) to political emancipation (especially in underdeveloped nations) all the way to sexuality as an end in itself as well as a central and defining feature of human life.

From a European, especially Austrian or German, point of view, one can view this narrative as part of a social-democratic story of progress including a rather un–American aspect—namely, that of planning, as in family planning (cf. Djerassi, *This Man's Pill* 17). From an American perspective, it is another version of the many American utopias promising perfection on the basis of the emancipation of the body, starting, in the modern sense, with Walt Whitman. Notions of the massiveness of the phenomenon—such as the facts that 80 percent of all women born after 1945 have used the pill and that it has become central to the American social "fabric"—are specifically American interpretations. That Djerassi's conceptual narratives fit both worlds is another confirmation of his status as a transatlantic visionary and thinker.

Demographic Trends and an Austrian Media Controversy

In the final decade of his life following the death of his wife Diane Middlebrook, Djerassi spent extended periods of time in his native city of Vienna and was confronted with the increasingly xenophobic attitude of certain segments of the population in view of the increasing immigration to Austria and Europe at large. Reacting to gains by the Austrian right-wing Freedom Party, he wrote an article which I translated for the leading Austrian daily, *Der Standard*. The article, the original English text of which I unfortunately lost, is included below in a re-retranslation. It shows the wide perspective Djerassi took of demographic questions by pointing out that the declining population in Europe could only be compensated by increased migration.

When Austrian Cardinal Schönborn referred to this article in an interview, "a veritable explosion of articles appeared in Europe and the USA, primarily under the aegis of Catholic press services, with headlines such as "Pill inventor slams Pill" or "Co-inventor of Birth Control Pill Now Calls It a Catastrophe" (quoted in Djerassi correspondence). In the appendix, I am including, in addition to the re-translated article, the original version of Djerassi's "Rebuttal" which he sent me in early 2009, and a small translated selection of—at times outrageous, at times funny—online comments on the article that were posted in the hours and days following the publication of the article. Of course, the latter include the fallacy of creating a causal relationship between birth control and demographic developments which

Djerassi rejects in his "Rebuttal." More significantly, however, they demonstrate the larger socio-cultural context in which the "co-inventor of the pill" had been operating—and battling—until the very end of his life.

WORKS CITED

Djerassi, Carl. "A Rebuttal to the Catholic Press articles About Carl Djerassi." 2009. (Ms. in a personal communication to author.)
_____. *Die Mutter der Pille. Eine Autobiographie.* Trans. Ursula-Maria Mössner. Zürich: Haffmans, 1992. Print.
_____. *In Retrospect: From the Pill to the Pen.* London: Imperial College Press, 2015. Print.
_____. *The Pill, Pigmy Chimps, and Degas' Horse.* New York: Basic Books, 1992. Print.
_____. *The Politics of Contraception.* New York: W.W. Norton, 1979. Print.
_____. *This Man's Pill: Reflections on the 50th Birthday of the Pill.* Oxford: Oxford University Press, 2001. Print.
_____. "Warum wir bald sehr alt ausschauen." Trans. Walter Grünzweig. *Der Standard*, 13 Dec. 2008. Web. 13 Oct. 2016.
Gehrke, Ingrid. *Der intellektuelle Polygamist. Carl Djerassis Grenzgänge in Autobiographie, Roman und Drama.* Münster: Lit, 2008. Print.
_____. "'If something like a next life exists, yes, I'd rather be a woman': Carl Djerassi's Science-in Fiction and the Regendering of the Natural Sciences." *The SciArtist: Carl Djerassi's Science-in-Literature in Transatlantic and Interdisciplinary Contexts.* Ed. Walter Grünzweig. Münster: Lit, 2012. 135–43. Print.
Grünzweig, Walter. "Carl Djerassi, Vater der Pille. Ein Jude als intellektueller Bigamist." *Das Jüdische Echo* 48, Oct. 1999, 244–50. Print.
_____, ed. *The SciArtist: Carl Djerassi's Science-in-Literature in Transatlantic and Interdisciplinary Contexts.* Münster: Lit, 2012. Print.
Lucid, Robert F. *Norman Mailer: The Man and His Work.* Boston: Little, Brown, 1971. Print.

APPENDIX A: "WHY WE ARE GOING TO LOOK REALLY OLD SOON," by CARL DJERASSI
(translated by Walter Grünzweig; originally published in Der Standard *[Vienna], December 13, 2008)*

The results of the last Austrian elections have brought great successes for political parties with a xenophobic bent. Even though the success of these parties cannot only be explained with xenophobic motivations, the strengthening of these tendencies has greatly surprised me, not only for moral reasons but because they reflect a simple-minded attitude. Some 30 percent of the population of this country have obviously received their training in schools which teach nothing on the demographic situation of our present world.

These Austrians still suffer from the illusion that their small country is not situated in the heart of Europe but on an island, where God permits them to live independently from the rest of the world and to enjoy their Schnitzel. Still more alarming is the observation that the majority of the voters of these xenophobic parties are below the age of 30. My contribution is designed as a wake-up call for these people.

I want to start with the realistic fact that in the future, sexuality and reproduction will be largely separated from each other. In Catholic Austria, in a country with an average of 1.4 children per family, this separation has essentially already occurred. Most Austrians enjoy sex without wanting to get a child—or without actually getting one. Since a country needs approximately 2.1 children per family merely to maintain the demographic status quo, it is obvious the population of a 1.4 children country will shrink in the course of this century. Instead of shocking the naive voters of xenophobic parties with a concrete horror scenario in Austria, I want to start with the situation of a neighboring country, which speaks more or less the same language, but which is ten times larger, namely Germany.

Both countries, just like most of the others in Europe, suffer from a serious illness, namely the rapid ageing of their populations, which can best be quantitatively expressed in the percentage of the population older than 65 years of age. In this respect, Germany is very ill because out of 195 nations in the world, it occupies the fourth place among the most aged. With "only" 16 percent of her population above 65, Austria is the 13th most aged country of these 195—not much different from fatally ill Germany. Of course, the population not only ages, it also shrinks. Estimates assume that Germany would need some 200,000 new immigrants annually in order to maintain its present population level.

What would happen if such a country had no immigration at all? Let us take Bulgaria, approximately the same size as Austria, with some 17 percent of the population above 65 years of age. According to forecasts, the population there will have shrunk by 34 percent compared to 2007! At this point in time, Austria already has more inhabitants above 65 than children below 15. In Japan, the second-oldest country in the world, it is estimated that 40 percent of the population in the next 50 years will be 65 years or above. One does not have to be an economist or a demographer to understand, that an impossible situation will arise in many countries in the course of this century. There will no longer be sufficient young employees to do the necessary social work and pay for retirement benefits.

This dramatic development can be demonstrated using demographic diagrams which show a demographic "belly" in the age group from 30 to 55 years of age, which in the course of the next 30 years will move toward a demographic "head." In this respect, Austria looks exactly like Germany, with the one difference that Germany is a giant and Austria a dwarf. Which means that the structure of the population of these two countries by the end of the century will look as bizarre as Sun City, Arizona.

This demographic obesity is even more threatening than the epidemic of obese people one meets with everywhere in America and Europe today. While individuals can actively fight their obesity through a diet or more physical activity, demographic obesity is much more threatening: It moves inevitably from the stomach to the head so that within half a century our demographic national body will consist of a giant set on very thin legs. It will take many decades to solve these problems with their complicated economic, political and social consequences. If we want to find a solution or at least slowdown of this process, we need to start in the next few years. As in the case of the environmental and climate crisis, we cannot afford to wait.

The solution is quite obvious: Either the majority of young Austrians immediately opts for at least three children per family (which is rather unlikely), or the country supports the arrival of young, capable migrants from other countries which are ready to assimilate culturally within a generation. Especially as this latter option is so realistic, the recent election results cannot be called anything but simple-minded.

Unless the new voters of anti-immigration parties do not immediately decide to start large families, the xenophobic rejection of an intelligent immigration policy is a recipe for national suicide. Since I am describing the election results as "simple-minded," I will try to explain what an "intelligent" immigration strategy might look like.

As immigration must be at least part of the solution, I would suggest to change to an active immigration policy, i.e., attempt to bring migrants to Austria who cannot only assimilate to the life style but to contribute to the economic and social development of the country. Eastern Europeans, who of course would have the best potential for cultural assimilation, have as few children as Germany and Austria and can hardly contribute to the solution of the demographic catastrophe.

India, Nigeria (mostly its Catholic sections) and Brazil seem to be more suitable to me. In all likelihood, these three countries will occupy places one, six and seven in the global population ranking in 2050. These three countries have many universities with many young people who are interested in migrating to Europe. The central problem of migrating to Germany and Austria is, of course, the language as German is not sufficiently taught abroad.

To study German only after immigrating would be a major hurdle. I would suggest that an Austrian organization, similar to the German Goethe Institute, establishes language and cultural centers in some of the most important university towns of these countries (e.g., Hyderabad, Bangalore, Ibadan, Ile-Ife, São Paulo and especially Rio Grande do Sul where there are many Germans) offering intensive language programs.

This would be a comparatively cheap experiment which would show whether Austria would be an attractive destination for younger immigrants wanting to start their families there. This strategy might enable a cultural and economic integration which would differ significantly from the situation of "guest workers" of earlier decades. The advantages of such an active immigration policy for educated immigrants has been proven in the United States since the 1960s when the very restrictive quotas for immigrants from Asia were dramatically increased for well-educated individuals.

In some American high-tech areas and at elite universities such as Stanford, more than a third of the researchers and students are foreigners; mostly from Asia. The United States are one of the few developed countries whose population is still growing rather than decreasing. The only reason for this trend is immigration, especially from Latin America. In 2050, there will be more Californians with a Latin American background than a European one.

As an American in Vienna—or an American Viennese—I consider it my obligation to make explicit these implications of the last elections, which are hardly ever addressed.

APPENDIX B: ONLINE COMMENTS TO DJERASSI'S ARTICLE

- Better old than Muslim!
- Oh dear! The birth rate in Austria and Germany will come back to normal eventually. We don't need immigrants, whether from India or from Nigeria. I love my Schnitzel!
- Where does it say that we are not supposed to shrink—there used to be fewer of us in the past a hundred years ago, there were only 1.65 billion people in this world and it seems to have worked—I would say not much worse than today, especially when you think of the natural resources or generally of the environment and Mother Nature. What if Austria instead of 8.348 millions only had 6 millions (1910–6.6 millions). I am certain nobody would be worse off than today.
- Djerassi's fight against xenophobia is a good one. I still don't agree with him. I would be interested what according to Djerassi the ideal population level for a country like Austria would be. Does he want 10 millions, or even 20 or 40 millions? Is he aiming at a population density like Bangla Desh for Austria?
- Dear Professor Djerassi! Don't feel insulted by the "intellectual" discussion in this Forum! As you can see, many fellow citizens require tons of brain food and not only Schnitzel!!

    Djerassi's manifesto in my view does not contain social romanticism but cool calculation. He is simply calculating for us that nobody will pay our (indeed: OUR) retirement benefits unless something happens.
- Dear Carl Djerassi, how badly off must people be in a country that they don't even get children any longer. Why can we not get our own children anymore? Why is there so little support in this country for getting children? Why do people who do not have children get the same retirement benefits as people with children? I don't see the problem that nobody wants to bring children into this world. I see the problem that those who dare to do so get to the financial limits of the system with the first child. Only those who are unemployed and stay at home have time for many children. I am calling on politicians to improve the support for working parents rather than bring in foreigners.
- The views proposed here are surprisingly quixotic…. We know well that the fanatics supporting a policy of multiculturalism want to swamp this country with foreigners. What is less well known is that Austria is three times overpopulated and that a healthy shrinkage would be more than necessary.
- Djerassi is a chemist which explains his thinking. Which elements combine well with each other (Austrians, Brazilians, Nigerians—because they are all Catholic). This is an innovative view and I personally

consider a "chemical" world view much more attractive than one derived from mechanistic physics, but Djerassi's approach also fails to do complete justice to the complexity of human life together.
- Carl has forgotten THE central point: Just as leading companies have to make themselves attractive for top employees, we need to clean our dusty place in order to be even considered by top immigrants. This does not only include a positive attitude toward foreigners but also the conviction that Austrian culture will automatically change massively. Because Brazilians and Indians for the most part don't go for Schnitzel and usually have wonderful alternatives: to remain at home in a growing market, the U.S., Canada, UK, Holland, etc.
- So Mr. Anti-Baby Pill also has a plan where the 200,000 jobs per year for the 200,000 migrants urgently desired by Germany will be created? Apart from the borderline ingenious idea that more inhabitants also consume more and therefore create more jobs which is unfortunately not true because otherwise countries like Nigeria would be rolling in jobs.
- If one would insist on a causality, one could also say Djerassi has invented the "pro-immigration pill."
- Now you see what you have done with your pill. The solutions offered are merely the admission of the author's bad conscience. This is brain drain, i.e., colonization of knowledge—the most important natural resource of a service society, education, is supposed to be exploited. This will never work.
- Without migration, Austria will become die out. Austria is already very colorful. In 50 years at the latest, 50% of Austria's population will have a migration background. And that this good because without migration, Austria's economic and social system would break down and the country would die out in 150 years.
- Indians, Brazilians, Filipinos? Sounds like positive racism. I can also do with Pakistanis!
- A problem which will be solved by itself after years or decades. In other words: the old folks will eventually die.
- What an instrumental—indeed inhuman—inhuman. What right do Europeans and Austrians have to select the rest of humankind under the criteria of "usefulness"? The fat and old Austrians are supposed to decide who guarantee their retirement benefits and their social system? Nigerians and Brazilians are allowed in, the others must unfortunately remain outside, they are "useless." One question is why bring children into this world? This requires optimism and belief in the future and economic opportunities. But there is little reason for optimism. And why is the state allowed to decree that it is "necessary" to have children? This sounds like fascism where the state also controlled families' decisions. Austria is not an island but the most narrow-minded backyard of Europe. Unfortunately, this includes text author of this text.

- This is a funny guy. First he invents the Pill and then he complains that the birthrate has fallen drastically.
- The way some commentators here simply vent their questionable feelings rather than address the arguments of a fact-based article is pathetic. To Mr. Djerassi, the future of Austria is fairly immaterial but he is constructive. One can disagree with him, but then please use counterarguments.
- So we should profit from young people whose training was financed by the Third World. This is also a version of imperialism.
- Why should the native Austrians not have three children? That would be a possibility.
- Most people cannot even afford one child. We don't know how to cope financially as it is. Plus, and that sounds terribly selfish: I like my job and I am very successful in it. With one child this is possible, with three children: never.
- I don't see a problem if Austria becomes extinct.
- Taking a long-term perspective, it makes more sense to migrate to Brazil or India than to Germany. Because in Brazil and India there will still be jobs in 30 years. In Germany and Austria, I am not so sure about that.
- Would these migrants come to a country where they know from the outset that they will be abused to safeguard people's retirement benefits. In earlier times, they used to get slaves to work. Now they get slaves for the retirement benefits. Sounds hard and brutal, but that's what it is.

APPENDIX C: A REBUTTAL TO THE CATHOLIC PRESS ARTICLES ABOUT CARL DJERASSI *(previously unpublished)*

According to the web site of the *Katholischer Nachrichtendienst*, Cardinal Schönborn referred to me in his 22 December 2008 *ORF Pressestunde* (Austrian Radio and TV Press Hour) in the following terms:

> The inventor of the "Anti-Baby Pille," Carl Djerassi, recently spoke about a "demographic catastrophe" in the *Standard* and confronted Austrians with the alternative to either have three children per family or to develop an improved immigration policy.

With one important exception, the Cardinal quoted me correctly. My recommendation for the 3 children per family was not addressed to all Austrians—a recommendation that would cause within a few decades a totally unsustainable population explosion that would be irresponsible from a demographic, economic, and environmental standpoint—but solely to the xenophobic component of the recent Austrian electorate that opposes immigration. A country needs an average of 2.1 children per family to maintain its population and since Austria's current average is 1.4 children (as is the case in all-Catholic Spain and Italy), if natural sexual reproduction were to become the only means of maintaining the country's current size, then the future parents of the anti-immigration persuasion would have to make up an ultimate "demographic catastrophe" by producing 3 children. But that is not the reason why I am writing this rebuttal.

Within days after the Cardinal's speech, a veritable explosion of articles appeared in Europe and the USA, primarily under the aegis of Catholic press services, with headlines such as "Pill Inventor Slams Pill" or "Co-inventor of Birth Control Pill Now Calls It a Catastrophe." These are slanderous calumnies that cannot remain unchallenged.

One of the most respected British newspapers, the *Guardian* (7 January 2009) under the headline "Church Grabs Chance to Attack Birth Control" started its article with the following sentence: "Roman Catholic leaders have pounced on a "confession" by one of the inventors of the birth control pill who has said the contraceptive he helped create was responsible for a "demographic catastrophe." The *Guardian* has now formally retracted these statements and has removed the entire article from its web site.

The source of all these calumnies—now having spread over hundreds of web sites throughout the world—is the claim that in my article (13 December 2008) in *Der Standard*, I attributed the decline in Austria's (and by inference Europe's) average low family size to the pill. Such a conclusion is absurd and I reject it categorically. It implies either deliberate disingenuousness or total ignorance on the part of these media—clearly unworthy of the Catholic Press Service—and thus requiring prompt retraction. People don't have smaller families because of the availability of birth control, but for personal, economic, cultural and other reasons, of which the changes in the status and lifestyles of women during the past 50 years is the most important. Telling support for my conclusion is provided by Japan, which has an even worse demographic problem than Western Europe; yet the pill was only legalized there in 1999 and is not used widely. Japan's rampant xenophobia makes the immigration solution practiced by the USA unlikely. It is not surprising, therefore, that it is estimated that by 2050, Japan's population will have decreased by a whopping 25 percent. By contrast, even though Japan's and Austria's family sizes are virtually identical, Austria's population is estimated to increase by 12 percent—all of it due to immigration.

Contraception, birth control, abortion, or the pill were nowhere mentioned in my article in *Der Standard*. I accused the startlingly large xenophobic segment of new Austrian voters of living under the illusion that their small country was not situated in the middle of Europe but rather on an island where God permits them to exist independently to enjoy their Schnitzels. Cardinal Schönborn in his *ORF Pressestunde* emphasized that "the birth rate among those attending Sunday mass in Austria is 2.66, while the national average is only 1.4." The presumed implication for this significant difference is that practicing Catholics exercise less birth control. However what is not stated is that it is precisely the condemnation by the Church of all contraception that is responsible for the increased secularization of European Catholics and the ever decreasing church attendance. The de facto separation of sex and reproduction throughout Europe (how else explain an average of 1.5 children through most of Europe or even of 2.66 among the church-going segment of Austrians?) is one that sooner or later the Catholic Church must face realistically and humanely. Falsely accusing the pill and its developers is not the answer nor will it disguise the fact that the Church's stand against contraception is largely responsible for all-Catholic Latin America displaying such huge illegal abortion rates.

About the Contributors

Jessica **Borge** is a doctoral candidate in the Department of Film, Media and Cultural Studies at Birkbeck College, University of London. Her dissertation is on "The London Rubber Company, the Condom and the Pill: 1932–1965," an interdisciplinary history of public relations strategy and competition in the British contraceptive marketplace.

Beth Widmaier **Capo** is a professor of English and gender and women's studies at Illinois College. She is the author of the monograph *Textual Contraception: Birth Control and Modern American Fiction* (2007). She has also published articles on Nella Larsen, eugenics in 1910s American literature, William Faulkner, Marilynne Robinson, Caresse Crosby, Kay Boyle, and feminist pedagogy.

Belinda **Carstens-Wickham** is a professor of German at Southern Illinois University, Edwardsville. Her teaching and research specialties are images of women and sexuality in Weimar and images of women and sexuality in German unification. She published one of the first articles about gender in German unification.

Shelley W. **Chan** is a professor of Chinese language and cultural studies at Wittenberg University. Her book, *A Subversive Voice in China* (2011) was the first English monograph about Mo Yan, 2010 Nobel Prize winner in Literature. Her articles, translations, and book/film reviews on Chinese literature and culture have appeared widely around the world.

Sofie **Decock** is an assistant professor of German at Ghent University. Her first monograph, *Papierfähnchen auf einer imaginären Weltkarte* (2010), examined the mythical topographies of Annemarie Schwarzenbach's travel writings about Asia and Africa. Besides several articles on travel writing and editions of Schwarzenbach's works, she has published on transnational and minority writing.

Walter **Grünzweig** is a professor of American studies and comparative literature at TU Dortmund University. He specializes in 19th-century American literature and transatlantic relations in literature, culture, and education. In 2010, he received the German National Prize in Excellence in University Teaching awarded by the German Rectors Conference.

Kirsten E. **Kumpf Baele** is a visiting assistant professor of German at the University of Iowa. Her research on the representation of hair in politics, art, and literature

224 About the Contributors

has been featured in LIT Verlag, and her work on German authors of non–German descent can be found in *Utah Foreign Language Review*. Her latest projects explore filmic responses to the refugee crisis in Austria and Anne Frank and her diary.

Waltraud **Maierhofer** is a professor of German and an affiliated faculty member of the Honors Program and International Programs at the University of Iowa. She is the author and editor of several monographs, collected volumes, and critical editions in German literary and cultural studies and a textbook for German literature since 1750.

Jonas **Nesselhauf** is a postdoctoral research associate in German and cultural studies at the University of Vechta. His research interests focus on serial narration on television, representations of the human body in literary works, and literature and the economy. He coauthored an introduction to serial narration on television with Markus Schleich, *Fernsehserien* (2016).

Manon S. **Parry** is an assistant professor of public history at the University of Amsterdam and the author of *Broadcasting Birth Control: Family Planning and Mass Media* (2013). She is researching a book on the social relevance of medical museums and organizing a festival of cultural responses to HIV/AIDS.

Regina **Range** is an assistant professor and language program director of German at the University of Alabama. She is the author of *Positioning Gina Kaus* (2012). She has published on German-speaking émigré writers and film professionals, autobiographical writing, exile literature, film and scriptwriting.

Markus **Schleich** is a doctoral candidate and research associate at Saarland University in the Department of Comparative Literature. His research interests focus on serial narration on television, popular music, theories of popular culture, intermediality, and thematology. With Jonas Nesselhauf he has coauthored and co-edited publications on quality television, including *Das andere Fernsehen* (2015).

Jamie **Wagman** is an assistant professor of history and gender and women's studies at St. Mary's College, Notre Dame, Indiana. Her research interests include topics related to sexuality, television's "mad men," and women reformers of the Depression era. Her work has appeared in the *Journal of Urban History* and *Nashim: A Journal of Jewish Women's Studies & Gender Issues*, among other places.

Index

abandonment, child 6, 87, 98, 124–5, 133, 142, 143, 174, 176–80, 184, 188
abortion 1, 5, 6, 39, 68, 156–173; advocacy for access 157, 168, 190; forced 6, 127, 176, 179, 180, 186; gender-selective 174, 177; "I had an abortion" 169; legality 2, 6, 101, 114, 117, 121, 156–70; with Misoprostol 168; pill 2, 157; self-induced 203
abstinence 2, 70, 156
Ad Council 75
adolescence 67–73, 100–114, 122, 163
adoption, forced 5, 82–116, 127
advertising 12–28; regulation 12–13; television 12
"Affordable Care Act" 137, 151
Africa 211
African-American 75, 201
anti-baby pill 29, 209–10, 218, 219
Australia 7, 30, 101, 102, 106, 114
Austria 5–7, 82–4, 93, 97–8, 206, 209–21
autobiography 29, 83, 86, 98, 207–13

Bagge, Peter 196; *Woman Rebel* 6, 190–201
Bedsider 73–76
Belgium 5, 100–114
birth control, advocacy 65, 70, 151, 192–94; failed 6, 38, 61, 137, 151; sabotaged 137, 151
birth-control pill (the pill) 14–26, 29–46, 66–77, 83, 138–46, 151, 192, 194, 206–21; access 22, 151; advertisement 48–62; criticism 208; dispenser 55–8, 62, 140; Enovid 30, 48, 51–2, 60; introduction 121; "male pill" 2; Ortho-Novum 777 57–60; Ovulen 55–7; prescription-only 14, 62, 139; trials 15, 48, 62; Yaz 61; *see also* oral contraceptive
blog 61, 69, 73, 194
Boardwalk Empire 195, 201

Brešan, Vinko 141–2; *The Priest's Children* 143, 151
Britain 2, 11–26, 101, 140–41, 209
British Board of Film Censors (BBFC) 11, 16–23
Brotherhood 33–6

Canada 103, 218
Catholicism 15, 23, 35, 45, 53; *Humanae Vitae* 23, 140
censorship 3, 11–26, 31–2, 118
certification (film) 11, 16–23
China 1, 6, 161, 174–89; *see also* one-child policy
Choices of the Heart: The Margaret Sanger Story 194–8
Clausen, Murmel 147–148
Clinton, Hillary 2, 190
comedy 6, 22–4, 32–3, 40–44, 136, 140–152
Comfort, Alex 25
comics 197–8; *see also* Bagge, Peter
communism 1, 101, 157, 161; post-communism 137, 141, 151, 162, 175, 184, 186, 209
Comstock, Anthony 50, 194
Comstock law 51
condoms 13, 18, 22, 25, 26, 45, 72, 74, 77, 137, 141, 143, 151, 152, 197
contraception 137; effectiveness 42, 45, 53, 61, 65, 71–4, 144, 146; emergency (Plan B) 61, 137, 145–50, 168; mechanical and chemical 13, right to 137, 151
Corinna, Heather 70–1
crime 13, 31, 119, 156, 159, 162–7, 195
The Crime of Father Amaro 6, 162–5, 167
Croatia 6, 136–7, 141–3, 151–2

death 42, 58–9, 70, 95, 107–8, 113, 136, 156, 177, 182–3, 190, 199–200, 213; death

225

penalty 158; death rate 143; maternal 164–5, 168, 187
demographics 175, 213–20
Desperate Housewives 42–3
detention center 5, 117–34
diaphragm 196, 200, 202
Djerassi, Carl 3, 4, 6, 29–30, 206–21; autobiographies 29, 207–13; *The Politics of Contraception* 206–8; "Rebuttal" 7, 219–21
documentary film 12, 14, 101, 148, 157, 192; *The Pill* 14
Dziuba, Helmut 117–118; *Jana and Jan* 114–34

eugenics 6, 191–4, 197, 199–202
Europe 30, 101, 137, 142, 143, 151, 157, 159, 160, 167, 200, 210, 211, 213–8

family planning 2–4, 11, 41–2, 44, 54, 67, 73, 77, 83, 87, 121, 137, 142–3, 178, 203, 213; clinics 49; experts 74; government programs 162, 174
Family Planning Association: British 12; Mexican 163
Family Planning Committee (China) 179–86, 186
FDA 48, 52–4, 62, 146
feminism 1, 147, 191, 193, 201, 208
fertility 1, 5, 15, 29, 30, 43, 73, 137, 148, 157, 175, 209; rate 163; treatment 39, 142
film rating 3, 16, 152; *see also* certification
film script 5, 15, 17, 83, 87–98, 138, 148–9
4 Months, 3 Weeks and 2 Days 6, 157–62

The Guardian 2
gender inequality 5, 85, 88, 137
gender roles 31, 33–6, 38–40, 45, 55–7, 62, 65, 77, 82–4, 93, 94, 96–9, 110–11, 124–5, 147, 164, 208
German Democratic Republic, East Germany (GDR) 5, 117–34
Germany 6, 83–6, 97–8, 101, 118, 136, 143, 147–52, 169, 213, 215–9
G♥rl 70
Go Ask Alice 70
graphic novel 191, 196–201

Haberlandt, Ludwig 207, 211
Härtel, Manfred 118; *Friedlose Herzen* 118
health 30, 44, 59, 65–78, 119–20, 158, 161, 163, 184, 190, 195, 217; global.
Here We Go Round the Mulberry Bush 25
HIV/AIDS 12, 67
Hollywood film 5, 16, 82, 85, 88–93, 96–9, 146, 156, 160
House of Cards (TV) 30–40, 44

human rights 24, 183, 185
humor 5, 6, 26, 73, 105, 136–152, 200

implant 72–5
India 216–9
infanticide 98, 136, 174, 177, 202
Ireland 2, 100, 101, 106, 114, 142, 162
IUD 2, 3, 66, 71–3, 75, 163

Jana and Jan 117–43
Japan 175, 180, 184, 187, 211, 215, 220
Joys of Fatherhood 147–51

Kaus, Gina 5, 82–98; *All Children* 87–8; *The Mother* 83–4; *Three Secrets* 88–97; *Toni* 85–6
Khoury, J.C. 6, 136; *The Pill* 143–7
Kim, Lil' 3
A Kind of Loving 18–21

legality 14, 65, 92, 100–2, 114, 138, 140, 143
Little Black Spiders 100–16
Lodge, David 152
Lynn, Loretta 3

Ma Yinchu 175
Mad Men 36–8
magazines 5, 48–55, 62, 88, 169; *Glamour* 61; *Look* 53–4; *The Mother* 83–4, 97; *Ms.* 169; *Sex, etc.* 71; *Stern* 169
Mao Zedong 175, 177
Marie Stopes clinics 14
melodrama 5, 59, 194
Mexico 6, 156, 162–7
migration 7, 143, 213, 215–20
Mill, John Stuart 18
Mills, Hugh 5, 136, 138; *Prudence and the Pill* (novel) 138–41, 158
Minaj, Nikki 3
minority 7, 48, 49, 53, 55, 85
Misoprostol 168
Mo Yan 6, 174–88, "Abandoned Child" 178, 184; "Explosions" 180–3; *Frog* 183–8; "Tunnel" 179, 185
morality 12, 17, 91, 113, 139, 147, 185
mother 1, 15, 34, 35, 39, 40, 82–98, 121, 125, 129, 138–40, 164, 166–7, 178–9, 191, 194, 196, 202, 207–9; anonymous 100, 114; foster 84; single 37, 88, 100–15; surrogate 184–5; Virgin Mary 109
Mother Nature 217
Motion Picture Association of America 16
Mungiu, Christian 141, 157, 159, 160; see also *4 Months, 3 Weeks and 2 Days*

National Campaign to Prevent Teen and Unplanned Pregnancy 67–8

"New Woman" 85
Nigeria 2, 8, 217–8
novel *see* Clausen, Murmel; Mills, Hugh; Mo Yan; Sanger, Margaret

one-child policy 6, 174–88
oral history 88

parenthood 141, 212; ambivalence toward 129, 137, 141
patch, contraceptive 1
pill *see* birth-control pill
The Pill (film) 14–16, 135, 143–7
The Pill (PBS American Experience) 54, 56
Pincus, Gregory 15, 207
Planned Parenthood 4, 7, 14, 78, 169, 174, 202
Poland 2, 142, 157, 169
policy 65, 124, 158, 217; immigration 216, 219; pro-family 117; pro-natalist 100, 161; social 5, 121; UN Population Policy Data Bank 114; *see also* one-child policy
poverty 49, 62, 167, 170, 211
pregnancy, unintended 2, 3, 68, 78, 83, 87–8, 97, 100, 102, 107, 114, 117, 136, 151, 157, 160, 168
The Priest's Children 143, 151
progesterone 30, 209
Prudence and the Pill 22–24
Punto y Aparte 6, 166–7

racism 6, 190, 202, 218
rape 32, 104, 121, 170
rate of children per woman 143
rating (film) 3, 16, 152
religion 5, 29, 31, 35, 87, 101–2, 113–4, 142, 162, 165, 167, 174, 190, 194
reproduction: choice 18, 24, 29, 36, 90, 100, 156, 161, 166, 175, 202; medically assisted 137; separation from sex 29, 31, 220
reproductive rights 1–7, 11, 17, 18, 23, 37, 41, 71, 82, 97, 122, 137, 138, 143, 156, 158, 160–1, 162, 190–3, 196–8, 200–2; Coalition for 162, 169; denial 5, 30, 43–4, 106
rhythm method 53, 127, 152
romance 55–6, 59, 97, 147, 149
Romania 1, 6, 156–62, 170

Sanger, Margaret 1, 6, 7, 190–203, 207–8; *The Birth Control Review* 195; *Choices of the Heart* 194–5, 198; *Margaret Sanger* 192, 195
satire 40, 40–5, 141–3, 180
Scarleteen 70–2
Schweighöfer, Matthias 5, 136; *Joys of Fatherhood* 147–51

Scrubs 40–2
Searle, G.D., & Company 30, 52–6
sex education 2, 4, 37, 50, 55, 65–78, 86, 121, 127, 142, 156, 161, 200
Sex Education (TV documentary) 14
sexual liberation 57, 138
sexually transmitted infection (STI) 13, 61, 76, 139, 152
The Simpsons 43–4
16 and Pregnant 67–9; social media 65–78
socialism 84, 86, 119–23, 127, 143, 175, 180, 188, 192
South America 168
Soviet Union 121, 161
sperm donation 148, 151; rights 152
Der Standard 7, 213–20
state institutions 5, 36, 49, 95–7, 101, 119, 175, 188
sterilization 137, 163, 178

Tamar hospital 102–3, 113
Teen Mom 67–8
teenager 2, 15, 16, 18, 20, 25, 71–2, 76; birth rate.
television 1, 3, 4, 6–7, 194, 197; British 11–26; U.S. 29–46, 65–9
Three Secrets 88–97
Toni 85–6
Toye, Patrice 5; *Little Black Spiders* 100–16
tragedy 33–8, 59, 125, 136, 142, 187
Trevelyan, John 18–23
Trump, Donald 2
Twitter 4, 62, 65, 75; #BirthControlHelpedMe 78; #ShoutYourAbortion 169

U.S. 2, 6, 26, 29–45, 48–62, 66–7, 75, 84, 87–97, 161, 218
Unmarried Mothers 14

vasectomy 151
violence 128, 182, 186, 195; sexual 138, 161

websites 4, 65–6; Bedsider 73–76; G♥rl 70; Go Ask Alice 70; Scarleteen 70–2; Women on Web 169
Wedekind, Frank 156
Wende (end of the GDR) 117–34
What Every Girl Should Know 195
withdrawal 73–5, 78, 127, 161
Women on Web 169
Women's Liberation Movement 11, 26, 213

Youth Detention Center 117, 119–20, 124–5

www.ingramcontent.com/pod-product-compliance
Ingram Content Group UK Ltd.
Pitfield, Milton Keynes, MK11 3LW, UK
UKHW041949140426
5217IPUK00014B/709